SIMPLY THE
BEST

SIMPLY THE
BEST

The Inside Story
of How Wigan Became
Rugby League's Greatest
Cup Team and Won
Eight in a Row

FRANK MALLEY

First published by Pitch Publishing, 2017

Pitch Publishing
A2 Yeoman Gate
Yeoman Way
Worthing
Sussex
BN13 3QZ
www.pitchpublishing.co.uk
info@pitchpublishing.co.uk

A CIP catalogue record is available for this book
from the British Library.

ISBN 978-1-78531-281-6

Typesetting and origination by Pitch Publishing
Printed in the UK by Bell & Bain, Glasgow, Scotland

Contents

'Sport has the power to change the world. It has the power to inspire. It speaks to youth in a language they understand. Sport can create hope where once there was only despair.' –

Nelson Mandela

For Carole and Michael

ALL ROYALTIES IN AID OF JOINING JACK

In October 2011, at the age of three, Jack Johnson was diagnosed with Duchenne Muscular Dystrophy, a terminal, incurable disease. It is a muscle-wasting condition which in time attacks every muscle in the body.

Jack's parents, former Wigan rugby league player Andy and his wife Alex, set up the Joining Jack charity to help fund research and trials in the hope of finding a cure or treatment for Jack and children like him. Sportsmen such as England rugby union player Owen Farrell and Wigan rugby league star Sam Tomkins have publicised the charity by linking the forefingers of both hands to make two 'Js', the charity symbol.

All royalties from this book are being donated directly to the charity. You can donate online through JustGiving, or by texting JOIN01 followed by the amount £1, £5, £10 etc., to 70070 or send cheques payable to Joining Jack at Joining Jack, c/o ADM, Unit 1, Appleton Street, Wigan, WN3 4BZ.

Acknowledgements

I WOULD like to say a big thank you to the following former players, coaches, backroom staff and journalists who sifted through their memory banks and gave their time, many in extended interviews, to supply the reminiscences contained in the following pages:

Joe Lydon, Mark Preston, Ian Lucas, Denis Betts, Steve Hampson, Mick Cassidy, Shaun Edwards, Phil Clarke, Barrie-Jon Mather, Andy Farrell, Nicky Kiss, Shaun Wane, Martin Offiah, Anne Mills, Peter Aspinall, Dave Hadfield, John Dorahy, Brian Noble, Bill Hartley, Billy McGinty, Jason Robinson, Gary Connolly.

A special thanks to Martin Dermott whose enthusiasm was invaluable in tracking down former team-mates, some halfway around the world. Thanks, too, to Ian Laybourn and Pete Coulson for their support and to Frank Orrell for his picture research.

Sincere thanks also to the *Wigan Evening Post* and *Wigan Observer* and to PA Images, who kindly supplied the photos. Above all, thanks to Paul at Pitch Publishing for having faith in the project.

Frank Malley, 2017

Prologue

THE crowd, some 200-strong, huddled together under their umbrellas in a tight circle, craning their necks and shifting their stance like emperor penguins in an attempt to see and keep warm and dry as the rain, heavy and unrelenting, swept in from the Irish Sea.

In the middle of the circle stood Billy Boston, in a blue suit and no raincoat, seemingly oblivious to the downpour as he obliged the attendant photographers by raising his hands in victory mode as they snapped him in front of the newly-unveiled bronze statue capturing him in his cherry and white jersey in his rugby league pomp.

It was 3 September 2016, almost half a century since Boston had played the last of his 488 matches for Wigan, the most famous rugby league club on the planet.

Yet the joy and affection was deep and tangible, as many who had watched him play and more, who had heard others speak so reverently of the man who scored a club record 478 tries in 15 years at Central Park, gathered on the foulest of autumn days to witness the tribute at the site of the statue in Wigan's Believe Square, at the top of Millgate and The Wiend, the town's highest point.

This book is not about Boston, who grew up in the Tiger Bay area of Cardiff, the son of a Welsh mother and a seaman father from Sierra Leone. The Boston story has been told on numerous occasions in the past half century. Yet in some ways it is all about Boston and his legacy, when it comes to the values and standards as a sportsman and as a man that he brought to the town when he signed at the age of 19 and deprived Wales of a potentially legendary rugby union star.

I first became aware of Boston at the age of four when my father would lead me and my older brother, Patrick, up to our bedroom in the terraced house above the shoe shop in which we lived on Wallgate, Wigan, 50 yards from the town's famous pier.

Looking out of that bedroom window, day or night, was like peering into an L.S. Lowry landscape. Barges sailing into dock on the canal to the right. Cotton mill girls clip-clopping along the pavement. Chimneys belching their industrial fumes from grimy, red-bricked factories. And, every so often, the local bobby checking in with the police station headquarters from a telephone housed in a little hut, with a blue light on top, which was strategically placed in a fork in the road.

'If you are good you can stay up for 20 minutes and watch Billy Boston when he walks through that door,' Dad would say, pointing to the front entrance of the Bridgewater Arms pub 30 yards across the road where Boston took a regular drink and which was situated in the shadow of the huge and imposing Trencherfield cotton mill.

We pressed our noses against the bedroom window and waited in excited anticipation for this man who Dad spoke about with respect and reverence approaching awe.

Like Roy of the Rovers. Like Superman, like every comic book hero a kid looks up to. And when we caught a glimpse of him it was the most thrilling moment, even though, or maybe because, my only knowledge of rugby at the time was via my father's sketchy stories of Boston's thundering tackles and rampaging runs, scattering all before him. This was a real-1life hero in our street.

I recited the tale to 'Billy B' when we spoke in a small restaurant close to Believe Square and he threw his head back and chuckled.

Days previously, Boston had revealed publicly and bravely on regional television that he was suffering from vascular dementia. At 82 his memory was failing. His ability to describe those halcyon days lacked detail and precision. But mention a team-mate, such as fellow legend Eric Ashton, or his love for Wigan, and the dark eyes twinkled and the years rolled away.

'I came from Tiger Bay in Cardiff where there were loads of coloured people and when I came to Wigan I was the only one,' Boston told me. 'But they treated me like a lord and I appreciated that. I wasn't the best player and it was a great honour to play for Wigan. I just carried on what the Ernie Ashcrofts and Jackie Cunliffes started. I didn't go back to Cardiff because Wigan is a wonderful place and I love the people here. If I had my time over I would do the same thing.'

That has always been the allure of Billy Boston MBE. Modesty and humility, with an ability to keep sport and life in perspective, even though there is no question he was the 'best player'.

Wigan gave Boston, who married Joan, a girl from the town whom he met on a blind date, a new life. Boston, in turn, helped Wigan to six Challenge Cup finals, winning three of them, and then threw the rest of his life into raising cash for charity and extolling the virtues of his adopted town as the club's finest ambassador while setting the standard for generations to come.

It was a tough act to follow but in the late 1980s and 1990s a team from Wigan did just that, winning eight Challenge Cups in a row between 1988 and 1995 with the sort of style and panache which evoked memories of Boston and Ashton and Cunliffe and Ashcroft.

This book essentially is the story of those eight-in-a-row years.

The Wembley years.

The story of a moment in time when the town's rugby club dared to dream of scaling the heights that Boston and co. had achieved more than a quarter of a century before.

A time when it dared to trust in a blend of the town's young local talent and audacious big-money signings.

A time when real-life sporting heroes, in turn inspiring a new generation, once more walked its streets.

1

Tough Love

T HE images running through my mind were sharp and clear despite the mist of more than a quarter of a century as I arrived at the west London apartment of Shaun Edwards.

There was the picture of Edwards lifting the Challenge Cup trophy to the Wembley skies in 1988, the youngest rugby league captain ever to do so.

There was the memory of an even younger Edwards as a fresh-faced teenaged altar boy at St Mary's Catholic Church on Standishgate, Wigan, a church I used to attend and which is located a hefty drop kick away from where the halfway line used to exist at Central Park, Wigan rugby's old and now spiritual home after the sacrilege of it making way for a Tesco car park.

Edwards, in his black cassock and white surplice, would serve at the 11am Mass on a Sunday and often, just a few hours later and less than 50 yards away, inspire Wigan to yet another victory in the afternoon, in front of many of the same faces from the morning congregation.

Also etched on the memory was the more recent image of Edwards, the international rugby union coach of maturity and renown, invariably seated high in the stand with a face emanating thunderous intensity.

My undertaking was clear. It was not to tell Edwards's story, although his influence on rugby league over two decades was so pervasive that to analyse Wigan in the 1980s and 1990s without reference to Edwards would be tantamount to tracing the career of Ernie Wise without mention of Eric Morecambe. The mission, via the considered reflection which comes when boots have been hanging undisturbed for a couple of decades, was to pinpoint the reasons behind the most spectacularly successful team in British rugby league history.

A team that played rugby which surged with life and conviction. A team that beguiled the sporting world to such an extent that many of its main characters became household names in parts where rugby league was neither played nor understood. A team that conquered all before them, going undefeated in 43 consecutive Challenge Cup matches, lifting the trophy eight times in succession from 1988 to 1995.

Only one man experienced the soaring exhilaration which accompanied playing for Wigan in every one of those 43 matches: Shaun Edwards.

Many other characters played crucial roles down those years. Of course they did.

There were men such as Jack Robinson, a lifelong supporter who joined the board in the late 1970s when Wigan were a shambles on and off the field and turned a 12-man boardroom, whose members would defer any decision more complex than whether they should take milk or cream in their coffee, into the famous 'Gang of Four', a streamlined board with an astute eye for a rugby player who championed homegrown stars and also signed cheques in the 1980s and 1990s which would have made past board members wince.

Maurice Lindsay was one of those dynamic directors and there is no doubt his relentless energy as chairman and his slick, sharp-witted public persona promoting a fresh, modern club in the 1980s, also invigorated the place.

Yet there were also people like fitness coach Bill Hartley, physio Keith Mills and kit man Derek 'Taffy' Jones who formed a backroom alliance built on respect and camaraderie, which is still cherished today by the players of that era.

On the playing front the stars of that dynasty read like a *Who's Who* of the game.

The supreme athlete who was Ellery Hanley, nicknamed the 'Black Pearl' by the Australians, a man whose feats spoke for themselves and a good job they did because he rarely, if ever, talked to the media.

The magical Martin Offiah, simply the most clinical and charismatic finisher in the game's history, even if he did once score ten tries in a game and still failed to win the man-of-the-match award.

The freak of nature named Jason Robinson, or 'Billy Whizz', a man who wriggled through gaps as if bones were not part of his anatomy.

The enigmatic Andy Gregory, whose withering one-liners are treasured in Wigan folklore as much as his ability to offload the perfect pass for every scenario.

There were more. Not least Joe Lydon, who fans dubbed 'Royce', as in 'Rolls-Royce', in tribute to his effortless and graceful running style.

Lydon's carefree nature also went some way to demonstrating that a serious, physically-punishing sport could still be fun.

There was Andy Goodway, nicknamed BA, as in 'Bad Attitude', on account of his grumpy demeanour but who was the epitome of professionalism whenever he crossed the whitewash.

Add Denis Betts, Andy Farrell, Dean Bell, Andy Platt and the Iro brothers, Kevin and Tony. The list is long. The reasons truly are many and varied when it comes to analysing the events which paved the way to the old Twin Towers of Wembley eight times in a row. Sporting phenomena rarely owe their existence to a single cause. Invariably, they are formed by a collision of events, each one building on the last before eventually exploding to burn brilliantly for a limited time like some giant supernova.

But first and foremost in Wigan's Challenge Cup history there is Edwards.

Every great sporting team needs a constant. Lionel Messi was Barcelona's go-to man for a decade. Dan Carter fulfilled that role for the All Blacks, Dan Marino was the quarterback supreme for 17 seasons with the Miami Dolphins.

In a sport with a profile not nearly so elevated, Edwards was Mr Wigan for 14 years, a man famed for his intensity. A man who gained his appreciation of the values associated with one of the toughest games on Earth from his father Jackie.

His relationship with his father forms my first question, after, that is, Edwards demonstrates the northern hospitality housed deep in his DNA by insisting on making me a steaming mug of tea and offering up a helping of his partner Maggie's fish pie.

'Better have some Daddie's sauce, it's a bit bland,' he warns, out of earshot of Maggie, before reminding me proudly that his dad was one of the top young rugby league stars of the 1950s, signing for Warrington on his 16th birthday in 1954 for a world record £1,000.

Within months he was the youngest player to captain a professional rugby league team and would have gone on almost certainly to be one of the enduring scrum half stars of the sport if he had not suffered a crippling, career-terminating spinal injury in a match in 1963.

At the age of 24 he was finished, never to work again, with four spinal operations necessary to spare him from life in a wheelchair. It is a measure of the Edwards family tenacity that it did not prevent him encouraging his son to take up the game.

'It had always been a regret of my dad's life, it still is really, that he never played for Wigan,' said Edwards, the Lancashire vowels clattering flat and purposefully from his lips as if wearing the clogs worn by the cotton mill girls of yesteryear.

'A couple of times he went on the transfer list for £10,000 and was persuaded to come off the list and a week later Wigan came in for him with a £10,000 offer but his chance had gone. It was always natural he wanted to play for Wigan.'

Instead, he became young Shaun's personal coach, a tough, no-nonsense taskmaster.

Was he hard on you?

'Yeah, yeah, very hard. I read a book recently about different places of excellence. It was about how Russian girls became good at tennis all of a sudden and how Kenya was the place for long-distance running.

'There was one common denominator and that was really pushy parents. It ended up being the right thing for me. It's tough love. That was the right way to bring up a young man, particularly at my size.

'I was only 12st and 5ft 8in. You are going to have to be a pretty determined person to make it against blokes, especially against Australia, six or seven stones heavier than you and half a foot taller.'

By 1983 his dad's 'tough love' had fashioned a teenager who was being touted as the brightest prospect in the world of rugby, having become the only player to captain England schoolboys at rugby union as well as rugby league.

The only doubt was which direction to take. Wigan were still in a moribund phase which had kept them bereft of league titles since 1960 and without a Challenge Cup appearance since 1970 when they had lost 7-2 to Castleford.

There was, however, £35,000 on the table at Central Park, a world record for a 17-year-old, if Edwards signed, at a time when the average price of a house in the UK, according to the Office for National Statistics, was just £24,000.

The size of that first cheque, seven times more than the ordinary highly-talented rookie player would have received and yet still £7,000 less than St Helens reportedly offered, clearly remains a source of pride to this day, perhaps mainly because it was vindication of the expert coaching he had received from his father.

'Actually, I got offered more, not just from St Helens, but from Leeds and from Widnes too,' said Edwards. 'At first I was thinking Widnes were the best team. That was the place to go. They had Joe Lydon and Andy Gregory playing for them.'

He was wrestling with the decision when he picked up the special notebook in which his dad used to compile hand-written match reports on his son's contribution to every game he played as an amateur or as a schoolboy. He flicked through the pages, searching eagerly for the latest critique.

'It used to say things such as, "Shaun was terrible today, too slow into position," said Edwards. 'Or, "Shaun did well today, his support play was excellent but needs to improve on his tackling."

'But this day it said, "Shaun has a big decision to make. Does he want to try to play at Wembley in front of 15,000 Widnesians or 35,000 Wiganers?" That was it. As soon as I read that my decision was made.'

The story made sense of one of the most touching quotes I have read about Edwards. When asked well into his 40s what inspired him to continue searching for success after winning 37 major rugby medals, he answered, 'Everything I do really is to try to make my mother and father proud of me.'

Thus he signed for his hometown club on his 17th birthday, 17 October 1983, making headlines next day on the back page of every national newspaper with Alex Murphy, Wigan's coach at the time, justifying all the hullabaloo by saying, 'If this lad was a horse, with his pedigree he would be worth £1m.'

His debut at scrum half came in a 30-13 triumph against York three weeks later.

A fellow debutant that day was full back Steve Hampson, who was four years older than Edwards and who picked up a more standard signing-on fee of £4,500.

The pair were pals and enjoyed mutual respect, much of which came from the fact that both of them trained under the tutelage of Shaun's dad.

'I knew Shaun picked up more than £30,000 when he signed and I got just £4,500. There was a massive difference but, do you know what, it really didn't bother me,' said Hampson when I met him at his Orrell home. 'Shaun was an international in both codes. When we played against York I got man of the match and I was so pleased with that.'

Hampson's delight did not last long. There was no sponsor in place so a whip-round was instituted among directors, etc., for a man-of-the-match prize and Hampson was duly presented with £25 in notes, whose condition could only be described as 'very well used'.

'I'd like to thank you all,' said the courteous Hampson, starting a short address to the gathered throng when a hand appeared from behind his head and reached down to snatch the fivers out of his grasp.

'It was skipper Graeme West,' recalled Hampson, who supplemented his rugby earnings in the early years with a job as a drayman. 'He said, "That goes into the players' kitty."

'I was a bit gutted about that. Nobody told me. My first game after converting from rugby union, where you got no cash, and I had my money taken off me.'

The next couple of years were something of a whirl for Edwards, who became the youngest player to feature in a Challenge Cup Final at Wembley in the 19-6 defeat against Widnes in 1984 before securing his first Challenge Cup winners' medal the following year in a final generally regarded as the best in Wembley history.

True, Wigan's 28-24 victory against Hull did contain ten sumptuous tries and Wigan stand off Brett Kenny did enhance his reputation as the best player in the world at that time, but while it was a match of thrilling entertainment there was a measure of defensive frailty on show which also presented British rugby league in a dubious light.

No matter, Wigan had won at Wembley for the first time in 15 years and Edwards is convinced it was the catalyst for the great things to come.

'People don't believe me but I am sure there were 110,000 people in Wembley stadium that day.

'I think all the blokes on the turnstiles were getting a bit of dropsy. There were loads of people on the pitch at the end. There was a lad who was in my year at school and he slipped one of the stewards 30 quid or so for his yellow jacket and he is on all the Wigan photographs with the players.

'Wigan had signed Brett Kenny and John Ferguson and decent players such as Graeme West. It gave us a taste of what was to come.'

The work of Lindsay was also gathering pace. He was the leader, the public face of the club.

Lindsay was a self-made man via the success of his plant hire company and his business as a bookmaker. He knew how and when to gamble big. Most importantly, he knew when the odds were stacked in his favour, a crucial quality when you are trading in big-money sporting signings that invariably depend on an element of fortune.

He also possessed a natural charm, a welcoming demeanour and a disarming manner, all of which hid inner steel.

As Edwards reflected, 'A lot of people underestimate Maurice. They see this small and gentle guy and don't realise he used to be a boxer when he was a kid.

'He could run 100 yards in 11 seconds. He was a good athlete in his own right. He is not a person to be underestimated, a real competitor. He was the figurehead, the spokesperson, in the eyes of the players.'

He was also from Wigan, or to be exact Horwich, a small conurbation nestling on the lower slopes of Winter Hill on the West Pennine moors.

Why was that important?

Maybe you have to be from Wigan to properly understand the nature of its heritage. Some people perhaps still form their opinion of the area from George Orwell's 1937 book *The Road to Wigan Pier*, which cast the town in a bleak, depressive light. A town of hardship and deprivation.

A town surrounded by slag heaps and cloaked in industrial grime and which was even more graphically described in Martin Cruz Smith's novel *Rose* as 'at first sight looking more like smouldering ruins than a town'.

All that was true back then. After all, there were 133 collieries in the Wigan area in 1880, a figure that had fallen to four in 1980, the year Lindsay came to the Wigan club.

Bickershaw, Parsonage, Parkside and Golborne were the only ones remaining, the latter making national headlines in 1979 when ten miners were killed in an underground explosion, a story I helped cover as a young reporter on the local evening newspaper, the *Post & Chronicle*.

The point is that the area, despite being cleaner and greener than once it was, remains steeped in hard graft and working class values. Edwards himself came from a family of pitmen and famously marched with them during the miners' strike of 1984. Wigan was no place for prima donnas as it struggled to come to terms with the death throes of an industry, which had been its life-blood for more than a century.

The irony, however, was that as Prime Minister Margaret Thatcher and the Tory government were snatching away the jobs and livelihoods of Wigan's hardest men, the town's rugby team, packed with local talent and a pleasing balance of overseas players, were on the rise.

2

Five Yards Closer
to Wembley

A S IF fate had decreed the worst should be first, Wigan's epic
Challenge Cup run began on a slate-grey afternoon on 30 January
1988, on a pitch that resembled the hippo enclosure at Chester
Zoo.

Dour was not the word for Wigan's first-round struggle against
Bradford Northern at Central Park that Saturday.

Dull. Laborious. Attritional. They were all nearer the mark. Which
is why when Joe Lydon picked up the muddied ball and wiped it down the
front of his even more muddied jersey and squinted through the murk at
the white H-shape of the rugby posts in the distance he was about to do
all 9,825 spectators a favour.

To the right and out of the corner of his eye he caught a glimpse of the
back of referee Brian Simpson's black shirt as the official tried to placate a
bunch of angry Bradford players near the halfway line, who were arguing
that the penalty he had just awarded should not have been given.

Mr Simpson had waved play on originally when Shaun Edwards was
tripped by second row Karl Fairbank, only to change his decision and
signal the penalty a few seconds later after the intervention of a touch
judge.

With red mist distracting Bradford's players, Lydon computed the
geometry of the forthcoming kick in an instant and took an instinctive
step forward. All laws of mathematics in mud said, at close to 50m, it was
marginally out of range.

Like a thief with his rugby ball swag under his arm, Lydon took
another more furtive step towards those posts. It was the 39th minute of

a match that had not yet yielded a single point and quite possibly never would do so, such was the glue-pot nature of the surface and the even-steven arm wrestle of two packs of mud-caked forwards.

Lydon took another sly step forward. Then another. Five steps in all before placing the ball on the mud and sculpting an elevated platform with the heel of his boot from which to take the kick.

As Mr Simpson broke away from the huddle of protest, Bradford hooker Brian Noble strained to point out Lydon's sleight of foot.

'Ref, ref, it's not from there, the penalty was back here,' screamed Noble, pointing to the site of the dubious infringement. 'He's nicked nearly ten yards.'

Mr Simpson, resolve hardened by Bradford's continued protestations, waved Noble away and Lydon steadied himself to launch the kick which saw the ball tumble end over end before stalling in the heavy conditions and practically kissing the woodwork as it cleared the crossbar. Inch perfect. Lydon was always good at geometry.

Wigan were 2-0 up, a lead they clung to for the entire scoreless second half. And when Mr Simpson finally blew the full-time whistle to put an instantly forgettable game out of its misery the greatest Challenge Cup run in the history of the sport had begun, courtesy of Lydon's spot of spontaneous gamesmanship.

Or cheating, depending on your perspective. There is no doubting Noble's point of view.

'Every time I see Joe, despite his proper and nice image and his lovely persona and his high intelligence, I remind him that he's an absolute cheat,' said Noble, a hint of fire in his voice despite the mellowing of the passing years and the fact that he and Lydon, almost 30 years later, are the best of pals.

'I remember me spitting chips and saying to the ref, "Take it back, take it back." You were allowed to speak to the referee in those days but if you did it too much you were sent off. My protestations fell on deaf ears.'

Lydon, whose only other moments of note during the course of the match involved dislocating the same finger on his right hand three times, has lived comfortably enough with his little ruse. It does not keep him awake at night. Yet, as he stirred the clouds atop his full-fat latte in a London coffee house, he did at least manage to sound a tad contrite.

'I confess I cheated,' said Lydon. 'I walked forward four or five yards, just enough for the ball to fall over the bar and I know Brian has never forgiven me. I should get some credit for the confession, though, shouldn't I?'

Not on the eastern side of the Pennines. Not in those parts where, without Lydon's chicanery, Wigan would have been heading for a midweek replay at Odsal, a prospect as welcome as Mrs Thatcher in the Yorkshire coalfields at that time.

The fact that Lydon kick-started, literally, Wigan's golden era was somehow appropriate.

For a start he is a Wiganer born and bred, hailing from the Pemberton suburb of the town, a player who came through the familiar route of the amateur ranks, playing for the renowned St Patrick's amateur club before being snapped up by Widnes in their heyday of the early 1980s.

'Snapped up' sounds dramatic. In a way it was. Dramatic and a shade clandestine.

Lydon the teenager, as was common at that time, was playing rugby league on a Sunday and rugby union on a Saturday and had been selected for the England schoolboy rugby union tour to Zimbabwe when Widnes coach Dougie Laughton offered him professional terms just before Widnes were due to play Hull in the 1982 Challenge Cup Final.

'It was a little underhand in a way but with no malice,' recalled Lydon. 'I remember Dougie rang me up and he said, "If you let me announce the signing and you don't go to Zimbabwe I'll play you at Wembley against Hull." I said I'm going on tour and I don't think I'm ready to play. He said, "Trust me, you are."

'In the end I went on the tour and waited until I came back to announce it and I was almost excommunicated from the rugby union family for turning professional.'

He admits his own family also found it a tad difficult to separate loyalties, especially two years later when he was at Wembley, destroying Wigan in the 1984 Challenge Cup Final at the age of 20, scoring two 75-yard tries that earned him the Lance Todd Trophy as man of the match.

It was the first time Wigan had returned to Wembley since 1970.

'There were three Wiganers playing for Widnes; me, Andy Gregory and Keiron O'Loughlin,' said Lydon. 'When I scored my second try "Greg" came up to me and swung me round to face the Wigan end. We were pretty pumped.

'There had been quite a lot of banter beforehand. Keiron scored one try and I scored two so there was a bit of animosity but to be honest I think people in Wigan were quite pleased just to go back to Wembley after so long. Me and Andy were the youngest in the team so weren't really frowned upon.'

Ironically, Lydon learned a lesson that day from Widnes coach Vince Karalius, one which was to become a mantra in the Wigan dressing room in years to come.

'In the changing rooms he said, "I don't want anyone waving to friends and family when you come out of the tunnel. Nobody waves." He said "Let

Wigan wave, we are coming to win. After we've won I'll stay here until it goes dark and you can wave to as many people as you want.'"

It was typical Karalius, a man nicknamed the 'Wild Bull of the Pampas' in his playing days for Widnes, St Helens and Great Britain by the Australian press in reference to his resemblance to the Argentine boxer Luis Angel Firpo, who had knocked world heavyweight champion Jack Dempsey out of the ring back in 1923.

Karalius, who had served three years at Central Park as coach between 1976 and 1979, possessed a fearsome reputation as a strong runner and destructive tackler.

Yet when Lydon and several team-mates returned to the team hotel the morning after their triumph, still in Wembley suits and sporting jackhammer hangovers, Karalius was waiting for them, refreshed and invigorated from a good night's sleep after a job well done.

'Come on, we're off to thank the Lord,' he proclaimed.

And with that he bundled the entire bunch into a taxi and headed off to the nearest Catholic church for morning Mass.

Lydon, in particular, had much to give thanks for, considering that year he also won the sport's most coveted individual honour, the Man of Steel, plus the Division One player and young player of the year awards.

Lydon was happy at Widnes. Why wouldn't he be? This was the club that had been to eight Wembley finals in nine years and won four of them. There was a team spirit, a camaraderie, a pleasing mix of youth and seasoned professionals, some of whom, such as Mick Adams, took it upon themselves to let the laid-back, carefree, fun-loving Lydon know what rugby league was really about.

After one defeat in which Lydon made a couple of crucial mistakes Adams took him aside.

'Play like that again and I can't pay my mortgage,' said Adams.

For the first time in a career that thus far had been focused almost exclusively on fun it registered with Lydon that rugby league was a job. A serious job, one which paid the bills and determined the futures of families.

Yet Lydon might have stayed at Widnes for the rest of his career if he had not received a telephone call one Thursday afternoon in 1986.

'How much would it take to bring you to Wigan?' said the man's voice on the other end of the line, without revealing his identity.

'Widnes won't sell me,' said Lydon, a tad affronted by the caller's presumptuous tone.

'They just have done,' replied the caller, who turned out to be Wigan director Jack Robinson.

And so they had. Without consulting Lydon. Without as much as a heads-up that his hometown club were interested.

What prompted the transfer? The first straight cash deal in excess of £100,000 in rugby league history was clearly a temptation the Widnes board could not resist. Yet the deal had significance beyond the folding stuff.

It confirmed Wigan were prepared to spend big to lure the top players. They were ready to embrace the dream. And in many ways it also heralded the changing of the guard, Widnes heading south on the rugby league compass of success with Wigan's needle sliding in a distinctly northerly direction.

It all left Lydon a shade bewildered, not to mention feeling a little hard done by.

'I was disappointed,' he admitted. 'I enjoyed my time at Widnes and we had some quality players there. But Tony Myler and myself were put up for sale mainly for ground improvements. I was told the money would go into health and safety to build a wall. That was the reason. It kind of grounds you when you are sold for a pile of bricks.'

Before you ask, Lydon never saw a penny of the £110,000 fee, a sum which was underwritten personally by Robinson, so desperate was he to land his man.

'There was an agreement at the time that if you played for a club for five years you would be eligible for five per cent of the transfer fee if you had not asked for the transfer,' he explained. 'I had been at Widnes four and a half years. I never got anything.'

Yet Lydon was home and the memory of a chance encounter following his Wembley triumph with Widnes helped convince him that the transfer, despite his initial disappointment, was for the best.

He had been dropped off by the Widnes team coach in Wigan town centre and caught a local bus to the Lydon family home in Pemberton. Still in his suit from Wembley, kit bag over his shoulder, he stepped off the bus into the path of an elderly local man who was waiting at the bus stop.

'He looked me up and down,' said Lydon. 'And without a trace of a smile said, "Are yer sure yer in the reet place, lad?"'

He wasn't then. He was now.

3

Lowe Intensity

I F THE cash paid for Lydon demonstrated Wigan were serious in their pursuit of the game's most prestigious trophies then there were two more inspired appointments hugely instrumental in accelerating that quest.

One was Ellery Hanley, who arrived from Bradford Northern in a £150,000 deal, which also included Steve Donlan and Phil Ford moving the other way in part exchange.

The other was Graham Lowe, a strong-willed Kiwi who had coached New Zealand and arrived at Central Park in 1986 to replace the joint coaching team of Colin Clarke and Alan McInnes, who had delivered Challenge Cup success in 1985, plus Lancashire Cup and John Player Cup triumphs. In 1986, however, Wigan lost to Castleford in the Challenge Cup quarter-final and that was goodnight for the double act.

Lindsay and the board wanted the best. They craved the hard-edged leadership which seemed to be the norm at the top clubs in the southern hemisphere. Lowe fitted the bill.

His first match in charge was a pre-season friendly at Workington, a nondescript, instantly forgettable encounter made memorable for the strangest reason. Lowe said nothing on the team bus on the 125-mile journey to Cumbria, not a word in the changing rooms at half-time nor full time and even less, if it were possible, on the way back to Wigan.

He sat there, silent, deep and inscrutable, with a jaw like granite as the usual banter and high spirits swirled around him on the team coach.

The next day at training, like a lion-tamer unleashing his whip, he discovered his tongue.

'I have seen how you lot operate,' he growled, before proceeding to deliver his considered, no-holds-barred opinion on the various factions comprising the Central Park personnel. It was a red-light warning to some. To Shaun Edwards it was everything he wanted to hear.

'He said, "I have got some guys who are pretty intense and some guys who, let's say, take it pretty lightly,"' recalled Edwards. '"From now on every fucking player will be intense. There is no more clowning around in the dressing room. From now on we will behave like a professional, organised outfit, which is here for one thing: to win."

'It was all right for me because I was already like that. In fact, me and Ellery looked at each other and said, "Great."'

Training sessions became more focused with Lowe insisting the players wore their full cherry and white match kit instead of the assortment of dishevelled training attire that had sufficed before. The emphasis was on discipline and professionalism and precision. Instantly, the Central Park corridors echoed to Lowe's favourite mantra, 'Practice does not make perfect. Perfect practice does.'

'He pushed us viciously fitness-wise and if you weren't in the right position at training, he used to shout to get the whole team to run around the pitch as a punishment,' said Edwards.

'You didn't want to stand in the wrong position for two seconds because it would be, "Fucking hell, you're in the wrong position, get round that pitch." So we'd all be running round the pitch and if it were you who was wrong all the rest would be having a crack at you, shouting, "You stupid prick."

'I think he wanted to set out his stall when he first came. He was saying, "This is a new era. You have to be working hard." He did mellow as he went along and you could have a beer and a chat with him in the Boar's Head pub where he used to go with his missus.

'He was a very, very good big-game coach and I could imagine him being fantastic with an international team. He made you feel like you could run through brick walls. Made you really, really intense. He had an edge to him. You were shitting yourself about losing.'

Yet lose is exactly what Wigan did in the first round proper of the Challenge Cup in 1987, beaten 10-8 by Oldham on a cold and calamitous day at windswept Watersheddings, a venue with a name alone that is enough to make a spectator pull on thermals and pack a woolly scarf.

Crucially, however, Lowe delivered the league championship that year, Wigan's first for 27 years, as he guided the team on a run of stupefying proportions.

Between February and October, Lowe's team won a record 29 matches in a row; 20 in Division One, three Premiership Trophy games, four Lancashire Cup ties, one Charity Shield Final and then the big one, a World Club Challenge Final.

That last match, in which Wigan beat Manly-Warringah 8-2 in a brutal contest without a single try in front of a crowd of 36,895 at Central Park, was the first time an English club side had beaten a team of Australians at rugby league since the 1978 Kangaroo tour.

It was tangible evidence that something irresistibly intoxicating was stirring in British rugby league's heartland. But Wembley glory remained an overriding ambition. Wembley was the showpiece final, even more than world championship matches against Manly. It was Wembley that sent pictures advertising the beauty and the brutality of the sport whirring around the planet.

True, there had not been much beauty about that 2-0 Challenge Cup first round win in the mud against Bradford in 1988, which owed its outcome to Lydon's self-confessed cheating.

There was not exactly perfect harmony in the Wigan squad, either, considering a training ground bust-up had manifested itself in a feud between Lowe and captain Hanley, reported as a 'personality rift', which saw the best player in the world sidelined for seven weeks, missing all the early rounds of that cup run and finding himself on the transfer list at a record £225,000.

With club skipper Graeme West not guaranteed his place at the time, it led to Lowe handing the captaincy to Edwards. Lowe made another shrewd move. With a harsh winter meaning poor and heavy pitches were the norm he ordered the team to train in the mud.

While most sides were moving inside into sports halls or on to artificial surfaces, Wigan were squelching their way to train on the muddiest, stickiest training pitches available.

The strength and stamina such training conveyed helped them fight back from 10-0 down to beat Leeds 34-14 on a quagmire at Central Park and then saw them overcome Salford on another mud-heap in the semi-final at Burnden Park, Bolton, the latter game seeing the return of Hanley from his feud-related exile following a reconciliation meeting with Lowe at his Shevington home.

'Graham's idea to train on the mud was key. Our legs were used to this heavy, gluey stuff and it helped us to outlast teams,' recalled Edwards.

'Graham was so determined to win the cup. He would say, "If we don't win I'm not going to any parties. I'm here for one thing, winning, nothing else."

'It was quite a traumatic time really with Ellery's bust-up. Ellery and Graeme West had been sharing the captaincy but Ellery was the main captain.

'Ellery and I had always been really tight. He was like a brother to me and we remain like that to this day.

'I was a bit uncomfortable taking the job as captain because I was only 21 and there were all these superstar players. But I was asked to do it.'

There are some things in life a sportsman just cannot turn down. For a rugby league player, captaining Wigan at Wembley is one of them.

4

It Started With a Kiss

CHARISMATIC. Determined. Skilful. Magical.
A special player with special banter. Generous to a fault.
A cocky little shit.

Just some of the descriptions used by team-mates to describe the mercurial and enigmatic Andy Gregory.

As Wigan prepared for a Wembley final in 1988 against Halifax, Gregory, or 'Greg' as he was known, was not the sort to sit with headphones on in the changing room, staring at the floor and ruminating over every potential scenario before kick-off.

Introspection was not in Gregory's make-up.

Gregory, who had joined Wigan for £130,000 from Warrington in 1986, was much more likely to be seeking an intense-free zone, in the boot room or the physio's room, having a laugh and telling jokes with physio Keith Mills and players such as Ged Byrne and Joe Lydon.

There is no doubt Gregory, who played in eight Wembley finals for Wigan and Widnes, winning seven of them, and six Ashes series against Australia, is one of the finest scrum halves ever to play rugby league, even if he was turned down as a youngster by Wigan because they deemed him too small.

Perhaps that instilled in him the feisty combination of iron will and devil-may-care attitude which saw him first visit Wembley in a dream debut season for Widnes as a 19-year-old in 1981, beating Hull Kingston Rovers 18-9.

The story behind that victory said much about Gregory's resilience, the scrum half having been plagued with raging toothache the night before the game, so painfully debilitating that the club doctor insisted he went to hospital where the molar was removed.

It meant Gregory managed just a couple of hours of sleep that disrupted night, but it did not prevent him turning in a brilliant playmaking display which saw him score a try between the posts to clinch the victory in the second half.

Yet among those rugby league veterans who fought alongside and against him it is the force of his personality which surfaces time after time in their recollections, powerful, relentless and frothy, like waves breaking on Bondi Beach.

They talk of his wit and his banter and his spiky, strutting demeanour as much as his ability to deliver the late, killer pass.

The stories are many and varied.

Such as the time Joe Lydon had ordered a new leather settee and chairs from Leatherland in Liverpool but was experiencing problems with delivery as the driver was struggling to locate his address.

Lydon was late for training so was forced to leave home before it was delivered, only to find a Leatherland furniture van on the Central Park car park when he arrived. Somewhat vexed, he hurried across to the van and was remonstrating with the driver for not turning up at his house when Gregory pushed open the changing room window, leaned out and shouted across the forecourt, 'Joe, what have I told you about taking suites from strange men?'

Sports teams benefit from such characters. In environments in which big egos and even larger insecurities are in constant collision, humour often clears a way to uncovering the truth without causing offence.

The targets of Gregory's humour were mostly anybody within his line of sight.

Most players called Edwards 'Gizmo', or 'Giz' for short. Gregory took to calling him 'Youngest Ever' because that was how he was invariably described in newspapers, having been the youngest to play at Wembley in the 1984 final.

'He would take the mick out of Shaun,' recalled Bill Hartley, who was the team's fitness and sprint coach and worked closely with all the players on an individual basis.

'He had a sharp brain on him and he was tough. He was ahead of the game, too clever for others to react. His thinking on the way he played was on a different level to some who played with him. But you wouldn't want to referee him, he never shut up at them.'

Huddersfield's Billy Thompson perhaps bore the brunt of Gregory's acidity more than most. Thompson was arguably the most colourful match official the game has seen, a man who regularly refereed the Challenge Cup Final and was happy to inform everyone that he received just £14 less tax in 1971, £20 less tax in 1978 and £50 in 1984 for the

Widnes v Wigan final, although his wife apparently was required to pay for her own ticket.

His most controversial decision was sending off Leeds captain Syd Hynes in the 1971 final for an alleged headbutt on Leigh's Alex Murphy. Hynes always maintained his innocence, insisting he never touched Murphy and that Thompson, on the advice of one of his touch judges, made a mistake.

It was Thompson's authoritative style and his ostentatious signals that often antagonised both sets of supporters, so much so that he always refused to leave his car in any space on the club car park which proclaimed 'Reserved for the referee' on the basis that he would rather the fans did not know where to find him and he preferred returning to his motor with all tyres intact.

'You park there and I'll park in your spot,' he used to tell officious stewards who tried to insist he took up his designated place.

Yet on the pitch Thompson was a forerunner to the Steve Ganson, Stuart Cummings and John Holdsworth school of refereeing, an accomplished communicator who respected the players and indulged in on-field banter when appropriate.

He also used his bottomless well of rugby league stories to fund a lucrative post-rugby career on the after-dinner speaking circuit, where he would lift the lid in pithy fashion on the humour and irreverence at the game's coal-face, such as the time Dennis Wheatley, a hard, uncompromising prop with Doncaster, Hunslet and Castleford, floored an opponent with a left hook immediately in front of him.

'Why did you hit him then?' asked a perplexed Thompson. 'He wasn't even looking your way.'

'That's exactly the time to hit him, Billy,' came the reply as Wheatley trudged by on his inevitable route to the changing rooms.

Thompson, however, was no match for the sharp-mouthed Gregory and Joe Lydon recalls one classic encounter.

Following a spate of dubious decisions Gregory approached Thompson and said, 'If I called you an effing bastard would you send me off?'

Billy replied, 'Yes I would. There's no place for that sort of language aimed at the referee.'

'If I think it to myself, though, there is nothing you could do, is there?' said Gregory with a smirk.

Billy considered for a moment and then said, 'No, I don't suppose so.'

'Well, then, I think you're an effing bastard,' said Gregory and trotted swiftly past him.

Such altercations earned Gregory the respect of his team-mates almost as much as his brilliant performances, although some viewed Gregory with a wariness bordering on trepidation, regardless of whether they were youngsters or established internationals.

Everything is funny as long as it is happening to someone else is probably the best way of describing how Denis Betts remembers the Gregory factor.

'You never really looked Greg in the eye,' said Betts. 'You always hoped that he got you to help him to back up on somebody else because then you were in his gang. He had that little man sharpness mentality about him where, no matter what, he had a go at you.

'He had small man disease and he was a cocky little shit. Sharp and witty. He had grown up on scrapyards and around those kind of blokes.'

He could be moody too.

One day at training the entire squad were warming up, running around the perimeter of a soccer pitch when they spotted Gregory slowly trudging around the centre circle in the middle of the pitch all by himself.

'He had a real monk on that day,' recalled Hartley. 'He had a strop on and he could go that way.'

Out on the pitch, the banter, the confidence, the spikiness, the will to win all combined, however, to make him arguably the most proficient exponent of creative scrum half play the British game has ever seen.

In 1988 Nicky Kiss, in particular, witnessed that close up as Wigan's long-established hooker.

Kiss was a Central Park stalwart, the son of Hungarian refugees who had arrived in the UK at the time of the Hungarian Uprising in 1956. He claims he never realised rugby league was a professional sport before signing for Wigan on his 16th birthday after being entranced by the 'beguiling' sight of the Central Park turf newly mown and glistening under the floodlights.

Down the years he played with such well-renowned Wigan figures as Bill Ashurst and Green Vigo and made a decent living to go alongside his plumbing business in Saddleworth. In truth, he would have played for nothing. He simply adored rugby league and everything that went with it. The training. The camaraderie. The discipline. He loved the fans too and never missed an opportunity to converse with them. On the pitch or in the bar or on the touchline. It did not really matter.

And they loved him, even though he was not one of the superstars. He was not in the Hanley, Edwards, Gregory and Lydon class of organising generals. He was one of the foot soldiers and proud to be so ranked, along with others such as Brian Case, Ian Potter and Shaun Wane.

For them rugby league, even in a side as successful as Wigan, was foremost about the essential donkey work, heaving their considerable weight up the middle time after time, especially in the heavy mud of midwinter, setting up the platforms for the more creative exponents of the sport outside them to exploit. It was a tough, uncompromising, unheralded job, but they relished doing it.

Kiss, when he wasn't plying his expertise as a hooker at a time when the scrum half was required to put the ball in straight and hookers actually had to strike with a boot to win it, was the man who tracked their progress, slotting in at dummy half, collecting the ball, passing it on to the creators, or sometimes darting through himself.

It required excellent ball-handling skills, a sense of rhythm and timing and a sharp rugby league instinct. A foot soldier with brains, ambition and vision, one might say.

Even so, while his name may have been a headline writer's dream, rarely did it appear in oversized print.

His relationship with Gregory was perhaps best illustrated by one typical cameo from that 1988 season, although first let Steve Hampson, who used to room with Gregory and was his best pal for a decade before the pair fell out spectacularly, set the scene.

'Some players really got it in the back of the neck from him on the pitch when they made a mistake,' recalled Hampson. 'He would give them some grief. Greg's the only player in the world who never made a mistake on the pitch. It was never his fault when he threw a bad pass, it was the guy who should have been coming on at 100mph. That was typical Greg. We used to take the piss out of him about it after the game.'

During one particularly close-fought match Wigan were on the attack and Kiss had struck a pleasing rhythm in the dummy half role with a luxurious wealth of talent lined up outside him. He could spin the ball to Hanley or Edwards or Gregory. Rather like shopping for a motor and choosing between a Maserati, a Ferrari or an Aston Martin.

At a break in play Gregory sidled up to Kiss and hissed in his ear, 'Don't give it to Ellery any more, give it to me because I can do something with it, other than just running with it.'

At the next play-the-ball, Kiss, trusting his positional sense and his rugby instinct, did the opposite, flipping the ball left to Hanley, who was immediately tackled without making much ground.

'Greg absolutely screamed at me,' recalled Kiss, deleting the inevitable expletives. 'He gave me a right rocket. He said, "It was on down my side of the pitch. It was on."'

Thirty seconds later Gregory again was screaming for the ball. This time Kiss went the other way and passed to Shaun Edwards, who he deemed to be in the best position. Again nothing came of it.

'Greg was spitting venom at me again, bawling, "What are you doing? Give it to me, give it to me every time I ask,"' said Kiss.

'At that point I lost it. I told him if he spoke like that to me again I was going to rip his head right off on the pitch there and then. I was so pissed off with his attitude.'

Needless to say the threat went unheeded. A couple of plays later the air was blue once more as Gregory screamed even more manically for the ball and this time, with a resigned flick of his arms, Kiss gave it to him.

'To be honest I thought he had no bloody chance,' said Kiss. 'But a couple of jinks and a couple of dummies later and he is walking in right under the sticks.'

As they jogged back to the halfway line Gregory ran over and jumped on Kiss from behind, ruffling his hair, enveloping him in a big bear hug and shouting, 'Brilliant, that was brilliant,' before adding, 'Does that mean you are not going to rip my head off?'

Kiss just shook his head and chuckled and replied, 'No Andy, you carry on, mither me as much as you want.'

That high-octane combination of sharp brain, lacerating tongue, simmering aggression, unwavering confidence, undisputed brilliance and cussed humour perhaps explained to some degree the personal problems, including drink and matters of the heart, which beset Gregory when his career finished.

But in 1988 the story was not about the 20 pints a day he subsequently admitted to downing as his life turned from glory days to daily haze.

It was about Gregory, the 5ft 5in superhero from Ince-in-Makerfield whose ability to organise those around him and deliver the ball with precision to line-breaking runners was a match-winning talent on a weekly basis.

Edwards, who dovetailed so astutely with Gregory in the half back positions, has just one regret about their partnership.

'We never really had a good crack at the Aussies for Great Britain when we were both in good form. In 1988 I was injured, in 1990 my form was poor and in 1992 Greg got injured,' said Edwards.

'He was brilliant at doing the runaround movement and hitting the right option off it. He had a good turn of pace too when his mind was right and he was fit and his weight was down and he was very explosive off the mark.

'And he was the finest exponent of a delayed pass in 120 years of rugby league. He would go straight up to the line and double pump it with perfect timing. I've not seen anyone come close to him. When he left I tried to copy him although I would never say I was as good as him at doing it.'

The evidence of that delayed pass, in particular, is there for all to see in that Wembley final against Halifax on a sunny afternoon when the full extent of the value added by Lowe's arrival was revealed to the nation.

Standing head and shoulders above the rest, metaphorically, not physically of course, was Gregory.

Wigan's first try came from a brilliant side-stepping break by the little man, who sent Edwards scampering away and when he was caught five yards from the line big Kiwi centre Kevin Iro had the easiest task of barging over from the play-the-ball.

There is only one word to describe Gregory's part in the second try: genius.

He ran straight at Halifax tackler Neil James, took the tackle and then flipped the short pass one-handed around his opponent's back to Dean Bell who fed Henderson Gill for a try in the corner, sparking the wing man's famous hip-swinging, arm-twirling, disco-style celebration.

Already the gulf in class was obvious and compounded when Kevin Iro went in for his second try and Lydon received a pass from the pirouetting Edwards to dive over under the posts.

The long floated pass from Gregory which followed and which landed with inch-perfect accuracy in the arms of Tony Iro for the next try doubtless clinched Gregory the Lance Todd Trophy in a match whose defining image was still to come.

When it did, just a minute or so later, it was a piece of intuitive magic, the sort which became Wigan's calling card over the next decade. Ironically, it emanated from coach Graham Lowe's demand for precise structure in all areas of the pitch.

Thus, from the Halifax kick-off following Tony Iro's touchdown, the ball was fielded low down by Gregory, who immediately fed it left to Joe Lydon who set off on a diagonal, arcing run across the pitch.

That adhered precisely to Lowe's geographical demands. But within Lowe's structure there was always scope for options. One of which was for the player with the ball to dummy and go himself. That was exactly the option chosen by Lydon, who took a step off his left foot, opened up the throttle, sped by two would-be tacklers and galloped elegantly into acres of Wembley space.

He was ten metres from the left touchline with the cover defence scrambling and Wigan players charging up in support. The chances are the Lydon surge would have made it all the way to the line but in those days it took a deaf, a foolish or a very brave man to ignore Ellery Hanley screaming for the ball.

So Lydon swung his hips and threw the ball inside to Hanley and then something quite preposterously brilliant occurred.

With Halifax winger Martin Meredith bearing down on him Hanley suddenly changed direction. Instead of taking the tiger line to the touchdown, on which almost certainly he would have been caught, he started to crab sideways, running at an angle so he could turn his head to see his pursuer and, most importantly, use that trademark left-arm fend to keep the tackler at bay.

His jig inside was a considerably longer route to the line but it was a short, sharp lesson in the art of improvisation and evasion where running rugby was concerned. Before eventually touching down under the posts, he even collided with the supporting Edwards who was in space and calling for the ball on his outside. In truth, there was more chance of Edwards walking on the moon than receiving the ball at that particular moment.

'Ellery, as usual, had not one thought of passing it to anyone else,' said Edwards, chuckling at the memory.

'We laugh about it all the time, Ellery and me. When he went to Leeds I became top try-scorer and I tell him it was because he used to get half of my tries before. We were pushing each other out of the way trying to get to the ball first. But I learned that great support line, which cuts the pitch down to size, off him.

'Warren Gatland, the Wales rugby union coach, told me he had watched me and Ellery and said it was exactly the support lines the great number sevens in rugby union run, like the great All Black Josh Kronfeld, when they go to clear the ruck.

'Ellery's running style was incredible. He had a great left-hand fend and was magical on his feet.'

Halifax did manage consolation tries from Tony Anderson and Neil James but Gregory rounded off an imperious performance, which included a drop goal and resulted in him winning the Lance Todd Trophy, with another slick dummy that initiated a break to put in Dean Bell for another touchdown.

Yet before Wigan had completed their 32-12 triumph, Edwards, the youngest winning Challenge Cup captain, had one more duty to perform before he picked up the cup. A duty which shone a light on the heart and soul of Wigan, the club and the town, at that moment.

With six minutes to go and no warning Edwards walked off the field.

He looked at coach Lowe and muttered something about a tight hamstring, but there was nothing wrong with his body. Edwards knew Lowe was a coach who did not always use his full complement of replacements and still squirming with frustration on the bench, yearning to be part of his first and only Challenge Cup Final, was the skipper's good friend and fellow Wiganer Ged Byrne.

Byrne jumped up from the bench faster than he ever ran up his ladder as a window cleaner after hanging up his boots and, according to Edwards, 'flattened three Halifax players he was so pumped'.

Shaun Wane, another proud Wiganer, who a quarter of a century later was to become a respected head coach of Wigan Warriors, was also introduced from the bench two minutes later for Ian Potter, at the insistence of Edwards, for his only Challenge Cup Final action as a player, although as coach he was to guide Wigan to their 16-0 Challenge Cup triumph against Hull in 2013.

True, the game was won, but the selfless nature of Edwards's gesture in sparking those substitutions was still impressive. It is a gesture Wane remembers with gratitude to this day.

'I was a bit upset with Graham Lowe for not putting me on earlier when we had won the game,' said Wane. 'But he didn't understand what it meant to a Wigan lad to get on the field.

'Shaun knew, he is a Wiganer and I will never forget what he did for me. I will always admire him for that. I was very disappointed at the time to get just three minutes or so. I was happy I got on and got a medal but I don't think I genuinely earned it.'

Nevertheless, he climbed the famous old Wembley steps proudly with the rest of the team as Edwards accepted the cup from Douglas McClelland, Australian High Commissioner to the United Kingdom, and shook it towards the Wigan supporters.

It was seven years before Edwards would repeat the feat as captain, the job he never sought, but as he reasoned, 'I must have done a half-decent job because we won the cup.'

All that was left was for Wigan's players to soak up the ambience of Wembley as winners, something every player who has performed there remembers for the rest of their days.

Nicky Kiss, for one, would concur with such a sentiment. Kiss could not tell you where he keeps his three Challenge Cup winners' medals nor probably who scored the tries on the day, yet, almost 30 years later, every moment of that celebration is etched on his memory.

'I loved soaking in all the emotion and looking at all the different faces,' he said. 'I'd had a good time. We'd done the job. I fancied a fag.'

He shouted into the ocean of cherry and white, 'Anybody got a tab?'

Immediately the Wembley sky was filled with 30 or more cigarettes raining down like ticker tape.

Kiss picked one up and put it to his lips before gesturing again to the crowd while wiggling the top joint of his thumb.

'Excuse me, anyone got a lighter?'

You've guessed it. Half a dozen lighters thudded all around him.

'I loved that interaction with the fans,' said Kiss. 'That was better than all the medals. I still get excited thinking about it now. It was a massive milestone in my life.'

Kiss took a deep drag and sucked in the euphoria and the enormity of the moment. There was one more ritual, however, for Kiss to undertake, one he had first performed in 1985 when Wigan beat Hull.

'I never found out where to go for a butty or anything like that at Wembley,' said Kiss. 'Every time I was there I just remember supping a bottle and a half of champagne in the bath and then wandering out on to the pitch pissed when everyone had left and shouting at the top of my voice so I could hear it echo all around the ground.

'We won the cup…we won the cup…we won the cup…we won the cup!'

5

The Pecking Order

WITH big-money signings on the field, cups and medals filling the trophy cabinet, average attendances steadily rising and Wembley once more the warmest of memories, a feel-good factor was returning to the Central Park terraces.

Yet something even more important was building in the changing rooms.

A winning culture, impregnated with loyalty and excellence, not dissimilar from the one that created the Boot Room mentality at Anfield in the days of the great Bill Shankly and beyond.

That had produced the 'Liverpool way', a template instructing coaches down the years, many of them former players who would sit and chat tactics on rickety chairs and tables while stripping bare problems and sipping the odd glass of gin or Guinness as well as instructing Liverpool managers of the future in the values of the football club.

Bob Paisley, Joe Fagan, Ronnie Moran, Roy Evans, Kenny Dalglish. They all participated in preserving and nurturing the Shankly legacy. It brought success and stability for the best part of 35 years and has gone down in football folklore.

The 'Wigan way' was not instituted formally, nor by a cohort of coaches, more by the leading players and at its heart was the notion that entrance to the first team changing room was by invitation only.

Thus there were precocious stars such as Denis Betts who played more than 40 first team matches before he was allowed to use the first team changing room on training nights.

'I got changed in the second team room until Graham Lowe invited me in and gave me a peg,' recalled Betts. 'And if he hadn't told me where I could sit I wouldn't have sat there. I looked round and saw faces that to me said, "You think you can sit next to me?" Sport is different now, you can't do that sort of thing, but then it was an unwritten rule that you had to be invited in. You had to be given the right to go straight in. I got given a space next to Shaun Wane next to the boot room.

'We all understood where we stood in the pecking order. You walked into the changing rooms and they had "Millionaires' corner" and you knew you hadn't to sit there. In that group you had Ellery and Andy Goodway and Andy Gregory and Shaun Edwards. There was a serious point to it. Everybody knew where they sat within that group.'

It was a policy that remained in place for the entirety of Wigan's golden era, one that had the additional bonus of ensuring the reserves and Alliance team youngsters arrived at training on time.

By chance the boot room was situated inside the first team changing room, which posed a tricky problem for any unpunctual youngsters while providing mischievous merriment for some first-teamers.

'If you didn't get to training early enough they wouldn't let you into the first team dressing room to get your boots,' Mick Cassidy recalled.

'So if training started at 6pm you had to be there at 5pm to make sure. You would knock on the door and they would ask who it was. They would then ask how many first team games you had played. They'd just think of a number that you could never have achieved and then say, "No, you can't come in."

'The architects of that were Andy Gregory and Andy Platt. It was all done in a jokey manner. You knew that you had really gained their respect when you were let into the dressing room and then you were treated just like one of the other fellas.'

Psychologists these days would pin a label on such actions. Something incomprehensible doubtless, such as 'Value-based performance measurement system accountability'.

Others might view it as a form of bullying. In reality, it was much more simple. Respect. That was the nugget at its core.

The sort of respect Joe Lydon had paid his team-mates when he first joined from Widnes following his £110,000 transfer.

Despite the record size of the fee and the fact that Lydon had already won a Lance Todd Trophy and was a Man of Steel winner he was concerned about upsetting any of his new team-mates by entering the first team changing room and sitting in someone else's position.

Lydon explained, 'When I had signed years before at Widnes I didn't know where to sit or where to go.

'I remember going straight into the first team and walking into the changing rooms and feeling uncomfortable that I had taken a shirt without really justifying it.'

So on his first training day at Wigan he arrived early, before any of the other players, armed with a screw, a screwdriver and a clothes peg of his own that he had bought from a hardware shop.

'I screwed it into the Wigan changing room wall, two pegs round from the door. That way I made sure people knew I wasn't taking anybody else's peg.'

It was a simple act, quaint in its sensitivity, but the forethought and humility at the heart of that story go a long way to explaining the secret of Wigan's success.

So does the experience of Martin Dermott who, as a teenager, did not possess the awareness of the screwdriver-packing Lydon and whose first match in the first team changing rooms only served to prove just that.

Dermott walked through the door, sat down, started to get changed and then saw Brett Kenny, the Australian stand off who at that time was arguably the best rugby league player in the world, standing by the far wall staring at him with a perplexed expression.

For years Dermott had regarded Kenny as his sporting hero so was understandably a shade star-struck, a feeling which only heightened as Kenny began to walk across to him.

'He was the first player to come over to me and he immediately shook my hand,' said Dermott.

'He then said, "You are sitting in my place. Don't worry, you can stay where you are. You can stay there, but just for today." He was brilliant about it and laughed it off, but I was sat there with Brett Kenny's number six shirt on my peg for 20 minutes. It was surreal.

'I will always remember he made me feel at ease, though, and I tried to do the same thing with other players down the years. For such a high-ranking player, who was like a god to me, to come over and say, "How are you doing, are you all right?" even if I was sitting in his spot was impressive.'

The unwritten rule, however, was that respect was never dispensed cheaply. The most important credentials were not the size of a transfer fee but values such as trust and loyalty and total commitment, all of which were non-negotiable and required to be demonstrated.

The job of guardianship of the pecking order most often fell to Dean Bell, a New Zealander whose organisational skills were as renowned as his teak-hard toughness. He also watched the first team door like a hawk and was liable to pounce on anyone whose credentials were unproven.

A precocious Andy Farrell once found his clothes deposited in the shower when he inadvertently sat in Bell's place.

Another such victim was Neil Cowie, an all-purpose prop who registered on the Bell radar on his arrival from Rochdale.

'He had just signed and walked straight into the dressing room,' said Steve Hampson. 'Dean made him go into the second team changing room and said, "You've got to earn your respect here and your place in the first team changing room. We'll invite you in when we think you are ready." Three or four weeks later Dean invited Neil back in because he had proved himself out on the pitch.

'That happened to everybody. We all went through that process. I think that attitude was exclusive to Wigan at the time. You had to earn your peg.'

Not that anyone wanted one anywhere close to Hampson at the time.

Hampo, as he is universally known, was one of those sportsmen who struggled with the nervous turmoil, which invariably accompanies a big match in front of a packed crowd of paying customers.

Everyone deals with PMT, pre-match tension, differently. Andy Gregory would disappear into the physio's room to tell jokes and have a laugh with players such as Joe Lydon, Ged Byrne and Martin Dermott.

Lydon could not play a match on an empty stomach and no one took the first part of the aphorism on the training room wall, 'Eat big, train big, play big', more seriously. He was always eating, so much so that once famously he was spotted in the team line-up trotting in carefree fashion down the tunnel at Central Park moments before kick-off, cramming into his mouth a large pasty he had pilfered from the boardroom.

Hampson was the exact opposite. A worrier. The sort of player who Aussie coach Wayne Bennett might have had in mind when he said, 'Worry is like a rocking chair. It gives you something to do but gets you nowhere.'

Nerves consumed Hampson before a match. They led to him suffering bouts of projectile vomiting on the changing room floor, so spontaneous it meant those around him were advised to be careful where they left their boots.

Hampson can chuckle at the memory nowadays while reflecting on the paradox of a changing room where unity somehow thrived despite the presence of so many disparate forces.

'I was always quiet and never said owt in the changing room. I always had the same routine, put my left sock on, then my right and then throw up an hour before kick-off. We are all different and we never had an issue with the lads who wanted a laugh. They did it away from the rest of us, although occasionally you could hear them laughing and joking and taking the mickey out of each other.

'But we never had an issue with it. There was no backstabbing, no calling each other. We were all grown men and enjoyed each other's company. We were like brothers. We watched out for each other and watched each other's backs as well, on and off the pitch.'

6

The Silent Hit-Man

THERE was one man who didn't drink, never joked, rarely smiled and who seemed impervious to big-match tensions, but who retained the total respect and admiration of the Wigan dressing room. Ellery Cuthwyn Hanley.

Hanley did not lead his players out of the tunnel fist-pumping and cajoling in an attempt to exert them to higher levels of intensity.

He took slow, deliberate, powerful strides, like a general on his way to deliver a meaningful address. It was a walk of authority.

A walk that became something of a trademark in a 19-year career in which, as well as Wigan, he played for Bradford Northern, Balmain, Western Suburbs and Leeds before going on to coach Great Britain, St Helens and Doncaster.

A walk, too, that rarely ended up in the press conference room, even though he was captain for most of his time at Wigan and convention decrees that a captain's duty is to be the spokesperson for the team.

There is no doubt Hanley, born in Leeds of immigrant parents from St Kitts, was a complex character, a hard player and an uncompromising self-contained individual of few words, but he was also one who possessed the ability to communicate the beguiling nature of rugby league in deeds like no other.

The following story concerning former Wigan Warriors full back Kris Radlinski is a case in point.

Radlinski, who made 322 appearances for the club, including winning the Lance Todd Trophy in 2002, and went on to become Wigan's general manager, refers to his 'magical childhood memories' of Hanley in his autobiography, *Simply Rad*. Radlinski admits he was not blessed with natural rugby league ability, just a desire to work hard and a passion for the game which, as a schoolboy, was nurtured by watching Hanley in action at Central Park.

Radlinski worshipped Hanley, literally. He created a shrine to him in a shed at the bottom of his family's garden where he would lift weights and train for hours as a teenaged rugby hopeful while looking at pictures of his idol.

Even his class speech at the town's St Thomas More school was an exhaustively researched study of Hanley.

That is the effect sportsmen capable of extraordinary feats can have on impressionable youngsters with dreams in their head and the ability and desire to make them reality. That is why, like it or not, successful sportsmen carry the weight of responsibility as role models for the next generation.

Some carry that burden lightly. Others less so.

Hanley's influence was undeniable. A brilliant player without question and an accomplished leader, too, which is why the following pages are sprinkled with examples of how his presence raised the expectations and standards of those around him.

In fact, when Radlinski retired in 2006, following a career of outstanding service, he used the difficult interregnum months coming to terms with the dying of his sporting light by hand-writing his memoir.

There was no intention to publish at the time but when it was finished he had three copies printed, two of them leather-bound. He gave one to his dad John, and sent the other to Hanley, who he had never played with and never even met apart from in his garden shed dreams.

It was Radlinski's way of saying thank you to the man who, albeit unwittingly, had inspired him to realise his potential. It is a heartwarming story and one that paints sport and rugby league in a favourable light.

Hanley's reaction to receiving that gift is also illuminating in that, in one of his rare interviews in 2008, he described it as 'the greatest thing that has ever happened to me'.

Respect from his peers, it seems, was Hanley's driving force, more so than medals and trophies or Great Britain caps.

'I was speechless and struggled to explain to him how much his gesture meant to me,' Hanley told rugby league journalist Richard de la Riviere in a magazine interview brokered by Doncaster, a club he coached for a total of 35 matches. 'He told me that I'd been inspirational in his life and that, to me, was bigger than any award. It's the biggest honour I've ever received.'

Radlinski was not the only Wigan youngster at the time to fall under the spell of Hanley, whose talents when he retired extended to coaching former world number one squash player John White in mental aspects of sport.

Andy Farrell remembers as a schoolboy playing incessantly a video set to music of the world's great loose forwards, most of whom were from Australia, but the best of all in Farrell's eyes was Hanley.

Like Radlinski, Farrell never played with Hanley, although he trained with him in his early days at Wigan and the pair feature together now in the club's hall of fame.

'I used to look up to Ellery massively,' said Farrell. 'He had an effect on everyone at the club because everyone wanted to live up to his standards. The competition was fierce.

'Ellery probably wouldn't remember me as a kid but when he left I was gutted that I didn't get to play with him. He went to Leeds and every time we went to Leeds I thought it was a privilege to play against him.

'You used to judge yourself on how you played against Ellery, that's as big a compliment as you can pay anyone. I used to try to get tackled by him.

'He was way in front in professionalism before he was even fully professional. When I signed as a 14-year-old, Maurice Lindsay told me that Ellery made sure he trained every Christmas Day. After that I trained every Christmas Day too throughout my career.'

Hanley exerted his influence on the pitch, in the changing room and on the training field, sometimes even in the boardroom He was a player of natural balance and strength, even though he was rarely to be found in the gym lifting weights.

That was part of his mystery, as was the talismanic nature of his performances.

In one season at Wigan after being signed from Bradford Northern he scored 63 tries, the highest total ever by a non-winger. For Great Britain he played in four different positions, centre, stand off, wing and loose forward, bringing to mind that famous observation by Brazilian football coach Joao Saldanha when asked by a journalist who was the best goalkeeper in his squad.

'Pele,' he replied, because he believed the striker, arguably the greatest footballer who ever lived, was so talented, so athletic, so accomplished in all aspects of his sport, that he was the best man for every position.

Hanley perhaps fell a shade short of such universal excellence but there was no doubt he was equally adept as a back or as a forward. His greatest asset, undoubtedly, was an uncanny sense of positioning which enabled him to track the flow of play and arrive as the break was made, allowing him so often to finish off with bursts over 30 or 40 metres.

Perhaps Martin Dermott summed up his influence best.

'When Ellery was playing there was always a feeling that we can't lose today. Just for him to be on the same team sheet lifted you. It could be the

79th minute and he would be talking to you and motivating you as though he had just come on the field.

'He was such a naturally fit athlete. I would be blowing out of my arse with sweat and blood everywhere and Ellery would be like he had just come on.

'He could run 80 yards and score a try and appear not to be out of breath. When he was playing you had to be on your "A" game because he would tell you to sort things out and you just did it.

'He commanded respect because you knew he always gave 100 per cent. When he had a word with you during a game you had to act, you had to change your game. He had that authority about him.

'He was a very focused, private man. No one knew what he did after a game, he just went off. He never drank. He wasn't a social type of fellow.

'I think he frowned on us going out on a Thursday night for a few beers after a training session. It was more of a business for him. We enjoyed the training and the comradeship but with Ellery it was more get the training done and go home.

'It was only after I had finished playing that I found out he was so good at squash. He was such a private man. But that was probably why he was so fit. He never did weights with us but he had lots of other things going on we didn't know about. We really didn't know him.

'I couldn't believe it when he turned up on *Dancing on Ice* on television a few years ago. He actually smiled and I had never seen Ellery smile.'

Dermott cites an incident in the 1994 Challenge Cup Final when Hanley was playing for Leeds as typical of the man.

Dermott went to tackle him and ended up accidentally elbowing him in the shoulder which made him drop the ball, leading to a Wigan try. Hanley was forced off the field by the injury.

After the game Hanley, wearing his wounded arm in a sling, sought out Dermott and shook him firmly by the hand and proffered a few words which have stayed with Dermott ever since.

'No problems Derms,' said Hanley. 'I would have done the same. Spot on. Congratulations.'

Not long after, when Hanley was head coach of Great Britain, he called up Dermott for an important Test.

'He pulled me aside and I wondered what he wanted,' said Dermott. 'He said, "One of the reasons I picked you was because of that incident at Wembley. You didn't care who I was and you did what you had to do to win."

'I thought fair play, it was the measure of the man really. Yeah, it was kind of embarrassing in a way the way he snubbed the press, but he was just a focused man. I just feel lucky to have played both with and against him. I learned a lot from him.'

Wherever you turn, it seems, there was a rugby league player at that time whose career or life was touched by Hanley.

Martin Offiah, whose rugby league journey took him from Widnes to Wigan to London Broncos to Salford City Reds, never played with Hanley at club level, but they forged a close relationship from their days on tour with Great Britain.

They were room-mates on the 1988 Great Britain tour of Australia and Offiah admits that Hanley 'became more of another older brother, a mentor from whom I learned a lot'.

Offiah admits it was Hanley who taught him how to be ruthless as a player, but also how to relax before matches in order to conserve energy. He also impressed upon Offiah the short and fickle nature of a sportsman's career and the necessity to plan for the future with wise financial investments.

Hanley also introduced Offiah to the famous Manchester house music club, The Hacienda.

'He opened my eyes up to a whole new world of jumping to the front of queues, getting into clubs free and rubbing shoulders and socialising with celebrities like Boy George, Mark Moore from S'Express, Mike Pickering from M People and Mick Hucknall from Simply Red,' wrote Offiah in *50 Of The Best*, a book which charts the top tries in rugby league.

'We were out so much together that people still come up to me today and ask, "Where's Ell?"'

'He taught me that you can have fun on a night out, stay sober and still get up in the morning and train hard. It's something I carried on doing for most of my career.'

The Hanley statistics are breathtaking. He scored 428 tries in 498 games and won 36 Great Britain caps. He was voted Man of Steel three times, won the Lance Todd Trophy and was awarded the Adidas Golden Boot as the world's most outstanding player.

It is part of the mystery how someone with such unique talents, a man with such obvious charisma when leading his peers, could have such a sour relationship with the press.

The fact is that during Wigan's most glorious years Hanley refused just about every interview request, not just with the national press, but with the local reporters covering the team on a daily basis.

More pertinently, the awkward, unnecessary stand-off was allowed to continue by administrators and board members who appeared to be in awe of a man with such spectacular talent.

Hanley's silence did not reflect well on the sport. How can a sport expect to expand its frontiers, reach out to new markets, sell itself as an attractive and entertaining product, in a world where the message is dominated by the media, when its leading practitioner is forever giving an impression of Howard Hughes?

Could football's David Beckham or Wayne Rooney or rugby union's Will Carling or Martin Johnson or cricket's Alastair Cook have been allowed to get away with not talking to the media when they were captains of England? Not a chance.

The pity is that Hanley, judging by that 2008 magazine interview in which he revealed how touched he had been by the gift of Radlinski's autobiography, was clearly a cogent and gifted thinker with astute perception about his chosen sport. Ideal qualities, in fact, to make a perfect ambassador.

Addressing the subject of his silence, however, he was intractable.

'Can I tell you about journalists?' he said. 'I'm not interested in journalists. The reason I'm not interested in journalists is that 99 per cent of them haven't played rugby league and have no idea what it's like to step over the whitewash and actually play.

'It doesn't matter what level you play at, amateur or professional, they have no idea. All they do is write a report and give their opinion. Any person from the public can do that so, for me, what they say holds no bearing on me whatsoever.'

Of course he is entitled to that opinion but isn't that a philosophy which ignores one of the primary roles of a sports reporter, to report the views of the most influential players in order to give news and insight to the fans who, after all, help to pay their wages? When a sportsman refuses to speak to the press he is also refusing to speak to the fans.

It became a lingering issue at Wigan and with Great Britain, culminating perhaps when one national newspaper reacted to yet another episode of the silent treatment with a banner headline proclaiming 'THE INCREDIBLE SULK'.

Yet Hanley's feats on the pitch did not go unreported. Quite the opposite. They demanded column inches and Dave Hadfield, the respected rugby league correspondent of *The Independent* for a quarter of a century, wrote many of them.

He remembers the Hanley era with a mixture of admiration and frustration.

'Hanley rarely spoke to the press after a certain point,' said Hadfield. 'After Bradford he became impossible to deal with to be honest. People used to ask him for interviews and he just knocked them all back. A great player, but a strange character.

'My argument was that he shouldn't be Great Britain captain unless he was prepared to do the full job, including being upfront with the media.

'I think Maurice Lindsay was a bit in awe of him to be honest. Ellery doesn't talk and he could create quite a hostile atmosphere around himself as well, but a tremendous player. In some respects, the best I've seen, not necessarily the most skilful but the most driven. You could drop him from the moon and land him on his head in Central Park and spin him round 20 times and he would still know where the try line was.

'He wasn't the fastest, wasn't the best passer of a ball. There were a lot of things about him that weren't perfect, but the whole thing added up. He had mental toughness and mental discipline unlike anyone I have ever seen.

'There was this triumvirate of Hanley, Shaun Edwards and Andy Gregory and they were all in competition with each other to an extent, although they played superbly well together. Keeping the three of those happy and with egos massaged was a major feat.'

The prizes for doing so, however, were also destined to be major.

7

A Drop of Cheer

WIGAN in Wembley week invariably went to town. Flags and scarves would flutter in the breeze from first floor windows. Cake shops enjoyed a roaring trade in red and white icing and fancy celebration sponges sculpted in the shape of a ball or a rugby pitch, while the town's famous pie trade inevitably turned out crusts proclaiming, 'Good luck Wigan'.

After training on the Thursday lunchtime before the 1989 final against St Helens and before the team coach arrived for the journey south Andy Platt and Joe Lydon took a short stroll up Standishgate, the town centre's main thoroughfare.

The purpose, apart from killing some time, was for the two Wigan-born players to soak in the warmth and anticipation which emanated from pretty much every shop front, as well as to stock up with some food for the journey.

A few heads stirred as the two locally famous faces accepted 'good luck' wishes from passers-by before sidling into a baker's.

They selected an assortment of sandwiches and a couple of pies and were about to exit when a woman shopper of mature years touched Lydon on the forearm, looked him straight in the eyes, and said with mock warning tone, 'Don't forget to win!'

Lydon responded with, 'Don't worry,' and a reassuring smile, and Platt leaned over when they were out of earshot and said, 'Do you think we'll ever forget to win?'

'If it gets to that stage we've definitely done something wrong,' replied Lydon, who recalled the tale not because it was extraordinary but because it was the exact opposite, an ordinary and simple example of the affinity Wigan's players, especially the homegrown ones, enjoyed at that time with townsfolk who had an innate sense of pride and ownership in their rugby club.

'It was a way of saying, "Best wishes",' said Lydon. 'But it was all wrapped up in don't let us down, we trust you, bring the cup back. There was so much of that and I enjoyed that feeling of trust and belonging.'

There was good reason for the growing sense of well-being as Wigan prepared to defend their Challenge Cup crown against St Helens, their nearest and fiercest rivals and the team their supporters loved to hate.

Despite a complex cocktail of underlying respect between the clubs, it was an antipathy that had coursed through generations and one mischievous put-down, attributed to Billy Boston, perhaps sums up one of the most enduring arm-wrestles for supremacy in the whole of sport.

'You can't have a team of Wigan legends, there are too many of them. You can't have a team of Saints legends, there aren't enough of them.'

In 1989, Wigan were definitely in the ascendancy. They had already won the John Player Trophy, beating Widnes 12-6 at Bolton. They finished runners-up to Widnes in the league championship while St Helens drifted in mid-table.

There was a growing confidence and a pleasing style about Lowe's team and resilience, too, which had seen them progress to Wembley despite being drawn away in every round of the Challenge Cup.

They had beaten Doncaster 38-6 in round one with Lydon scoring four of their seven tries, then beat Bradford 17-4 at Odsal in round two without playmaker Andy Gregory, who was in dispute with Lowe and had been left on the substitutes' bench for the previous three matches. Against Bradford, Gregory refused to sit on the bench for the fourth time so was dropped from the squad, proving once more how complex it must have been to juggle the egos at Central Park. Oldham were then overcome 12-4 in the quarter-final.

The semi-final against Warrington, in front of 26,529 spectators at Manchester's Maine Road, was one of those matches that helps explain why sport has secured such a place of influence in the lives and aspirations of ordinary people and why it is invariably at its best when the tension is high, the scoreline tight and the outcome unpredictable.

Wigan's early lack of discipline that Easter Saturday afternoon allowed John Woods to kick two early penalties and give Warrington a 4-0 lead they retained until the 38th minute when Dean Bell evaded an attempted tackle by Paul Cullen and slipped the ball to Lydon who touched down in the corner. The teams went in with the score 4-4 at half-time.

The tackling was brutal and chances were scarce until Woods put Warrington in front once more with a third penalty in the 59th minute. Nine minutes later and with both teams reticent to take unnecessary risks with a Wembley prize at stake, Lydon kicked a penalty for Wigan to level the scores. It seemed a replay might be required to separate the teams. Until, that is, with less than eight minutes remaining, something quite extraordinary happened in the world of rugby league, which had never been done before and which has never come close to being repeated since in the Challenge Cup, or in the sport for that matter.

Wigan's forwards carried the ball away from their line, taking a central route up the Maine Road pitch until a scampering Shaun Edwards was brought down on the fifth tackle around the halfway line. Hooker Nicky Kiss, at dummy half, passed the ball back swiftly and precisely to Joe Lydon for what everyone expected would be a kick downfield to pin Warrington back on their own line.

Lydon had other ideas. With a composure bordering on the casual he took one look at the posts in the distance, dropped the ball and with an elegant but powerful swish of his right leg he sent the ball soaring between the uprights.

The kick was measured at 56 metres, or 61 yards in old imperial measurements, the longest successful drop goal in rugby league history according to *Guinness World Records*.

It is not the longest drop goal in history as it is sometimes referred to, although that particular record is shrouded in some confusion.

The longest successful drop goal, again according to *Guinness World Records*, is 77.7 metres (85 yards) by rugby union's Gerald Hamilton Brand for South Africa in their 7-0 victory against England at Twickenham on 2 January 1932.

That measurement, however, apparently was taken from the point of impact on the halfway line, close to the touchline, to where the ball landed in the stands. There is brief footage of the match on *British Pathe*, with straw around the touchlines and touch judges in long trousers and heavy jackets and there does not appear to be a gale blowing which might have explained such a long kick, but sadly there does not appear to be footage of the kick in question.

South Africa's Francois Steyn was also renowned for the ability to drop goals in rugby union from his own half and on YouTube you can check out his effort in 2010 for Racing Metro against Clermont, one of the most beautifully-executed long drop goals in the history of the game. But rugby union awards three points for drop goals. There is more incentive for players to 'have a go' than in rugby league in modern times where a solitary point is the meagre reward for a successful drop kick.

It was not always that way. In fact, the first points ever scored in a Challenge Cup Final came from a drop goal by Batley stand off Joe Oakland on 24 April 1897 in his side's 10-3 victory against St Helens at

Headingley in front of 13,492 spectators when four points were awarded for a successful drop kick.

Lydon's effort edged Wigan just one point in front. It was, however, a game changer. A moment of instinctive individual brilliance that shifted the balance of momentum in the tightest of matches. It is a rugby league record of some renown.

Wigan did score a last-minute try at Maine Road when Hanley broke down the right wing before kicking forward for Edwards to touch down with Lydon adding the conversion for a 13-6 scoreline.

But it was the drop goal that shredded the Warrington resolve. A spontaneous cameo of artistry with its roots planted in dedicated preparation and practice, which included competitions on the training ground after the main sessions had concluded in landing drop kicks from all manner of angles and distances. As Lowe would have said, 'Perfect practice makes perfect.'

'I found I could hit a ball,' recalled Lydon. 'So when I heard Steve Hampson say "Hit it", I just did. To be honest, Warrington had a big set of forwards who I didn't fancy running into, so I let it go. The Maine Road pitch had a good surface, the bounce was uniform.

'Even so, if I had tried it again ten times it wouldn't have gone that straight or that far.

'Talking to Warrington's Mike Gregory after that game it was obvious that drop goal set the tone. It was a fluke thing to happen but it broke the deadlock.'

It also set up the much-anticipated final against St Helens.

But while Platt and Lydon clambered aboard the team coach with their lunch provisions and a sizeable army of excited Wigan fans waved the team off from Central Park on their journey to the capital, this was one sporting occasion which would be kept in sharp perspective.

The reason? It came exactly two weeks after the Hillsborough disaster.

The world of sport, and rugby league is no exception, is prone to a touch of hyperbole. It is full of 'Super Sundays' or 'Super Leagues' or 'Magic Weekends'. It is rife with trite aphorisms such as, 'Winning isn't everything, it's the only thing'. It talks about 'war' on the pitch when it means little more than a hissy fit between two players who have indulged in a spot of name-calling. It takes itself too seriously, too often.

Then along comes an afternoon such as 15 April 1989, the day when 96 people left home to watch a football match between Liverpool and Nottingham Forest and never returned, crushed to death in Britain's worst and most harrowing sporting tragedy.

Little did anyone realise then, when the heartbreaking funerals were taking place on almost a daily basis, that it would take 27 years and the admirable tenacity of the families in their pursuit of justice for the truth about Hillsborough to emerge.

A fresh inquest in 2016 overturned an earlier ruling that the deaths were accidental and recorded a verdict of unlawful killing, exonerating the fans and instead blaming police blunders.

Back in 1989 in the close-knit north-west there was just the desperate grief and a solidarity among the Wigan and St Helens fans, many of whom might have known someone affected by the tragedy, that there were more important things in life than sport.

8

Hampo Breaks the Jinx

THE man who led out Wigan at Wembley in 1989 had more reason than most to hope for a triumph.

As a young man and a committed rugby league fan Jack Robinson had travelled to the Twin Towers on 21 May 1966, only to see Wigan humiliated 21-2 in the Challenge Cup Final by St Helens, just weeks before England defeated West Germany there in football's World Cup Final.

John Mantle, Tommy Bishop and Len Killeen, three auspicious names of rugby league, had scored tries for St Helens that day with Wigan's only score coming via a penalty from Laurie Gilfedder.

The disappointment of losing to the club's chief rivals had stayed with Robinson ever since. The joy of winning is temporary. The pain of losing so often is permanent. It has a way of burrowing into the psyche. It ate away at Robinson for years afterwards, partly fuelling his desire to see Wigan back where they belonged as a dominant force in the game.

The most crucial part of that determination, however, had come years later when, armed with the confidence and savvy he had gained from owning and running a successful business, he decided to mount a takeover for the club after returning from Yorkshire and another painful defeat, this time a 38-1 demolition by Leeds on Saturday 8 December 1979, during which full back George Fairbairn scored Wigan's only point with a drop goal.

Wigan were not just losers that day. They were a shambles, a club sliding inexorably towards relegation. Robinson, by contrast, was a thrusting entrepreneur with energy and vision who was well on his way to making a fortune courtesy of an antiques business selling to the American market.

Antiques were his living, but rugby league was his passion, as you might expect from a man who was born at 17 The Wiend, Wigan town centre's highest point and coincidentally the exact spot where Billy Boston's statue now stands.

Within months Robinson, the lifelong fan, had found a way of blending his work and his passion, outflanking the existing 12-man board, rounding up support from hostile shareholders outraged by the manner in which the club had been allowed to drift, to engineer a bloodless coup which allowed him to eventually replace the old guard in 1982 with a more efficient board of four comprising himself, Maurice Lindsay, Tom Rathbone and Jack Hilton, the latter being chairman at the time as well as having played on the wing for the club. 'The Four Just Men' was how the *Wigan Observer*'s headline once described them.

Leading the team out at Wembley after a decade which had seen a meteoric transformation in Wigan's fortunes was Robinson's reward. But it would have counted for little if the team had not avenged the memory of 23 years earlier.

As it turned out Wigan took more than revenge in Robinson's name. In effect they took all the past defeats against St Helens, including and especially 1966 at Wembley, wrapped them up in a box with cherry and white bows and engraved it with the numerals 27-0.

That was the spectacular and humbling scoreline. To put that in perspective it was 24 years before another club was 'nilled' at Wembley, that dubious honour going to Hull in a 16-0 defeat, again at the hands of Wigan in 2013.

For St Helens, however, a quick glance at the statistics explains the extent of the humiliation.

In the history of the tournament, dating back to 1897 when Batley beat St Helens 10-3 in the first Challenge Cup Final, it is the only time St Helens have failed to score in a Wembley final. And they had played in 21 finals up to and including 2016, winning 12 of them.

By contrast, Wigan featured in 30 finals up to 2016 and won 19, failing to score in just one of them, against Broughton Rangers in a 4-0 defeat in their first final in 1911. They did lose the away match at Odsal against Bradford Northern 8-0 in 1944, after winning the first leg 3-0 at Central Park when the trophy was decided on aggregate score during the Second World War.

The 1989 final, however, could not be explained away by such grey statistics. Instead it revolved around a catalogue of intriguing personal stories, the sort sport appears to throw up unfailingly whenever the stakes are highest. One of them concerned the precocious Saints full back Gary Connolly, a local lad born and bred in St Helens, who was playing just his

12th professional match. Six months earlier he had been playing for the under-17s at amateur side Blackbrook Royals.

He had left school barely 12 months before and was working on a building site as an apprentice bricklayer.

But Alex Murphy, the St Helens head coach at the time, saw raw and rich potential and Murphy was never shy when it came to backing his opinion.

So it was that Connolly, with his boyish looks, coltish gait and shock of blond hair, was thrown into the frantic swirl of pressure, physical intimidation and unrealistic expectation, which so often constitutes professional sport at the top level.

It helped that St Helens had travelled to Central Park and beaten an under-strength Wigan side 4-2 the week before in the first round of the Premiership Trophy. It gave Connolly a chance to familiarise himself with exactly what was entailed in facing men such as Wigan's huge centre Kevin Iro at close quarters.

After that game Murphy had taken Connolly aside and broken the news he had been waiting to hear since he was little more than a toddler. He told him he was playing at Wembley.

'You've got us here and played in every round of the Challenge Cup so why should I drop you?' Murphy said. 'You deserve your spot.'

Connolly believes Murphy's faith and the experience of that trip to Wembley paved the way for his trophy-laden career, much of it ironically with Wigan. He was young and fearless and he admits he enjoyed the occasion despite the result. In fact, he has drawn strength from that day ever since.

'Before the game I felt like the luckiest kid in the country. But being a Saints lad and being beaten 27-0 by your arch rivals and not having the best of games it was hard to take. It was an emotional 20 minutes after that match with everyone down and depressed but it's part of what made me the player I became. I thought then that I was not going to get into that situation again. I vowed to try to put right the wrongs we did. It was a really good learning experience for me. There were 78,000 people there. How could you not enjoy that?'

Connolly's 'wrongs' mostly came down to what BBC match commentator Ray French referred to as 'rank bad tackling'. Easy for him to say sat on the television gantry and easy to reflect on a quarter of a century later.

The bottom line was that Connolly, with a dozen professional matches in his young life for experience, was the last line of St Helens defence that day with the job of stopping two of rugby league's all-time most destructive runners.

One was Kevin Iro, nicknamed The Beast, just turned 21 and 6ft 3in and around 15st of muscle. It took Iro two minutes to demonstrate the power contained in that considerable frame, taking a pass from Ellery Hanley and bulldozing down the right, through opposing centre Paul Loughlin and then simply brushing aside prop Tony Burke and the slight frame of Connolly to touch down for Wigan's first try.

Watch it these days and the ease with which Iro scatters the St Helens defence is reminiscent of another New Zealand rugby player who pushed back the boundaries, albeit in the rugby union code. Jonah Lomu.

Lomu scored four tries against England in the semi-final of the rugby union World Cup in 1995, famously trampling over Mike Catt on the way to one touchdown as the full back curled up on the turf to protect himself like an unseated jockey amid thundering hooves at Becher's Brook. By the final whistle, Lomu was on his way to becoming the first truly global rugby superstar.

He might even have graced Super League if an audacious move by Sheffield Eagles and their chairman Gary Hetherington to bring him to British rugby league during that World Cup had come to fruition. It didn't. Neither did attempts by Wigan and Leeds at that time, nor again in 1998 when Lomu met then Wigan chief executive Phil Clarke to discuss a deal.

Lomu, who tragically died at the age of 40 from a heart attack in November 2015, brought on by the chronic kidney disease from which he suffered, remained an All Black and the sight of him galloping down the wing with opponents bouncing off him is one of the most captivating sights in rugby history.

Iro was not in that class. Not as quick, nor as imposing, but the man who went on to play for and coach the Cook Islands and then founded the Cook Islands marine park in his work as an environmentalist was a devastating finisher, scoring six tries in his first three Wembley outings for Wigan.

Imagine how Connolly must have felt to have experienced the might of Iro bursting through his would-be tackle one minute for a try and then not much later being faced with the sight of Ellery Hanley in full flow, laying waste to what seemed like half the St Helens defence.

Hanley scored some remarkable tries in his career, evading Martin Meredith and the rest of the Halifax defence in crab-like fashion in 1988 being one of them. Yet the way he weaved and swerved and sidestepped and fended off St Helens tacklers in the 25th minute at Wembley a year later was beyond remarkable. It was out of the one-man battering ram school of attacking rugby.

Balance was a key component. So was an innate sense of evasive running, switching direction randomly and instinctively, like a gazelle escaping the clutches of a predator. But, most of all, it was strength, the sort of inner core power which is a gift of nature rather than a product of gym sessions, which took him the 40 metres or so to the St Helens line on a run that saw him burst through Paul Vautin and Paul Forber, brush off Phil Veivers and explode past another ineffective Connolly attempt at a last-ditch tackle.

When Andy Gregory dropped a goal just after half-time to take Wigan three scores clear the match was all but over as a genuine contest. Connolly's learning curve, however, was becoming steeper and more embarrassing by the minute.

Iro ran in for another try after 46 minutes, again leaving Connolly grasping Wembley fresh air and then 18 minutes later Shaun Edwards made a scything break from the halfway line, beating the unfortunate Connolly before being hauled down just a couple of yards out by Forber.

In the act of falling, however, Edwards managed to offload the pass and the supporting Gregory ran in for the easiest of touchdowns.

It was turning into one of the most one-sided finals in the tournament's history and yet there was one more personal story, which gave the final minutes a heartwarming hue.

Full back Steve Hampson had missed Wigan's 1984 final against Widnes after breaking a leg the month before. He had missed the following year's final too, that wonderfully thrilling spectacle against Hull, with a broken arm.

In 1988 Hampson's lot was becoming more than unfortunate. It was becoming positively freakish when, after having pulled on the cherry and white jersey more times than any other player that season, just two matches before the final he again broke an arm. No wonder then, and it is obvious if you watch the video of that 1989 final against St Helens, Hampson was close to tears when he walked out of the tunnel as the emotions engulfed him. As soon as the match kicked off, however, there was a wide and toothy grin on his face which would not have been out of place coming around Tattenham Corner. He was there, all in one piece, at Wembley, actually playing in his first Challenge Cup Final.

It was why the biggest cheer of the entire match reverberated around the grand old stadium after 75 minutes when Gregory threw out a raking long ball to Lydon, who timed his pass perfectly to send Hampson racing for the corner.

As Hampson caught the ball, five years of rotten luck and bitter disappointment appeared to melt away, his excitement and delight apparent as he raised an arm and punched the air before grounding the ball as he slid in for the touchdown. The try was of no real consequence as the match was already won. But one by one the Wigan players came over, Lydon, Dean Bell, Edwards and the rest, to wrap him in a series of warm and congratulatory hugs as the supporters waved their flags and scarves and, more surreally, their enormous Norweb Power plastic light bulbs.

A few minutes later the players had climbed the famous Wembley steps, captain Hanley had received the Challenge Cup from Viscount Whitelaw and passed it to Hampson, who was second in line. Before receiving it Hampson dragged his palms down his jersey so as not to tarnish the famous silver trophy with dirty fingerprints, then he raised it high in the air and kissed it tenderly.

That was the kiss that underlined the jinx was broken. Hampson had joined the cup winners' club. All was well at Wembley and his place in history was assured. The memory rekindles a feeling somewhere between relief and satisfaction. Naturally, there is also the widest of grins.

'I admit I did feel a bit jinxed by the time I had missed three finals. My overriding memory is scoring that try. Joe Lydon could have scored it, but he had been to Wembley on numerous occasions so he just popped it up to me.

'I have got my arm up in celebration before I go over and normally you get a right telling off if you do that but I was so excited and there was no way I was going to lose that ball. I nearly popped it I had hold of it that tight.

'I'll never forget that try because, after missing three finals, scoring in that one was something special.

'I wasn't the biggest contracted player. The money was a bonus but the medals were most important.'

The man immediately behind Hampson in the royal box, with a trademark thin black-taped band around his head, also kissed the cup as he raised it to the skies. For Nicky Kiss it turned out to be a farewell kiss to Wembley. Kiss, who spent his entire 12-year professional career at Central Park, playing 259 matches and scoring 36 tries, was to play just six more times in the cherry and white jersey before a serious arm injury while playing and then a neck injury sustained in a car crash forced him to retire on medical advice at the end of the following season.

He suffered a brain haemorrhage soon after retiring, which was not related to the road accident. Happily, he made a full recovery and works as a self-employed builder and plumber in the Oldham area where he used to coach the under-11s at Saddleworth Rangers, the amateur club which nurtured his own passion in rugby league as a teenager and where he has become something of a local hero.

He is often asked what it was like playing at Wembley and there is a wistful catch in his voice as he answers.

'As you're getting ready it's like you are stood in a subway and trains are rattling above you,' he says.

'That intensifies nearer to kick-off time. You come out, line up, noise intensifies again. As you get closer to the mouth of the tunnel the noise intensifies once more until when you get to the top you can't hear anything. Silence. It's a weird sensation. Ticker tape and a sea of red and white. Just a marvellous, elating sensation.'

No prizes then for guessing the subject matter of the picture hanging on the wall and dominating the main room of the Saddleworth Rangers' clubhouse. Kiss kissing the Challenge Cup at Wembley, of course.

9

A Clown, Queen and a Poor Lad

'WHEN a man is tired of London he is tired of life.'
That quotation from renowned 18th-century writer and literary critic Samuel Johnson equally could be applied to the few acres in north London known as Wembley Stadium.

With the massacre of St Helens, Wigan fans had seen their team lift the Challenge Cup there in 1988 and 1989, as well as in 1985. They had also been to Wembley in 1984, despite suffering a loss to Widnes.

Like the players, the supporters were developing a taste for it.

The old stadium was not in the best of repair. It was showing its age. The toilets were dilapidated, the bars cramped and the concrete bowels positively Dickensian. The views, too, were often severely restricted by unfortunately positioned pillars.

But somehow it did not matter, because the place was overflowing with memories of sporting legends and magnificent achievements.

There are too many to list comprehensively and yet everyone will treasure their personal favourites with England's victory against West Germany in the 1966 football World Cup, when Geoff Hurst scored the only hat-trick in a final in the history of the tournament, when Nobby Stiles was dancing and when Bobby Moore famously cleaned his hands before receiving the Jules Rimet Trophy from the Queen, being up there with the best, at least with people old enough to remember the last time England's footballers won a major prize.

Even those who aren't old enough to have witnessed it will have seen and heard about 1966 and all that so many times on television and in the media, every time a World Cup comes around, that it has become a cultural constant in the sporting consciousness. A landmark occasion conferring pride and glory and reminding us of what was once possible and might be again if only the perfect collision of hard work, talent, commitment and good fortune could be engineered.

Football, the nation's most popular sport, features heavily in any portfolio featuring cherished moments at the national stadium. Yet one of the most iconic images is not of a ball flying into the net or an exquisite moment of skill or even players amid ecstatic celebration. It is of a horse. A horse called Billy who happened to be white and thus stands out in the old sepia newsreel as his police rider attempts to control the crowd in the FA Cup Final in 1923 between Bolton and West Ham United when it is estimated 300,000 people gained entrance to a stadium with a 125,000 capacity and the terraces overflowed with spectators spilling on to the areas around the pitch.

Billy waded through the throng and his image was so memorable that the match, won 2-0 by Bolton, has become known as 'The White Horse Final', a bridge at the new Wembley being christened 'The White Horse Bridge' in his memory.

The 'Matthews Final' of 1953, in which the bewildering wing play of Stanley Matthews inspired Blackpool to a 4-3 win against Bolton, must also be included in Wembley folklore.

So must Charlie George's extra-time winner for Arsenal against Liverpool in 1971, famous for his unusual celebration when he lay flat on his back with his arms aloft after securing Arsenal's first Double triumph.

So must Ricky Villa's strike for Tottenham in the 1981 replay when the bearded Argentine slalomed like a downhill skier through the Manchester City defence to score the winner.

So, too, must Wigan Athletic's 1-0 victory, again against Manchester City but this time the 'moneybags' version, at the new Wembley in 2013 when Ben Watson's late header turned sporting logic on its head.

Great moments. Wonderful achievements. And a healthy preponderance of teams from the north-west hotbed of British sport contributing to the nation's sporting history.

Some might remember other events beneath the Twin Towers, such as the Live Aid concert in 1985 which Status Quo kicked off with 'Rockin' All Over the World' and during which Queen provided a 20-minute set which began with 'Bohemian Rhapsody' and closed with 'We Are the Champions' and has been hailed since by many music critics as the greatest live performance in rock music history.

But the Twin Towers did not always witness triumph. Sometimes the defining performances were framed around failure and tears. They were just as memorable. Just as moving.

Such as the night England failed to qualify for the 1974 World Cup when they drew 1-1 with Poland, partly because of an eccentric goalkeeper named Jan Tomaszewski, who was called a 'circus clown in gloves' by football manager and television pundit Brian Clough but who went on to make a series of outstanding saves to deny England the victory they required.

That night, Poland coach Kazimierz Gorski had told his team before the game, 'You can play football for 20 years and play 1,000 times for the national team and nobody will remember you. But tonight, in one game, you have the chance to put your names in the history books.'

In many ways, that summed up the allure of Wembley, which had a crass soubriquet in the shape of 'Venue of Legends', but also had a very real ability to shape and shred reputations. Even reputations of men as charismatic and likeable as former England manager Kevin Keegan.

So often Keegan as a player had been a talismanic presence for his clubs, Liverpool, Hamburg, Southampton and Newcastle, as well as England, but a wonderful playing career and a likeable demeanour did not help him when he trudged down the Wembley tunnel, head bowed, to jeers and worse after the last football match at the old stadium on 7 October 2000, following England's abject 1-0 World Cup qualifying defeat against Germany.

Keegan promptly resigned in one of Wembley's toilets, convinced by the suffocating vitriol that he was no longer up to the job. What a dreadful way for a decent man's international career to come to an end.

Keegan did not deserve that. But then sport and fate have a cruel way of combining to single out undeserving causes for merciless treatment in the harshest glare and on the biggest stage.

There can be no more pertinent example of that than what happened to Don Fox, or 'The Poor Lad' as he became known to the wider public, following the heartbreaking closing moments of the 1968 Challenge Cup Final between Wakefield Trinity and Leeds.

This was the final that should never have been played. The Wembley pitch was turned into something resembling a waterslide park, courtesy of a monsoon downpour following a week of heavy rain. Players struggled to keep their footing as vast puddles formed all over the pitch. All three tries scored came via mistakes associated with the conditions.

Ken Hirst touched down in the first half for Wakefield but it was in the last five minutes, with the pooling water causing comical chaos, when the real drama arrived.

John Atkinson was awarded a try for Leeds for obstruction following a mad melee with players falling and sliding and generally careering around like penguins on ice.

Bev Risman added the conversion and then slotted over a penalty with two minutes remaining to give Leeds an 11-7 lead.

From the restart Hirst cashed in on a Leeds mistake to hack the ball forward a couple of times towards the Leeds line before diving on the ball under the posts, the three points available for a try at that time taking Trinity one point behind at 11-10 with the conversion to come.

Up stepped Don Fox. Fifteen yards from the posts. Dead centre. In normal circumstances, Fox would have slotted over that conversion and wheeled away in victory mode 1,000 times out of 1,000.

But it was the last kick of the game. All the pressure, all the eyes, all the weight of history were on him. The conditions did not help. The surface was slippery, his kit and boots were squelching with the volume of water they had absorbed. All of which culminated in the ball slicing off his boot and squirting wide of the posts. A dreadful, calamitous, career-shattering shank. Fox dropped to his knees in desolation and pounded the offending Wembley turf with one of his fists.

'He's a poor lad,' said BBC commentator Eddie Waring with genuine concern, echoing the thoughts of the Wembley crowd and a sympathetic nation.

As if fate had one more act of cruel irony to perform, Fox, who had just lost the match, was then awarded the Lance Todd Trophy as man of the match. Truly, Wembley works in mysterious ways.

The more you go, of course, the more chance there is of something good, bad, ugly or just plain outrageous happening.

Which is one of the reasons Wigan feature so prominently in the annals of Wembley history and record so many 'firsts'.

They kicked off rugby league's tradition at the national stadium in the first Challenge Cup Final to be played there with a 13-2 victory against Dewsbury in 1929, in front of a crowd of 41,500.

Syd Abram, Lou Brown and Roy Muir Kinnear scored Wigan's tries with the legendary Jim Sullivan supplying a penalty goal and a conversion.

In 1948 Wigan defeated Bradford Northern 8-3 in the first all-ticket final watched by a then record crowd of 91,465, plus King George VI, the first time a reigning monarch had attended, or at least admitted to attending, a rugby league game.

This final was also the first to be televised, although with outside broadcast TV in its infancy, it was available only to viewers in the London area.

Wigan also made history in 1970, despite being defeated 7-2 by Castleford. After 16 minutes Castleford scrum half Keith Hepworth broke the jaw of Wigan full back Colin Tyrer with a swinging arm, laying him out with blood pouring from his mouth.

Tyrer was led from the field and on came the first substitute in a Challenge Cup Final in the shape of Wigan's Cliff Hill.

The 1965 final between Wigan and Hunslet was the last played under the unlimited tackle rule and it turned out to be a thriller, an end-to-end encounter which ended 20-16 in Wigan's favour, courtesy of two tries from flying winger Trevor Lake and touchdowns from Keith Holden and Laurie Gilfedder.

The sense of history was accentuated when it came to announcing the Lance Todd Trophy winner, or in this case winners, Wigan's Ray Ashby and Hunslet stand off Brian Gabbitas becoming the only players to share the award in the tournament's history.

We can add to Wigan's collection of historical superlatives that expansive 1985 triumph against Hull, plus the greatest try, Martin Offiah's solo spectacular against Leeds in 1994 and much more of that later.

But then we must also include the biggest upset, the 17-8 defeat by John Kear's Sheffield Eagles in 1998, which was a triumph for dogged determination and organised teamwork by a side who had been written off by most of the critics but on whom Sheffield chairman Tim Adams had famously wagered £1,000 at 33/1.

Adams picked up £33,000 and came up with the best quote of the contest as many of Wigan's young fans, including my 12-year-old son Michael, brought up believing there was little more to rugby league than traipsing down to London every year, watching the cup being handed to the Wigan captain and then singing Tina Turner's 'Simply The Best', were shedding tears of anguish after seeing their beloved Wigan lose at Wembley for the first time in their lifetime.

'They said that we were underdogs. They didn't realise that we had a pack full of rottweilers, backs who were Yorkshire terriers, 13 bulldogs and every one could run like a bloody greyhound.'

10

If You're Conscious,
You Can Tackle

L IKE most self-made men, Maurice Lindsay, in his administrative
prime, possessed many talents.

No one rises to run a major sport, as Lindsay did when he was
chief executive of the Rugby Football League and then of Super League,
without displaying a flair for business, organisation, diplomacy and
promotion.

There are those who would argue not everything he did was entirely
by the book or politically correct and there is no doubt his softly-spoken
and measured demeanour masked a steely will and a ruthless edge.

Yet there was a generosity of spirit about Lindsay that endeared him
to many, myself included.

On one occasion when the rugby league correspondent of the *Daily
Express*, Alan Thomas, was retiring, Lindsay made a special trip from the
north, where he ran the RFL in Leeds, to the Express HQ, as it was then,
on the south side of Blackfriars Bridge in London, to deliver a thoughtful
gift and make a speech of genuine kindness and appreciation which lifted
the occasion before joining in an afternoon of champagne quaffing of
champion proportions.

Another time, when I was northern sports editor of the *Daily Express*,
we were chewing over ways of spreading rugby league's gospel along
with bangers and mash at Langan's Brasserie in Mayfair when he asked
about my family and I told him my seven-year-old son Michael was one
of Wigan's most ardent fans, watched the cup games endlessly on video
and could recite every team and try-scorer from the glory years, his only
regret being that he lived 200 miles from Central Park.

A few days later, entirely unsolicited and even though Lindsay was no longer at Wigan, I received a telephone call from a secretary at the club asking could Michael be at Central Park the following Sunday for the match against Salford. Oh and, by the way, could he turn up dressed in full cherry and white kit because he would be running out as mascot, which he duly did, swapping passes with Shaun Edwards as the team ran out of the tunnel.

That was the other side of Lindsay the hard-nosed negotiator. That was Lindsay the dream maker.

But perhaps Lindsay's greatest gift of all in a career which, among a multitude of other things, saw him build his own plant hire company, work as a rails bookmaker, oversee Wigan's rise after the ignominy of relegation in 1980 and manage two Great Britain tours, was that of persistence.

Never was that demonstrated quite so starkly as in the way he lured John Monie to Central Park when Lowe returned Down Under to coach Manly-Warringah at the end of his contract.

Actually, lured is not entirely accurate. It was more like tortured. More like pushing a man's head under water time and time again until he surfaces one last time and screams, 'Yes, I'll do it,' if only to make the dread of drowning go away.

For persistent dunking substitute a phone call virtually every other day from Lindsay, then Wigan chairman, to Monie's home in Australia where he had just finished a five-year stint with the Parramatta Eels, which included winning a Grand Final.

'I'm talking to the next Wigan coach,' was how Lindsay would begin every conversation and Monie would calmly reply that he had no intention of coming to England, that he wanted to take a year out from rugby league to do something more relaxing, such as surfing on the Gold Coast in Queensland.

Lindsay would not let it go. Monie was his man, his mission. He related tales of Wigan's rich history as a town and as a hotbed of rugby league. He conjured up pictures of past greats such as Billy Boston and Eric Ashton and current superstars such as Joe Lydon, Andy Gregory and Ellery Hanley, the latter being generally regarded as the best rugby player in the world at the time. And he crafted a famous line about Wigan Pier being almost as good for surfing as Queensland.

There is no doubt about it. Lindsay could charm the barges out of the canal and eventually Monie fell for it. He said yes and Wigan had acquired a man of verve and vision who was to prove to be one of the greatest coaches in their history.

The first thing Monie did after agreeing the move demonstrated his class and style as well as his acumen as a manager of men. He sent out an invite to the small contingent of Wigan players plying their post-season summer trade at that time in the suburbs of Sydney and took them all to lunch.

Monie wanted to know how Wigan played. He wanted the inside track on the coaching structure, the backroom set-up, the strength of the opposition and the level of support. He wanted, in rugby terms, to know his way around Wigan, what London cab drivers would deem 'The Knowledge'.

That lunch set the tone for a relationship of mutual respect and admiration between coach and players and also meant he had met and picked the brains of influential characters such as Joe Lydon, Andy Gregory, Andy Goodway and Steve Hampson before he had even set foot on English turf as the new man at the helm at Central Park.

There are those, of course, who take the view that anyone could have coached a team of superstar players, many of whom had been assembled for big money by the board and then blended together expertly by Graham Lowe.

But sport is not like that. It never has been. Why did the Manchester United team implode spectacularly following Sir Alex Ferguson's retirement at Old Trafford, despite having just won the Premier League for the 13th time?

Why did Jose Mourinho's reign in his second spell at Chelsea come to such a juddering halt when players, again who had won the Premier League title the season before, simply stopped playing for him?

Coaching sports teams is not an exact science. Assembling talented players is one thing. Turning them into a team capable of producing a conveyor belt of major trophies is the difficult part, the bit which relies on intuitive art and experienced craft with a spot of science thrown in.

There was one strategy, however, which became abundantly clear as soon as Monie walked through the door at Central Park. Success was destined to be founded on defence.

Lowe had already concentrated on that department and made impressive strides with the defensive structures and Shaun Edwards, for one, recognised a kindred spirit when Monie arrived. Edwards had just returned from a summer stint in Australia with Balmain Tigers.

'John wasn't probably as confrontational as Graham Lowe,' said Edwards. 'But his laid-back, laconic style belied underneath a massive competitive streak which I could buy into because I had just been in Australia for four or five months. I think I played some of my best rugby in the months that followed.'

That competitive streak was often hidden behind a winning smile but invariably it was wrapped in a cloak of steel. Perhaps the best illustration of the Monie ethos was captured in one of his training team talks a year or so after he joined following a Sunday match during which an injured Frano Botica had received treatment on the pitch.

The following is a verbatim passage from that speech as published by author Neil Hanson, who was given access to all areas at Central Park in 1990/91 for the acclaimed fly-on-the-wall book *Blood, Mud and Glory*.

'It doesn't matter what's wrong with you when you're injured. I want you on your feet and in the defensive line.

'Now, the incident on Sunday when Frano stayed down hurt and they ran the ball up and they were inside our 22. I don't care if the physio's out there and he wants to examine you and all that stuff. That's not important. What's important is, this is for everybody, you've got 12 team-mates tackling their guts out, defending like anything inside the 22, and we've got the physio telling a guy to see if he can straighten his knee out.

'I don't care what's wrong with you; it doesn't matter what's wrong with you: if the opposition's got the ball, I want you on your feet and in the defensive line. As soon as we get a break in play, if you've got a broken leg you get off the field and we'll replace you, but whenever you can get on your feet, whenever you're conscious, I want you on your feet and faking it in the defensive line. As soon as there's a break, if you're injured, get off the field and we'll replace you.

'There are no exceptions to this rule. So, from now on, the only reason you stay down hurt and get attention from the sideline is because there's a break in play or you are unconscious. No other reasons will be accepted. I want everybody on their feet in the defence all the time. Bill or the physio will come out with water and, if you're hurt, tell him you need to be replaced and we'll use our replacements.'

The word uncompromising comes to mind. But then is it not the same coaching ethos which saw Jose Mourinho famously fall out with the Chelsea doctor, Eva Carneiro, when she came on the field to treat his main playmaker Eden Hazard, putting his already-depleted side temporarily down to nine men against Swansea in the first match of the 2015/16 Premier League season?

The fall-out from the resulting row cast Mourinho in a ruthless and arrogant light and probably cost him his job as disaffection spread through the Chelsea camp, but Monie doubtless would have understood Mourinho's unforgiving mindset.

As Denis Betts confirmed, Monie's training talk was by no means a one-off.

'We had rules about not being off the floor last,' said Betts. 'If you were in contact and felt that you were almost knocked out it was something that drove you to get to your feet first, so the lads couldn't take the piss out of you because you were on the floor last.

'I remember clashing heads with Andy Platt and being dazed almost to the point of being knocked out but thinking, "I am going to get up before that bastard gets up or I will never live it down." It was something that was driven into the team. As a coach I have said the same things myself as Monie said then.'

Iron defence was the one thing strictly non-negotiable on Monie's planet.

Which is why on occasions during Monie's four years in charge the Wigan defensive line resembled A&E at the nearby infirmary with casualties such as Martin Dermott battling on with a dislocated elbow, arm flapping by his side like a bird's broken wing. But he was on his feet in the line, plugging a gap. Helping his team-mates. That is what counted. That is what was demanded.

Not that Monie was all about passion and sacrifice and physicality. He was more rounded than that, more tactical, more in touch with the complexities involved in running a team of strong characters.

Fitness coach Bill Hartley worked closely with Monie from the moment he arrived and swiftly decided that Lindsay had done a good month's work.

'Graham Lowe appealed to the heart and John Monie appealed to the head,' said Hartley. 'Monie was far more cerebral, a deep thinker of the game, who was big on skills and preparation. At the end of Graham's reign, I think they were absolutely ready for someone like John to come in.

'It was interesting for me as a lover of the game to see certain players who didn't thrive under Lowe who absolutely did under Monie. A good example was Andy Goodway. I was best man at his wedding and he was best man at mine. I don't think Graham recognised what Andy was best at. I remember Monie saying to me, "I know you are a mate of his, but I have heard some bad reports about him."

'I told him, "He'll be as good as gold for you. Whatever you want him to do, he'll do it. If you appreciate what he does he will do anything for you." Guess what, he was players' player of the year that first season under Monie.'

Monie's secret, if he had one, was probably that he understood people. I met him just once but spoke to him on several occasions when I commissioned him to write ten columns for the *Daily Express* on the world of rugby league. He was approachable, flexible, studious and likeable.

An astute and cogent communicator. A people's person. Which was why during his time in the UK on occasions he also used to contribute lively comment to the BBC's coverage of the game.

When the Wigan glory years were done, Betts ended up at Auckland Warriors with him and so has a unique perspective on how his qualities translated on both sides of the world.

'John brought in a couple of things without changing everything,' said Betts. 'He didn't want to make the team look completely different. He understood the team had lots of good players who just needed guiding and nurturing. He did his job subtly, changing small things which made a difference. John in the early days could get you to do most things.

'He had an openness which made you want to play for him. I didn't really care what he knew because I believed him. Whether he was right or wrong I believed what he was telling me. That's a gift.

'He was of his time, in the right place at the right time with the right group of players. One of the things you learn as a coach is that your reputation is built on being in the right place with the right group of players.

'I remember John coming into the dressing rooms at half-time once when we were losing against Salford and saying, "What we need to do now is run from dummy half and we will win the game."

'So we ran from dummy half and won the game. It was pissing down with rain and we had probably thought it was going to be easier than it was, but he got us to realise where we were and that by running from dummy half twice as much as we had been we'd win and we did. All of a sudden we were thinking, "This fella's not bad."'

Those are the tangible successes in the world of a professional sportsman that sow the seeds of respect.

Monie's man-management was also more nuanced than Lowe's in the sense that he would warn players that they were in danger of being dropped because their form was sliding, whereas with Lowe the initial discovery was usually harsher and via the team sheet with no opportunity to right the wrong.

Monie also possessed humour. Sharp, sometimes acerbic, but the sort of humour which allowed criticism to strike home without giving offence.

On one occasion when the team were losing at half-time he told all the players to sit down in the changing room because he wanted to talk about tackling and what they were doing wrong.

'He looked at Shaun,' recalled Bill Hartley. 'And he said, "You can fuck off in there," pointing to the kit room, "because you don't do any."

'Shaun put his head down and trudged off and I looked across at Platty and his shoulders were shaking up and down as he tried to stop himself laughing. But fair play to Shaun, he was the top tackler in the second half so Monie knew what he was doing. He had done his job.'

Monie used to call Andy Gregory 'the speed bump' because he reckoned he never actually stopped anybody in the tackle, he just slowed down opponents for others to 'clean them out'.

Getting the better of Gregory, however, was not so easy. And there is one classic tale, recounted by many of the players, of the time Monie rounded on Gregory at half-time for not having made a single tackle in a match Wigan were losing.

Gregory had stripped off his jersey as usual at the interval and was sitting with little leather protector pads poking out at strange angles around his shoulders.

Betts, who was sitting opposite, remembers the surreal sight.

'Greg had this sort of dwarfish kind of shape to him,' recalled Betts. 'He had a little belly on him and he was whiter than white and because he had been running he was blotchy all over.

'John Monie pointed at him and said, "Greg, you've not made one tackle, not one, we're behind on the scoreboard and you're not doing the job I asked you to."

'Greg just looked up at John, whose face was earnest and intense, put his hands out palm upwards in front of him, stuck his belly out just a tad more and said, "Honest, John, would you run at me, though?" Everyone just chuckled, including John, and it killed the intensity of the moment and we went out and won the game.'

Monie's gift was his ability to ride such moments with natural ease and use them to the team's advantage.

Call it psychology or man-management. Call it thinking outside the box. Call it what you want. It was all about extracting the maximum possible from every team member. The little things mattered. Such as Hartley's idea to warm up on the pitch before kick-off to allow the players to attune to the surface as well as to set the blood racing for the battle ahead.

It sounds so obvious when you see all manner of sporting teams doing that every weekend of the year nowadays, but rugby league players at the time were still in the habit of warming up with little more than a rub of Fiery Jack and a few gentle stretches in the changing room five minutes before kick-off and then jogging out on to the field and ripping straight into each other with stiff joints and tight tendons.

At first Monie was not entirely convinced. He did not want to lose precious time for last-minute instructions. But a compromise was reached with the players required to be back inside the changing room at least a quarter of an hour before kick-off.

That was the Monie way. Balanced, even-handed management. Massaging egos occasionally. Calming the impetuous.

And working with individuals to make them better, such as Steve Hampson, who remembers taking his advice on tackling technique and how best to gather the loose ball in defence, all dispensed with easy-going authority.

'He knew how to treat his players. He was never rude or violent and he came out and had a drink with us. He was a person you could trust and if you trust somebody you will have him in your gang, won't you? All the players trusted him. We had open arms for him but he was the leader when he stepped out of the ring.'

Monie, as you might expect, never took complete credit for his success. He admitted the training techniques he brought across from Sydney, which he refreshed during each close season he spent Down Under, 'got us a jump on the other clubs for a few years'.

But he put down the glories to a fear of failure and the willingness to work harder and longer than the rest.

'People always focused on the fact that we had a lot of great players but they busted a gut,' Monie always said. 'They didn't take any shortcuts.'

They might, however, have taken a drink or two along the way. Even then Monie had a mature and measured way of dealing with it.

Take the time it came to his attention that certain players who travelled to training over the Pennines from Yorkshire were indulging a little too heavily on their day off following Sunday matches. So much so that Monday apparently had become known as 'Schooner Monday'.

Concerned that it might get out of hand and fuel some adverse publicity, Monie summoned Kelvin Skerrett, a Great Britain prop and a flamboyant character, into his office.

Skerrett was known as 'SuperKel', mainly because of his penchant for flying to the rescue whenever one of his team-mates was in physical danger from an opponent or if a fight broke out on the pitch.

Fans even had a 'SuperKel' T-shirt made in his honour, incorporating his image wearing a Superman cape, following one particularly spectacular 'rescue' when he took a galloping run-up and launched himself over a scrum of flailing fists to administer his own retribution.

He entered Monie's office as the head coach was in discussion with Bill Hartley.

'Ah, Kelvin, what are all these stories I've heard about you drinking all day on Mondays?' said Monie, looking up from his desk at the big Yorkshire-born Welshman.

'Who me?' replied Skerrett, pointing a forefinger to his chest and affecting a tone of bewildered innocence.

'I'm not saying don't have a drink,' said Monie, with a knowing smile and a genuine air of appeasement. 'But be sensible Kelvin. If you'd have five or six pints normally, just have two or three.'

'Okay John, no problem,' said Skerrett, nodding his head. As Skerrett walked out, closing the door behind him, Monie's eyebrows lifted and he rolled his eyes before returning to his discussion with Hartley.

Five seconds later there was a tap on the door and it creaked slowly open a foot or two and Skerrett craned his head around the frame.

'Coach, if I normally have 20, is it okay if I have nine or ten!'

11

'Just Give Me Five Minutes'

S PARE time is something sportsmen often have too much of and do not know what to do with, so much so that it becomes their enemy and not their friend.

Take England's footballers who checked in to their palatial headquarters in Rustenburg during the 2010 World Cup in South Africa and within a few days were complaining, despite the luxury, the table tennis, the copious video games and film hall, that they had nothing to do.

Hardly surprising then that disharmony spread like dengue fever and coach Fabio Capello was left with a mutiny on his hands which directly led to England's early exit.

The toughest time for a coach is not when he is taking a training session or talking the team through the tactics in the video room, or even when trying to rouse underachievers in the dressing room, as in all these places he has a measure of control.

It is time to worry when players have time on their hands and boredom burrowing a hole in their brains.

It was thus that following morning training at Wembley on 27 April 1990, before the Challenge Cup Final kick-off the next afternoon, Bill Hartley as usual was handed the task of looking after the team.

'You will keep an eye on the boys this afternoon and tonight, Bill, won't you?' said John Monie. It sounded like a request. It wasn't.

Inevitably, this led to Hartley accompanying a bunch of characters, including Andy Gregory, Steve Hampson and Andy Platt, to the nearby bookmakers where it had become something of a tradition to bet on every race involving that day's dog and horse meetings. Nothing too extravagant. Nothing in the realms of famous footballing gambler

Keith Gillespie, of Manchester United and Newcastle, who reckoned his addiction cost him £7m; or former Sunderland striker Michael Chopra who admitted spending more than £2m on betting during his career; or Matthew Etherington, of West Ham and Stoke, who blew a £1.5m fortune on poker, greyhounds and horse racing. For Gregory and co. it was more like £5 each way. A bit of fun.

It was after evening dinner that Hartley dreaded the call from Gregory and, sure enough, in 1990 it came right on cue at the team's Woodford Green hotel.

'Billy, I can't stay here all night,' Gregory whispered conspiratorially. 'Are you coming out for a beer?'

The irony contained in the fact that he chose the team's fitness coach as his prospective drinking companion hours before the biggest showpiece match of the year was lost on Gregory. It also set Hartley something of a conundrum.

'I'm thinking in my own little tin-pot way, should I stay or should I go? I decided I might be better going out with him and bringing him back safe and sound rather than leaving him by himself,' said Hartley.

'So we went and had a couple of beers, just a couple, and we were back at the hotel by ten o'clock. Greg was quite happy then because he liked the thought of beating the system a bit. Then Greg would say, "Billy, we need some mints", and I would be dispatched to find some in case he ran into John Monie.'

If Gregory awoke the next morning with just a hint of fuzziness then his half back partner Shaun Edwards stirred that 28 April with a clear-headed determination, which even in his world of obsessional focus was staggering in its intensity.

To borrow a phrase often used by controversial boxing promoter Don King at the time, there were two chances of Edwards indulging in a few beers the night before a big match: fat and slim. And slim just left town.

Edwards's night had been filled, not with drink, but with thoughts and dreams of how the day before him might unfold.

At just 23 it was the fifth time Edwards had prepared for a Challenge Cup Final at Wembley. He was becoming one of the venue's fixtures and fittings, like 'Abide with Me' and 'Jerusalem'.

Every Wembley appearance had been strewn with unforgettable memories, even the loss against Widnes in 1984, but there was an additional edge to this one against Warrington, an extra frisson of anticipation.

Partly that was because this particular cup run had been challenging. The magical run, which had now reached 14 undefeated matches, had almost come unstuck on yet another mud heap in round one against Hull Kingston Rovers.

Cold, a low sun, a biting wind, a sticky pitch and a hostile crowd packed into the new Craven Park. All the ingredients for a cup shock. Joe Lydon missed a penalty kick from 15 metres, dragging the ball wide from right in front of the posts, so turbulent were the conditions.

At times like that there is no hiding place. True characters are revealed and champion qualities are laid bare.

Even so, despite a heroic defensive performance from Wigan, the result was in doubt until the final whistle after Rovers' Mike Fletcher had landed two penalties and Wigan winger David Marshall dived on the ball following a kick-through for the only try of the match, which Lydon converted.

The second half was scoreless, Wigan's continued record owing much to a covering tackle by Edwards who brought down Hull KR winger Anthony Sullivan when he seemed certain to score.

It was an ugly 6-4 victory but winning ugly is preferable to the alternative: losing ugly.

A home romp against Dewsbury followed in round two before Wigan showed their true class, prevailing in a 26-14 struggle at Wakefield Trinity and defeating St Helens 20-14 in the semi-final at Old Trafford with tries from Steve Hampson, Ged Byrne and Andy Goodway.

Most of Edwards's heightened focus, however, emanated from the fact that he had broken a hand just three weeks before in the championship decider against Leeds. For most players, especially one whose playmaking role involved an extensive range of passing, that would have been the end of the dream.

Edwards was not most players. Which is why the day after suffering the injury he had embarked on an obsessive rehabilitation and fitness regime that quite possibly was the most punishing of his career.

He was unable to lift weights with his fractured hand. Instead he doubled the amount of leg weights sessions in the gym. Day after day he ran up hills or volunteered for additional sprint work with Bill Hartley, while following a strict diet regime designed to deliver him at Wembley in peak condition.

Day after day he was driven on by two reasons. One was the thought that his dad Jackie had missed his dream of playing at Wembley, first through misfortune in a couple of semi-finals and then by his debilitating spinal injury.

'People had kept telling me how unlucky my dad was never to have played at Wembley,' said Edwards. 'So it was in my mind all the time in the build-up what a privilege it was for me to be there for the fifth time at 23.'

The second reason was more selfish. Edwards was desperate to win the Lance Todd Trophy, the man-of-the-match prize voted for by the nation's rugby league writers and named after New Zealander Lancelot Beaumont Todd, who played for Wigan 185 times between 1908 and 1913, scoring 126 tries and seven goals.

Todd had been signed for £400 and was a member of Wigan's first Challenge Cup Final side when they lost 4-0 to Broughton Rangers in 1911. He went on to play for Dewsbury and to manage Salford to three league championships, four Lancashire Cups and the Challenge Cup in 1938, beating Barrow 7-4.

He also became the rugby league commentator for BBC Radio before dying in a road accident in 1942 at the age of 68 when he swerved his car to avoid a tram in Oldham and crashed into a lamp post.

Todd is buried in Wigan's Ince cemetery, but it was not the association with his hometown club that drove on Edwards. It was much more to do with individual achievement. At 23, Edwards had already won just about every prize the game had to offer. The Lance Todd Trophy conferred a cache that had proved elusive.

Maybe the Warrington team detected Edwards was a man on a mission. Perhaps they realised that, despite the healing bone in his hand, he was in rude fitness and desperate to be the pivotal cog in Wigan's pursuit of a third consecutive final triumph. Whatever the reason, Edwards was hit by a late tackle after five minutes.

'I thought, "That wasn't by accident,"' said Edwards. 'You get a feeling sometimes. Then I did a little grubber kick through and, "Bang", I got hit late again, this time by the top of Bob Jackson's head straight into my cheek.'

A blackness descended. But almost immediately the pain, excruciating, grievous pain, tore through the daze and Edwards knew he was in serious trouble.

At first he thought he had broken his jaw. In fact, his right cheekbone was so badly depressed that he could not speak. He peered around Wembley, at the crowd, at his team-mates. There were two of everything. He put his hand to his right eye to try to block out the double vision. The pain, if anything, was becoming worse. Lesser players would have succumbed at such a moment, happy to be carried off on a stretcher to the sanctuary of the dressing room and a blast of pure oxygen and a shot of morphine from the club doctor.

Edwards's veins, however, were pumping adrenaline while a stubborn streak as wide as Wembley Way was stumbling its way to the foreground of his mind.

'Excuse my language,' says Edwards as he runs a finger over his cheekbone, the heat and rage of that moment long gone suddenly returning in a flush of energy and expletives.

'I was thinking, "I've done all this fucking training, dedicated myself completely, I'm not coming off after nine fucking minutes." My dad's never played at Wembley went through my mind. And I thought, "I can play through this. I have to play through this."'

These days, with injury and concussion protocols rightly much stricter, a doctor would have been on hand and doubtless diagnosed that the eye socket was fractured and the cheekbone broken and emergency hospital treatment was imperative. No way would he have been allowed to continue.

Back then, when on-pitch treatment amounted to little more than the mythical 'magic sponge', Edwards blinked through his blurry vision at Keith Mills, the trainer who had come on to tend to him.

'Just give me five minutes,' Edwards grunted gutturally through a haze of incoherence, at the same time holding up five fingers to relay his wish.

Mills was a friend and had always been one of Edwards's biggest supporters.

'Knowing Keith he probably thought, "Let the mad bastard have a go." Millsy was the man who used to inspire me massively before matches. He always used to come up to me and say, "C'mon, when Edwards buzzes Wigan buzz." Little things like that to get me going.'

So Edwards played on, although for the next five minutes he staggered around with one hand like a pirate's eye patch over the shattered right side of his face to alleviate the double vision, not tackling and struggling to perform his playmaking duties.

It was not something even the most celebrated players could get away with for long in the Wigan set-up. The team, not the individual, always came first. There were no exceptions.

Which is why his ears felt almost as painful as his eye when Dean Bell, a New Zealander hewn quite possibly from Auckland steel, noticed his continuing discomfort and immediately administered some tough love.

'He just screamed at me, "Get back on your game or get off the effing pitch,"' recalled Edwards. 'That was exactly what I needed. I didn't need anyone being soppy or soft.

'I didn't do much tackling after that but it wasn't as if I had torn my hamstring and couldn't run. It was just really, really bad pain. It eased off a bit in the second half or maybe I just got used to it, but I felt I could still orchestrate the team with Greg.'

The truly astonishing aspect of Edwards's part in that 1990 final is that, despite his horrendous injury, he was involved in so much of Wigan's creativity.

It was his impish dart and brave leap that charged down Warrington full back David Lyon's kick, which led to Denis Betts diving over for Wigan's first try.

It was his trademark support play that saw him on hand to flip the ball up for Mark Preston to score his second try of the match after the strong running of Steve Hampson and Ellery Hanley had seen Wigan sweep 80 metres from deep in their own half for a score which BBC co-commentator Alex Murphy famously described as 'one of the tries of the century'.

Wigan also scored two tries from bulldozing centre Kevin Iro and a typically rumbustious effort from Hanley but it was the memory of that try which saw Edwards point to his bookshelf where, propped up against a line of novels, was the order of service for the funeral in 2007 of Wigan-born Mike Gregory, who captained Warrington in that 36-14 final defeat, scoring a try and pulling down Edwards five yards from the line when it seemed he was certain to score before he flipped the ball to Preston.

Gregory played for the Sacred Heart team in Wigan in his schoolboy days and should have played in the Wembley curtain-raiser in 1975, aged just ten, alongside Joe Lydon, but was taken sick on the bus on the way to the Twin Towers.

He went on to coach Wigan in 2003 and 2004 until an illness, later diagnosed as progressive muscular atrophy, a form of motor neurone disease, led to him losing his job. His death at the age of 43 shocked the world of rugby and the sight of his order of service helps Edwards keep rugby matters in perspective.

'It always reminds me how lucky we are to be doing the things we love doing, such as coaching, because that is what he loved to do,' said Edwards.

The match finished on a sour note, Iro and Warrington's Des Drummond swapping punches following the final try, an incident sparked by Iro needlessly throwing the ball at Drummond once the touchdown was complete.

Thankfully, it was a fleeting skirmish, no bones broken, no blood spilled, and once the cup had been lifted and Andy Gregory had received the Lance Todd Trophy for another brilliant performance, which was encapsulated by his mesmerising overhead pass for Hanley's try, Edwards was dispatched to hospital in an ambulance.

That is when the pain really kicked in. The journey from Wembley to the Harrow-on-the-Hill private hospital where Edwards was headed was no more than four miles.

The gridlock caused by the match traffic and 77,729 spectators leaving Wembley at the same time, plus a winding route, made it feel more like 40.

'I'm not a good traveller in the back of a car at the best of times but the ambulance was rattling and rolling and I felt horrendous,' said Edwards. 'I thought my head was going to explode so when I arrived I thought, "Thank God, they'll put me out, do the operation and everything will be okay."'

Not quite. Once the medical staff ascertained he had suffered double vision and almost certainly concussion the operation was delayed for 24 hours.

'Can you give me some painkillers?' Edwards asked, hoping for a morphine drip or similar, but in reality being handed two Paracetamol.

'That's all I had. I don't think I had one second sleep all night.'

He did receive some visitors that night, however, as the Wigan team bus made a detour to call on its way to the post-match celebration.

Maurice Lindsay and coach John Monie, who along with the players had learned of the seriousness of the injury only after the game, stepped off and went in to see Edwards, as did captain Hanley who made a point of telling Edwards how proud the team were of him.

On the bus, as they waited for the visitors to return, trust Andy Gregory to put Edwards's misfortune into perspective in his own inimitable fashion.

Gregory sauntered down the aisle of the bus in that cocky manner for which he was famed and leant over Bill Hartley, his drinking partner/ guardian angel of the previous night, before dispensing the following wisdom softly in his ear.

'Strange, isn't it, Bill, Giz [Edwards] has not had a drink all weekend, he's looked after himself all week. He's trained like stink for weeks and me, I've had a few pints. Guess what, he's gone to the hospital and I've got man of the match. Funny life, isn't it?'

With that he turned and sauntered back down the bus, whistling as he went.

Edwards stayed in hospital for two nights, taking a walk, at last pain-free, around the area on the Monday with his most vivid memory being seeing the pupils from the famous Harrow school in their morning suits and straw boaters.

'It's a different world down here,' he remembers telling his mum, Phyllis, when he rang home that night.

The school is famous for educating Lord Byron and prime ministers such as Winston Churchill, Robert Peel, Lord Palmerston and Stanley Baldwin. Little was Edwards to know that 20 years later he would revisit the area when his son, James Small-Edwards, whose mother is M People singer Heather Small, was offered a scholarship at the school and attended for four or five months before leaving because he did not like the full-time boarding.

The lasting regret for Edwards is that he failed to pick up the Lance Todd Trophy, the prize he coveted, that day at Wembley and it eluded him for the rest of his career. It was, however, the year he was voted as rugby league's Man of Steel for the only time.

Admittedly, that was partly due to his stand-out performances in two Tests to win the man of the series honour for Great Britain against New Zealand. But his performance at Wembley, which evoked J.M. Barrie's old rallying cry, 'Courage is the thing. All goes if courage goes', cannot have gone unseen.

Perhaps Martin Dermott put it most succinctly when he said, 'People ask me who is the hardest player I have played with or against and I have played against the best and the biggest around the world but Shaun was definitely the hardest man bar none.

'Everybody was trying to knock his head off from the age of 17. But in all those major finals for Wigan and Great Britain, for mental toughness no one got near him.'

Edwards does not require medals or videos to remember his heroics. He bears the scars and has been left with an unwanted legacy.

'It still bothers me to this day,' he said. 'I still get double vision in my right eye. I don't get headaches but sometimes I get migraines and double vision. After the injury I'd get that after night games about three or four times a season.'

12

The Man with the Golden Run

THE name is Preston. Mark Preston. Aka James Bond. Or more simply 'Bondy' to his team-mates.

Preston does not have a scar or double vision or a nightmare ambulance journey or a son who went to Harrow like Edwards to keep that 1990 Challenge Cup Final forever in his thoughts.

He did not enjoy a career laden with medals and trophies like Edwards and if you Google him you are much more likely to hit on the British landscape painter of the same name or perhaps the football team which was a founder member of the Football League and the first English football champions.

But he does have a DVD at home in Lytham St Annes which he takes out periodically to prove to himself, as well as his three daughters, that he could cut it in the rarefied echelons of rugby and that he did once score two of the greatest tries in Wembley history.

The reason Preston was nicknamed Bond goes back to the first time he walked into the Wigan changing room in March 1988. He was wearing a suit and tie, carrying a briefcase and sporting a sharp, slicked-back haircut, having arrived direct from his day job as an underwriter and claims manager at an insurance firm.

Considering most of his team-mates turned up in flip-flops and jogging bottoms, he caused something of a stir.

Preston, who actually does happen to hail from Preston, was different.

He had harboured an ambition to play for Wigan ever since he had been a season ticket holder as a schoolboy when he used to stand in the pen at Central Park, close to the entrance to the players' tunnel. His route to the first team had come via rugby union, playing for Fylde as well as England B and he had arrived at the club under the stewardship of Graham Lowe after directors Jack Robinson and Maurice Lindsay had backed a hunch and travelled to see him play at Fylde.

Preston could run. No doubt about that. He was a flier and he soon carved out a place in the affections of the spectators when he made his debut on Good Friday against St Helens and then scored five tries against Hunslet at home. He also lived up to his 'James Bond' soubriquet by invariably looking as immaculate when he walked off the pitch as he did when he stepped on to it. Not a spot of mud or a hair out of place.

The problem was that when Lowe left, John Monie did not fancy him. Not from the moment he set foot in Central Park. Monie preferred his wingers big and muscular and powerful as well as fast and resourceful. Preston, tall but slight and rangy, ticked only one of those five boxes. He was fast.

'I knew from day one he wasn't my biggest fan,' said Preston. 'He was very direct. If you didn't play well, he absolutely told you in front of everybody else.

'You knew where you stood. I got dropped quite early in the season and played in the reserves. He told me what he wanted me to do and I tried to vary my game. But if you try to bulk up and become one of these big Aussie wingers maybe you lose your speed, which was my game gone. I'd neither be a big winger, nor a quick winger.'

It is a familiar problem in team sports, often faced by players who can be regarded as essential match-winners by one coach and disposable luxury items by another coach.

Think Stan Bowles, Rodney Marsh, Matthew Le Tissier, Mario Balotelli in football. Think Danny Cipriani in rugby union. The fact that it is a struggle to think of many in the sport of rugby league probably is as good a measure as any of the challenge Preston faced under Monie at Wigan.

Yet there is no doubt he gave it his best shot, scoring five tries against Barrow in a rare first team outing to kick-start his 1989/90 season.

By the time Wembley came around he had scored 32 tries and with his handsome, suave demeanour and 'James Bond' nickname the media jumped all over him.

On the eve of the final he appeared on the back page of the *Daily Express*, dressed in black dinner suit and bow tie, holding a revolver, posing as Roger Moore's Bond character in *The Man with the Golden Gun* with his wife Debbie playing the role of Miss Moneypenny at his feet cuddling his legs.

Not that he demonstrated the nerveless trait of a master spy that night.

'I roomed with Bobbie Goulding because he said he wanted me to keep him calm,' recalled Preston. 'But when we went to bed at about 10.30pm he went to sleep and was snoring away while I couldn't sleep at all.

'I sat there watching the late-night snooker on the television with the sound down.'

His lack of sleep perhaps explains his anything-but-euphoric reaction when he scored his first try the next afternoon in a dramatic sprint to the line, which was a sporting cameo of genuine beauty.

The opportunity came after 33 minutes via a mis-kick from Warrington's Gary Mercer, which landed directly and somewhat fortunately in Preston's arms. When he looked up he saw acres of empty Wembley green space in front of him and around 80 metres separating him from the try line.

There are few more enticing prospects for a winger, especially one who at that time would by no means have been embarrassed at the start line in an Olympic 100m heat.

Out of the corner of his right eye Preston noted the hint of panic in the gait of Warrington full back David Lyon as he scrambled desperately across the field having recognised the imminent danger.

Then Preston was off, hugging the touchline and backing his raw speed, which by some distance was the most potent weapon in his sporting toolbox.

As I sat in the Wembley press box, marvelling at the balletic run of Preston on the far side of the pitch as he eluded Lyon's last-ditch attempt at a tap tackle, I could hear snatches of the BBC commentary of Ray French somewhere close at hand, competing with the swelling roar of the crowd.

'Preston, he can go the full length of the field,' screamed French in those excitable northern tones. 'I don't think Lyon will catch this lad. He's a flier, that's a try and a half.'

The reason there was no celebration is simple.

'I was nearly sick,' said Preston. 'I felt like you do in pre-season when you have been asked to do 400 metres flat out in training. It was the heat, the nervous tension and it was the first long run I had done in the game at speed.

'I was knackered and if I didn't look happy I was really trying to cover up how bad I felt. I kept calling the trainer on to cover me in water. I was not unfit but all that nervous energy, the heat, the run, no sleep, it just all caught up with me.'

If that spectacular race to the line justifiably ranks as a sparkling Wembley moment, one which regularly graces compilations of memorable Challenge Cup tries, then Preston's second touchdown in the second half earned him the Eddie Waring Memorial Trophy for the try of the season.

This time he did not run 80 metres with the ball, just five. And he owed that to the bravery of Edwards, who despite his broken cheekbone and eye socket had supported the combined 75-metre break of Steve Hampson and then Ellery Hanley to carry on the move, eventually flipping the ball into Preston's grasp for the easiest of touchdowns.

What did Monie do next? He took Preston off, substituting him at what turned out to be the zenith of his career. That is the ruthless nature of elite sport. Coaches do not deal in emotions. They regard sentiment as another word for weakness. They deal in cold, stark facts.

Perhaps the most telling example of that came just two weeks later on the same Wembley pitch when Manchester United manager Alex Ferguson dropped goalkeeper Jim Leighton for the 1990 FA Cup Final replay against Crystal Palace. Leighton had conceded three goals in erratic fashion in the initial 3-3 draw and while Ferguson enjoyed a close bond with Leighton from their days at Aberdeen he brought in Les Sealey for the replay.

United won 1-0 and Leighton, his confidence shattered and career at Old Trafford undermined by his humiliation, appeared just once more in a United shirt.

What is best for the team always comes first with the top coaches. The fact that Preston had an opportunity to become the first man to score a hat-trick of tries in a Wembley final, a chance to make history, simply was not a consideration that interrupted Monie's thought process.

In the days that followed, and it almost seems churlish to mention it when Edwards was lying in a hospital bed with a shattered face for his efforts, Preston mulled over that Monie decision. Not in a good way.

'That's the one thing that grates with me when I think about it,' said Preston. 'Nobody had scored three tries at Wembley and I was in a reasonable position to do that. Three days later when it really hit me I thought, "Bloody hell, I could have been the first. I could have made history."

'Still, if someone had said when I was seven that in 14 years' time I would play for this club and score two tries at Wembley I would have said, "Not a chance."'

Preston did enjoy one more fleeting taste of fame when the post-cup parade culminated at Wigan town hall and his father-in-law arrived to pick him up.

As Preston attempted to leave the building he was mobbed by a sea of fans and stranded somewhere between the steps of the town hall and the waiting vehicle, requiring a police escort to come to the rescue.

'Daniel Craig gets it all the time. It only happened to me once,' said Wigan's own James Bond.

The start of the next season saw Preston back in the reserves and he knew his days at the club were effectively over around Christmas time when every wing at the club, bar him, was injured. When the team sheet went up for the weekend match, instead of Preston receiving the expected recall, Phil Clarke, a second row or loose forward, was named on the left wing. Short of flying a banner proclaiming, 'Preston out', above the main stand, Monie's intent could not have been clearer.

'No disrespect to Phil but that's when I knew it was time to move on,' said Preston. 'I knew my days were numbered. I did have a conversation with John Monie but I was not the sort of player who chucked his toys out of the pram or caused trouble.

'Maybe you should do that, but it's not my style. When I rang Monie he said I had no future at the club. Not in a horrible way and in the end we parted on reasonable terms. I remember being in the boardroom just before I left and everybody thanked me and said I had conducted myself very well.

'Part of me thinks, "Does that really count for much?"

'I was a little bit bitter when I left Wigan after having had that feeling of supporting the club since I was young. I loved the club and wanted the club to win everything. It went from that to not really being interested in the club. It took me a few years to get over that. I never wanted Wigan to lose but I wasn't that bothered.

'It is only really in the last couple of years that I have returned to wanting them to win. I watch them on telly when I can and when I went down to the DW Stadium once I did the Golden Gamble at half-time and I got a nice reception.'

To some, Preston will be viewed as a one-season wonder, perhaps even a one-hit Wembley wonder. Viewed in isolation his Wigan career does appear that way.

But what a hit! Preston can still reach for that DVD and savour the time when he was the toast of Wembley.

It should also be remembered that he went on to play for Halifax for five seasons.

'When I went to Halifax I scored 20-odd tries a season and I won player of the year in my first season there. If I hadn't done that people could perhaps say I was a one-season wonder but I am pretty confident that what I did at Halifax showed I could do it.'

It would be wrong to leave 1990 without remembering one Wigan player who played for the third and last time at Wembley against Warrington, New Zealander Adrian Shelford.

Shelford, cousin of All Black Wayne Shelford, was a prop who had arrived at Wigan in 1987 amid controversy which culminated in a High Court battle when St Helens contested his registration.

Wigan won the legal wrangle and Shelford repaid them by racking up the hard yards with no complaint and little trumpet blowing until his career was ended early at 27 by a knee injury.

His commendable reaction was to launch into a new career, studying at Edge Hill University in Ormskirk, graduating with honours and taking a teaching post at a local high school. He had just gained promotion when he died of a heart attack on 19 September 2003, aged just 39.

13

Unsung Heroes

THE players are the most important assets in any successful sports club. That goes almost without saying. Without talented and committed players prepared to put their bodies on the line, as Shaun Edwards did in the 1990 final, greatness is impossible.

But great players require great support, which is where men such as Bill Hartley come in.

Hartley, an international athlete of some repute, was well into his 30s when he became besotted with rugby league and the memory still sets his eyes twinkling and brings a respectful hush to his voice.

'The thumping of the table. The effing and blinding. The noise of the aluminium studs on the concrete. The smell of Vaseline. The look on their faces. They were going to war, to do battle. I'll never forget that.'

Hartley was sitting sipping tea amid the radiant blooms and verdant greenery of his horticultural business in Lydiate, Merseyside, but for a moment he was transported back to the day he stood outside the Widnes dressing room at Naughton Park, where he had been invited by coach Vince Karalius in the 1980s.

'Believe me, for someone whose life had been spent in an athletics dressing room you could hardly have got anything further apart,' he said. 'It was such an education. I have always had a massive respect for the players ever since. Anyone who walks across that whitewash is brave in my eyes.'

Hartley was smitten from that first encounter, which is how he ended up spending six years at Wigan, helping to hone the fitness and sprinting talents of some of rugby's finest athletes, and why he ranks that time as among the most enjoyable and professionally rewarding years of his career.

For those not around before Ben Johnson, the most infamous drug cheat of them all, turned athletics into the sport that nobody could believe, Hartley was one of Britain's good guys.

Athletics was his gift as well as his passion, so much so that by 18 he held the under-19 record for 400m hurdles, recording 52.9 seconds.

He went on to win a silver medal for Great Britain at the Commonwealth Games in Christchurch in 1974 in the 400m relay and then a gold medal at the European Championships in Rome the same year at the same event, along with Alan Pascoe, David Jenkins and Jim Aukett.

Hartley could run fast. Very fast. His achievements on the running track are a source of national as well as personal pride.

But there is no doubt it is Wigan and rugby which remain in his blood.

He arrived as fitness and sprint coach at Central Park in 1986, having had a spell with Widnes following that eye-opener with Karalius outside the dressing rooms.

His appointment was another sign that Wigan were going places. Another stepping stone on the journey towards full professionalism.

Few clubs at that time would have assembled a backroom staff that amounted to anything more than a part-time kit man, a matchday physio and a groundsman and in some cases all three were the same man.

Hartley's arrival ensured that supreme fitness shared the agenda with other essential qualities such as talent and commitment. It was everything. The first priority when it came to pursuing the upper slopes of athletic excellence. He brought in drinks and energy supplements from his athletics days and from the world of cycling. He extolled the merits of good hydration and diet and the benefits of post-match rehabilitation.

He ensured the players had the necessary pre-season miles in their legs, many of which were captured in lung-bursting, sweat-dripping hill runs up to Haigh Hall country house, a locally famous and historic building in Wigan which was built by James Lindsay, seventh Earl of Balcarres, between 1827 and 1840 and was the seat of the Earls of Crawford and Balcarres for several generations.

That was how the imposing property was always described in the glossy promotional brochures at any rate.

Many Wiganers would have played in the landscaped grounds of the estate as children and ridden the train behind the steam traction engine which linked the hall from the Plantation Gates on Wigan Lane, or simply taken in the spectacular views it affords of the town and surrounding countryside to the west.

Many might remember stopping to watch as the Wigan team sprinted by.

In the late 1980s and early 1990s the grounds were a familiar sight to the Wigan first-teamers, not that they would have appreciated the hall's grand architecture at the time. The long and winding hill leading to it, through an extensive plantation of trees and rhododendrons, is a match for any athlete. A perfect challenge to sift the weak from the strong.

On top of that the squad underwent conditioning work at the Robin Park training centre in Wigan, where players would pull sledges with weights attached. It was energy sapping and character building.

'The more you sweat in training, the less you bleed in battle.' That summed up Hartley's contribution and the players responded fully and eagerly to his professional approach and inclusive manner.

Hartley said, 'Nearly all of them were very good trainers. They were easy to work with. Some of them played for the money, some of them played because they liked the game and some of them loved the training.

'Andy Goodway loved the training. Denis Betts was a good trainer. Often we would be going back from training and he would say, "Bill, come down early tomorrow and we'll do some extra sprints."

'He and Steve Hampson would do a sprint session along the concrete walkway at the bottom of the stand at Central Park before training even started.

'They wanted to be better. Andy Platt, Dean Bell, what fantastic professionals. We trained Tuesday, Thursday, Saturday with a game on Sunday, but on the other days, without fail, such as Betts and Platt and Bell would be in the gym.

'If I picked a back and a forward from my time there who epitomised the essence of that side it would be Dean Bell in the backs, you just could not fault him, and in the forwards probably Andy Platt. A top pro.

'Bell was uncompromising. Very tough. Very committed. He was prepared to put his body on the line all the time and prepared to lead by example.

'When he first joined the club from Leeds we used to go back there and the fans used to chant, "Judas, Judas", at him. Dean said he was sure they were chanting, "Genius, genius". I don't think he was joking.'

It was a dressing room full of powerful characters prepared to go the extra mile to ensure they remained fit and in the first team.

'I remember Andy Goodway had made a record number of consecutive appearances,' said Hartley. 'But he played one Sunday and received a dead leg. There was another game on the Wednesday and he was desperate to keep his run going. So he didn't sleep on the Sunday night, but stayed up all night to put an ice pack on his injury every 20 minutes. The next day he sat for hours with his leg raised up on a settee so he could play. He wanted the run to continue. He wanted the money too.'

Such dedication was a hallmark of the Wembley glory years and while much of Hartley's fitness work would be carried out on a group basis, the sprint element was often undertaken with individuals.

'I worked a lot with Shaun Edwards, Steve Hampson and Denis Betts on an individual basis,' said Hartley.

'Shaun was a good pro, had a great understanding of the game. It was in his body. Gregory was the same. Shaun had a massive will inside him to improve. He wanted to play good football. He wanted to entertain. They all realised pace was something you could not neglect and if you were not doing something to improve, others would steal a march on you.'

Everything that was cutting edge in the athletics world, Hartley was looking to pass on.

Much of it involved trying to improve stride length and the technicalities and mechanics of running at speed.

'Obviously, when you have a ball under your arm and someone is trying to take your head off it is a different situation from just thinking about your style. Generally, however, we did make improvements with all the players. The aims and ambitions to go forward were very strong. I really enjoyed contributing in that atmosphere.'

The contribution of Derek 'Taffy' Jones was simple: to make sure the players had whatever they needed. He was the go-to man for kit, tie-ups and shoulder pads and tape for strapping.

He was also the man who treated the Central Park pitch as if it was Centre Court at Wimbledon. Nothing came between Taffy and his desire to produce a pleasing surface for fans to admire and players to appreciate.

Once he jumped on his sit-on mower as the team were halfway through a longer-than-expected final preparation before leaving for Wembley on a Thursday morning.

'I went over to him and said, "Taffy, can't you knock it off, we are going down to Wembley, our biggest match of the season,"' recalled Joe Lydon. 'He said, "Joe, I'm getting the pitch ready for next week's Premiership final, my biggest match of the season, and you should have gone by now."'

If Hartley and Taffy were key members of the coaching team, to be followed later by fitness coach Chris Butler and physio Dave Fevre, then no one epitomised the all-for-one, one-for-all mentality that went to the core of Wigan's success during that golden era more than Keith Mills.

Millsy, as he was known, served as physio, kit man, matchday host and lottery manager during his five decades at the club. He picked the players off the ground, sponged them down and sent them back into battle when they were injured, even sometimes with rearranged faces as in the case of Shaun Edwards in the 1990 Challenge Cup Final. That is how most fans would have known him, as the larger-than-life character who dashed on to the pitch with his bag of tricks designed to patch up the wounded, even if he had no formal medical training.

He applied psychological sticking plasters too, his enthusiasm, optimism and sheer *joie de vivre* being renowned for lifting spirits. He also understood the passion and idiosyncrasies of professionals, being himself a utility sportsman of some repute.

He played in the second row, starting 25 first team games and making nine substitute appearances for Wigan from 1967 to 1969, his debut unremarkable in the great scheme of the sport but an unforgettable personal milestone when he came on from the bench during an 11-10 defeat at Dewsbury on 9 September 1967. Not surprisingly, the Mills family cherish his Wigan heritage number, which is 655 by the way, and the fact that he scored three tries in the cherry and white jersey in teams which included such illustrious characters as Billy Boston, Eric Ashton and Doug Laughton.

In many ways Millsy was a throwback to a different era. A renowned local cricketer, he even boasted the distinction of having played for Wigan Athletic reserves three times as goalkeeper in 1970. In fact, he could not understand the simmering division between the fans of the town's rugby and football clubs, even suggesting at one stage that football's Latics should no longer play in blue, but also in rugby's cherry and white to consolidate the town's sporting identity.

Men like that are diamonds in any dressing room. Why? Because they care with a passion. Because they radiate positive energy. Because they dare to dream the impossible and often help carry those around them to destinations they would otherwise never have reached.

Hartley remembers Millsy bursting out of the changing rooms after one team talk by Graham Lowe, pumping up his chest and saying at the age of 45, 'I think I could put my kit on and play myself after listening to that.'

He was only half joking.

When Millsy died aged 67 on 16 April 2012, it was no surprise that there was a stampede of top rugby internationals, including Joe Lydon, Andy Gregory, Va'aiga Tuigamala, Jason Robinson and Shaun Edwards, anxious to recognise his inspiration and his enthusiasm and his part in their success.

'He was as important in his own way as any player at the time. I can hear his accent now just thinking about him and it brings back a flood of wonderful memories,' was Robinson's touching tribute.

Millsy's wife Anne also worked at the club after being asked to go down there one day to help out for a few hours 'because one of the girls was sick'.

Twenty-five years later she was still there, having made thousands of pots of tea and washed equally as many muddy jerseys and when the club moved from Central Park to the JJB Stadium, later named the DW Stadium, to share the ground with Wigan Athletic, she took to washing both rugby and football gear.

'It was home from home,' said Anne. 'We were all in it together. We were just one big family.'

That, essentially, sums up so much of the Wigan way. Not just at the rugby club, but in the town, where there is a pride, admittedly restrained rather than gushing, in the celebration of Wiganers, sung and unsung and not just rugby players, who have enjoyed success on their travels.

Notable ones such as Sir Ian McKellen, the actor who played Gandalf in *The Lord of the Rings* and *The Hobbit* trilogies and Magneto in the *X-Men* films.

By any stretch, the man whose childhood was spent in Parson's Walk, Wigan, playing in Mesnes Park and the grounds of Wigan Cricket Club, has done the town proud.

But then it was a two-way street. The town could also claim credit for stirring and nurturing his thespian soul. After all, he saw his first plays, Shakespeare's *Twelfth Night* and *Macbeth*, at Wigan Little Theatre, and his sister Jean, five years his senior, apparently took him to see Wigan High School for Girls' production of *A Midsummer Night's Dream,* in which she played the role of Bottom.

Other entertainers include George Formby, an actor, singer-songwriter and comedian whose films, such as *No Limit* in which he played a TT motorbike rider, and comical songs while playing the ukulele, such as 'Leaning on a Lamppost', made him the UK's highest-paid entertainer in the 1930s and 1940s.

Formby, who was born in Westminster Street, Wigan, often played the gormless, accident-prone but good-natured Lancastrian whose basic goodness was the embodiment of the friendly, approachable, working-class nature of the area, but also resonated with the nation in much the same way that many of its rugby stars did in years to come. A statue of Formby stands not that far away from Billy Boston's in the town's main shopping centre, complete with toothy grin and ukulele in hand.

McKellen and Formby were not renowned Central Park enthusiasts. But comic actor Roy Kinnear, who was born in Mesnes Road, Wigan, and is best remembered for his film appearance as Veruca Salt's father in *Willy Wonka & the Chocolate Factory,* was inextricably linked to the club.

His father, Roy Muir Kinnear, played and scored a try in that first Challenge Cup Final at Wembley in 1929 when Wigan beat Dewsbury. In fact, Kinnear Snr was a Scottish dual code international centre of some renown and played 182 matches, scoring 81 tries, for Wigan between 1927 and 1933.

Tragically, he suffered an untimely death, collapsing while playing rugby union with the RAF during the Second World War, aged just 38. By unhappy coincidence his son also died unexpectedly and relatively young at the age of 54 after suffering a heart attack brought on by a riding accident while filming the sequel to *The Three Musketeers.*

Another high-profile fan, and a man located at the epicentre of the town's working class culture, was Joe Gormley, the former president of the National Union of Mineworkers, who was born in Ashton-in-Makerfield in 1917. He led the miners in two strikes in the 1970s and is widely credited with bringing down the government of Prime Minister Ted Heath, although for many years he was a voice of reason and moderation, in stark contrast to his raucous successor Arthur Scargill.

Gormley became Baron of Ashton-in-Makerfield in the 1983 honours list and his son Ian played for Widnes and regularly shared lifts with Joe Lydon on their way to training.

Down the years the rugby club has attracted all manner of famous fans, with the most recent perhaps being 2012 Tour de France winner Sir Bradley Wiggins, who lives in the area and is a regular visitor to the DW Stadium.

But it is the ordinary fans, those who invariably take ownership of the players by insisting on using their christian names as if they know them personally when talking about them, who have been the lifeblood of the club.

In the eras of Sullivan and then Boston, many of those were working class heroes in their own humble ways.

Not least the brave men who spent 12 hours at a stretch bent double or crawling on their bellies in the grime of pits such as Albert, Maypole, Giants Hall, Landgate and Astley Green, so many of whom worked in daily peril from gas leakage, tunnel collapses and explosions.

Men such as my own grandfather, Peter McCarthy, who worked as a lasher-on at Douglas Bank colliery from the age of 14. One April morning in 1916, just three weeks after his 16th birthday, he suffered a hideous fracture of his left leg when it was trapped between a chain and a half-ton coal tub.

Gangrene set in and days later the decision was taken to amputate at the upper thigh.

Like so many whose lives at that time were damaged by the harsh environment underground he never complained. In fact, 19 days after his 18th birthday he signed up in the Royal Army Supply Corps as a driver in the Great War, even though he was wearing a false leg.

Shaun Edwards signs for Wigan on his 17th birthday on 17 October 1983, surrounded by (left to right) Wigan coach Alex Murphy, directors Tom Rathbone, Jack Robinson and Maurice Lindsay, and Shaun's dad Jackie. (Wigan Evening Post)

Ellery Hanley's famous left-hand fend in action to repel Martin Meredith on his way to scoring a try in the 1988 final against Halifax. (Wigan Evening Post)

Keith Mills, trainer, physio, lotto manager and Wigan's all-round back-room motivator, raises both arms aloft as Wigan's epic Wembley run begins. (Wigan Evening Post)

Shaun Edwards becomes youngest captain to lift the Challenge Cup, aged 21. (Wigan Evening Post)

Shaun Edwards flips a pass for Andy Gregory to score in 1989 final against St Helens. A 17-year-old Gary Connolly is lying prone after failing to make the tackle. (Wigan Evening Post)

Steve Hampson, who had missed three previous Wembley finals through injury, punches the air in delight before diving over to score the try which proved the 'jinx' was finally broken. (Wigan Evening Post)

Captain Ellery Hanley lifts the trophy in 1989 after receiving it from (left) the Earl of Derby. (PA Images)

Ellery Hanley is tackled by Warrington captain Mike Gregory in the 1990 final. (PA Images)

A flying Mike Gregory hauls down Shaun Edwards. (Wigan Evening Post)

Wigan prop Adrian Shelford is tackled by Warrington's Paul Bishop. (PA Images)

Winger Mark Preston eludes Warrington full-back David Lyon on his 80m sprint to the try line. (Wigan Evening Post)

Wigan line up for their medals as captain Hanley lifts the team's third Challenge Cup in a row with (left to right) Hanley, Hampson, Dermott, Edwards, Preston, Goulding, Betts, Kevin Iro. (PA Images)

Frano Botica dives over for a try against St Helens in 1991, evading the tackle of Gary Connolly. (Wigan Evening Post)

(Top) *Martin Offiah points the way as Edwards runs in a try against Castleford in 1992. (Wigan Evening Post)*

(Middle) *Offiah bursts through two Castleford defenders to score his second try. (Wigan Evening Post)*

(Bottom) *Prime Minister John Major congratulates Wigan captain Dean Bell in the Wembley changing room after the 28-12 victory against Castleford. (Wigan Evening Post)*

(Top) **Offiah joins the sea of faces at Central Park for Wigan's triumphant homecoming in 1992.** (Wigan Evening Post)

(Right) **Kelvin Skerrett shares a humorous moment with the fans after Wigan's 20-14 triumph against Widnes in 1993.** (Wigan Evening Post)

Andy Farrell slides in for a try under the posts against Leeds in 1994. (Wigan Evening Post)

(Top) **Offiah sprints away from the Leeds defence on his way to the most famous rugby league try scored at Wembley. (Wigan Evening Post)**

(Middle) **Offiah dives over the try line with Leeds full-back Alan Tait trailing. (PA Images)**

(Bottom) **Offiah's famous try-celebration pose, which is immortalised in bronze as part of the rugby league statue at Wembley. (PA Images)**

Edwards tackles his big pal and former colleague Hanley, now playing for Leeds. (PA Images)

Mick Cassidy, Gary Connolly and Barrie-Jon Mather relax in the Wembley dressing room.

Head coach John Dorahy holds up the infamous sign 'For All You Doubters: SUCK' on Wigan's homecoming at Central Park in 1994. (Wigan Evening Post)

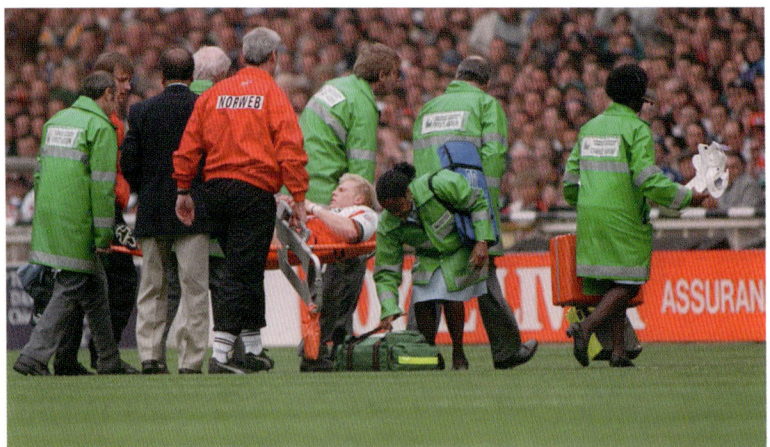

(Top) **Mick Cassidy is taken off on a stretcher with concussion after just nine minutes in the 1995 final against Leeds. (PA Images)**

(Right) **Denis Betts barging through the Leeds defence. (PA Images)**

Skerrett grabs hooker Martin Hall in celebration after he scored a try in the 1995 final, while Andy Farrell (right) is the picture of joy and Leeds's Garry Schofield (centre) the picture of despair. (PA Images)

Jason Robinson slides over for the first of his two tries in 1995.
(PA Images)

Wigan mascot Michael Malley, aged eight, with Barrie-Jon Mather.

Edwards and Offiah celebrate. (PA Images)

Francis Malley Jnr., Great Britain's shoe repairing champion, with Wigan's other big trophy, the prestigious Puritan Cup, won in 1958. Wigan won the Challenge Cup that year too, beating Workington 13-9.

Bill Hartley, Wigan fitness and sprint coach from 1986 to 1992, tending the flowers at his horticultural business in Lydiate.

Martin Dermott points to the ethos which could have summed up Wigan's golden era.

Martin Offiah sits in front of the picture gallery at his home in Ealing.

Billy Boston surrounded by fans at his statue unveiling in Wigan's Believe Square in September 2016.

Down the years Wigan has been a town in which tough men took life's hardships in their stride while their rugby heroes provided a weekly escape from the mundanity of working life.

Rugby was a talking point, a collective rallying force, the dissection of that week's game a daily ritual in the shops and pubs.

It still is today with the merits or otherwise of Sam Tomkins, Liam Farrell and Sean O'Loughlin top of the agenda where once it was Sullivan or Ernie Ashcroft or Eric Ashton or Shaun Edwards.

For my father and for me as a child it was invariably Boston.

My dad was in the shoe business and I can still recall the organic smell of leather and the thick scent of glue, remarkably similar to a quarter pound of pear drops, which permeated from his hot and heady cellar at 174 Wallgate, whenever I recall the 1950s and 1960s.

In those days Wallgate was, as it remains today, a major south-western thoroughfare into the town. Now, however, it is shorn of life, having been turned into an overspill area for industrial units, warehouses, car showrooms and faceless businesses. Progress? It doesn't seem like it.

Back in the day it was a bustling hubbub of daily activity, with commercial premises and family traders lining both sides of the street, all living above the shops, with terraced rows of houses behind, many of which were inhabited by the mill workers who plied their trade at Trencherfield Mill and other Victorian factories surrounding the Wigan Pier area of town. An honest, loyal, working-class community where there was no need to lock your door; where Shaun Edwards's parents lived; where Boston first chose to settle.

The inhabitants really never needed to venture into the town centre. Some streets were virtually self-sufficient such was the variety of shops plying their trade.

For example, circa 1960, on the north side of Wallgate, from Miry Lane to Clayton Street, a distance of no more than 100 metres, there was the Star pub, Ogilvie's sweet shop, a well-patronised butcher's, Malley's shoe shop, Young's sweet shop, a Post Office, Dr Petrie's surgery, Taylor's the newsagent, a chip shop, another pub, Dr Hall's surgery, Ashcroft's grocery, another chip shop, a clothing factory and yet another pub, the Grapes Hotel.

The streets were dusty, the carbon footprint huge as chimneys, domestic and industrial, spewed out their waste, pea-soupers were frequent and sulphurous and accompanied by an eerie quiet. Often the atmosphere was so dense that conductors would walk in front of the cherry and white Leyland buses run by Wigan Corporation waving a torch.

And whenever the shift patterns changed at the mills the clip-clop of clogs on the pavement resembled a hurrying herd of Shetland ponies.

These were days of outside lavatories, shire horses pulling dust carts, church walking days and the ABC Minors on a Saturday morning.

Hard days. Happy days. Business was brisk, family was paramount and the camaraderie was warm and tangible.

My father, Francis Malley Jnr, ran his shop with his brother Gerrard, making clogs and repairing and selling footwear. In some ways they were to shoes what Ian McKellen was to Shakespeare and Shaun Edwards was to scoring tries.

They had the trophies and diplomas to prove it. In fact, one of my earliest memories is holding aloft the replica of a solid silver trophy my dad won as national master shoe repairer of Great Britain in 1958.

The actual trophy looked uncannily similar to the Challenge Cup except that, if anything, it was even larger than the one Wigan won that season at Wembley for defeating Workington Town 13-9 in the final. It was also considerably more expensive, being insured for £400, equivalent to £6,500 in today's money. The story of the shoes merited a picture and a few paragraphs in the local press. The rugby, rightly, received many more column inches.

But, in truth, there were stories like my father's and grandfather's all over town. Ordinary hard-working men with extraordinary talents earning a modest living but setting the bar high in terms of honesty and integrity for all who followed. Many of them supporting the rugby team with a passion and providing a key ingredient for greatness to emerge.

I like to think of them all as Wigan's backroom boys, grafting behind the scenes just like Bill Hartley and Millsy and Taffy.

14

'Squeeze an Orange and You Get Orange Juice'

I T IS no secret. John Monie did not fancy Frano Botica. If it had been down to Monie he would not have allowed Botica anywhere near Central Park when the New Zealand All Black signed for Wigan in the latter half of 1990.

Monie was against trying to teach Botica a new art at the age of 26. He wanted tried and tested rugby league players, men steeped in the game from an early age.

There was no risk in that. What you saw was normally what you got in the rugby league world.

That was how Wigan had plied their trade for years; with stars possessing a proven track record. A hat-trick of consecutive Challenge Cups in the trophy cabinet said why change?

It is no thanks to Monie then and testament instead to the shrewd eye and ambitious instinct of director Jack Robinson that Botica came to Central Park and went on to rewrite the record books as a rugby league goal kicker.

Robinson had seen snippets of Botica in action on a video sent to him by one of the club's scouts and was entranced by the tidy running and jinking tricks of the Kiwi half back.

Botica had played 27 rugby union games for New Zealand. He was considered to be a better running half back than his counterpart at the time, the legendary fly half Grant Fox. He just was not as efficient in the kicking department.

Or at least that was the view Down Under, although that seems scarcely believable considering his dead-eye kicking feats while at Central

Park saw him become the fastest man in the history of the British game to reach 1,000 points.

Buying in talent from across the rugby Rubicon was not the usual Robinson way of working either. Robinson had always preferred home-grown or specialised assets. He wanted players who had lived and breathed rugby league almost from being a toddler, preferably British, Australian or New Zealand and even better if they had come through the local amateur ranks.

But there was a ripple of change occurring in the game, which mani-fested itself in an exodus of All Blacks players seeking the rewards of professionalism.

Full back Matthew Ridge went to Manly-Warringah where Graham Lowe was the new coach, John Gallagher turned up at Leeds with a million-dollar contract and John Schuster signed for Newcastle Knights in New South Wales. Botica arrived at Wigan, but only after he had been smuggled out of his New Zealand tour headquarters to be shown around the professional set-up he would be joining at Central Park.

In those days there remained a stigma to cross-code movements, which meant they were not entered into lightly or ostentatiously.

Yet even when Botica arrived, Monie still required convincing. He had wanted to sign Phil Blake, a tough, no-nonsense utility Australian, who could play at half back or centre or full back or even on occasion at hooker.

Blake had played 11 games for Wigan in 1989, scoring seven tries, in the off-season during a spell at South Sydney.

When Robinson opted for Botica it closed the door on any Blake deal. Monie was not pleased, even when fitness coach Bill Hartley reported his first impressions of Botica during a pre-season training run at Haigh Hall were positive.

'I was still running quite a bit myself in those days,' said Hartley. 'And I would take them on a really tough run. I would go off hard, really hard, but I could not shake off Botica.

'I told Monie, "He's stubborn. He has got something within that is special which makes him never give up."

'John said, "Yeah, whatever." But then he played him on the wing and what a career he had.'

A career during which he was equally adept at wing, stand off or full back and which saw him play 179 matches for Wigan, scoring 1,931 points, comprising 66 tries, 827 goals and 13 drop goals, putting him fourth on the all-time Wigan points list behind Jim Sullivan (4,483), Andy Farrell (3,135) and Pat Richards (2,468).

A total of 324 of those points came in his first season when he kicked 126 goals and scored 18 tries, statistics which turned even doubting John

Monie into doting John Monie. But that 1990/91 season and its inevitable finale, once again at Wembley, was not about one player, even one who added such obvious value as Botica with his nerveless and precision kicking.

Rarely has one season been more about the willingness of a group of individuals to overcome whatever mud, blood and ridiculous scheduling the rugby authorities were prepared to hurl at them.

The weather did not help with snow in February causing postponements, meaning Wigan played three league games in January and just two in February, with rearranged cup matches and international call-ups also combining to create a backlog which inevitably culminated in fixture gridlock as the final throes of the season approached.

So punishing was the programme once Easter was done that Monie dubbed Wigan's race for the championship title and Challenge Cup double 'Mission Impossible'.

At one stage, after the team had earned their Wembley place with a bruising 30-16 victory against Oldham in the semi-final at Burnden Park, they were required to play eight matches in 18 days. It left little scope for preparing and recovering.

Tuesday, Friday, Monday, Thursday, Sunday, Tuesday, Thursday, Saturday. That was the relentless match rota. Like hamsters on a wheel they just ploughed on as bodies creaked and minds began to fray.

Yet, in that spell, Wigan dropped just one point in an 18-18 draw at Bradford, after beating rivals Widnes 26-6 two days previously in a vital fixture at Central Park.

Much of that was down to mental toughness, an indefatigable will and the fact that during the spells of enforced inactivity Wigan worked harder than ever.

'We trained like stink,' recalled Bill Hartley.

'We did some fantastic sessions in the indoor area at Robin Park. I made them do some of the old sessions I used to do with the hurdles back in my running days. Put two hurdles down 35 metres apart and then run one way and then the other jumping the obstacles.

'The boys really bought into it and it was the fitness we were able to get into them during that time that allowed them to withstand all those games at the end. Collectively, they were also tougher mentally than a lot of the other sides.'

That mental strength is the quality that so often separates the very good from the greatest champions.

The mark of Monie the coach was that he was capable of taking all the separate examples of innate individual toughness and linking them together to make an almost unbreakable force. The starting point was always defence and one verbatim account of his half-time team talk in that 18-18 draw against Bradford demonstrates his leadership qualities at their most inspiring.

Wigan required a win to wrap up the title before their final match of the season against Leeds but they were trailing 12-2 at Central Park to a Bradford side who had already beaten them 31-30 at Odsal earlier in the season and also knocked them out of the Regal Trophy at Central Park.

It was beginning to resemble a match too far, but Monie was having none of it. Instead, he strode into the dressing room and, as the following excerpt from Neil Hanson's *Blood, Mud and Glory* suggests, rarely had the players seen the normally, calm, composed Australian so angry:

> 'We fought all this way to get here, the title is within our grasp and we're going down without a fight. To come all this way and then go out like cowards.
>
> 'This is like the Sydney grand final: win this game and we've won the championship, and we've got some players that I haven't even rated three out of ten on their first-half showing. Tell me you're tired and I'll take you off the field.
>
> 'This is a test of character. This is when you find out what's inside you. Squeeze an orange and you get orange juice out of it, because that's what's inside it. Now you've come to the squeeze and we're finding out what's inside you. I don't want players who are great when we're winning; I want players who'll dig deep into their guts when we're struggling.
>
> 'I hope you're angry. You've got a right to be angry; they've got ten more points than you. Don't worry about scoring the ten points. You'll score the points. Worry about not letting them score any more. It's defence that'll win this title. Stop them scoring this half and we'll win the title. Get into them.
>
> 'The Wembley team will be made up of tacklers. I won't take anybody to Wembley who won't put his body on the line tonight. There are 15 of you. Together as a team let's win the title.'

The true brilliance of that coaching soliloquy was that not only did Monie beat his team with a stick to rouse them for one more supreme effort to clinch the title, he also used the carrot of Wembley which was a fortnight away.

It was leadership at its finest.

Not that it looked that way when Bradford extended their lead to 18-2 with a try from Darrell Shelford five minutes after the interval. A stirring comeback, however, echoing Monie's words and including tries from Denis

Betts and Kelvin Skerrett, left Wigan just one point away from winning the title, a feat which was duly completed two days later with a 20-8 victory against Leeds at Headingley.

That was another momentous performance, perhaps more so because, prior to kick-off and at half-time, pain-killing injections were being administered almost as liberally as water bottles to wounded and battle-weary players in the Wigan dressing room.

When captain Hanley limped back on to the field at the final whistle, having gone off injured after contributing a rare drop goal, along with three from Bobbie Goulding, as well as tries from Andy Goodway, Martin Dermott and Denis Betts, the title and a sponsor's cheque for £44,000 were Wigan's.

Then something just as wonderful happened, which quite possibly would have occurred only in rugby league.

Harry Jepson, a Leeds director and also the president of the Rugby Football League at the time, entered the Wigan dressing room and delivered a fulsome tribute that said so much about the fairness and camaraderie inherent in him, his club and his sport.

'In the entire history of the game, I don't think a team has ever achieved what you have done,' Jepson told the mud-spattered faces.

'This will go down in the history of the game as the greatest championship feat ever. It reflects great credit on you and on Wigan. No other team in the world, and I mean in the world, could have done it.'

And so once more, wearily but wonderfully, to Wembley.

15

Pigs Might Fly

THE ODD shout from a groundsman echoed eerily around the naked void that Wembley always resembled when spectators were not present to dress it in ebullient life and vivid colour.

And as the breeze played blow football with a few scraps of paper on the concrete terraces, Ellery Hanley and Joe Lydon jogged down the old Wembley touchline, guarded as it was by the historic Twin Towers.

It was Friday morning, just 28 hours or so before Wigan were due to play St Helens in the 1991 Challenge Cup Final and the physically punishing denouement to the 'Mission Impossible' season looked like claiming two high-profile victims as Lydon and Hanley cautiously negotiated a 20-minute fitness test.

Both were doubtful, seriously doubtful, having been suffering from knee and hamstring problems.

They broke into a series of 20-metre sprints and then slowed to a jog again before stopping at the corner of the pitch and completing a few gentle stretching exercises, desperately hoping to exorcise the aches and pains they were both experiencing.

Lydon grimaced as he mustered one final stretch before glancing across at Hanley and saying, 'I'm not right. It just doesn't feel right. What about you?'

Hanley shook his head and Lydon recalls him saying he felt exactly the same. He was not fit.

The injury, which had seen Hanley come off early against Leeds, was still causing problems. The pair rose to their feet and began trudging resignedly across to the other side of the pitch to break the bad news to John Monie who had been watching the test studiously, together with a couple of the Wigan directors.

Monie was the sort of coach who trusted his players to determine the measure of their own fitness but he began walking towards the pair, anxious to know the verdict.

'Okay lads, how are you both?'

Lydon's lips tightened and he shook his head.

'I'm not right. I'm worried I might let the team down if I played,' he said.

Monie then turned to Hanley and asked, 'How about you?'

A quarter of a century later Hanley's response still brings a look of incredulity to Lydon's face.

'Ellery looked him straight in the eye and said, "I'm all right. I'm fine,"' gasped Lydon, his voice rising half an octave as he recalled the incident.

'I turned to Ellery and said, "You bastard!" Then I looked at John Monie and said, "Can I change my opinion?" and he just shook his head and said "No".

'When Ellery ran out the next day he couldn't beat the band, but in some ways it epitomised Ellery. He was so competitive that he just didn't want to give up playing at Wembley. I felt I couldn't have done the team justice. For me the team came first.'

Lydon strode off and as he walked back to the changing rooms, trying to reconcile the decision he had just made with that of Hanley's, one of the Wigan directors, who had been studying the fitness test, caught up with him and said, 'Don't worry Joe, we will look after you.'

'He meant financially,' explained Lydon. 'By withdrawing myself it meant I wouldn't pick up my winning money for Wembley, which was quite lucrative at that time. Needless to say, however, they didn't look after me. They looked after the lads who played. But I had too much fun and too many good things happen to me at that time to worry about money.'

The next day began as usual. It had reached that stage. So consistent had the trips south in spring become that there really was a 'usual' custom and practice attached to Wigan at Wembley.

The team rose early and assembled in the car park of their Woodford Green hotel. There was a head count and a check to make sure no one was sick or missing and then a light training session was held which involved little more than a runaround among the cars.

The players and staff would head off to Wembley after noon and stick to the normal routine, which meant a couple of card tables at the back of the coach.

Some players would play cards, others were more introspective, musing privately on what the day might hold in store. Clarifying their particular job. Familiarising themselves with moves and calls.

Some were losers before they even reached the ground.

'I wasn't a very good card player,' admitted Lydon. 'But Frano Botica was the worst card player I have ever known. He never worked out in all the years he was at Wigan that the reflection in the window he always sat at showed all his cards.

'Some people, such as Phil Clarke, would never play cards. He was a bit of a worrier. He worried if we were ten minutes late. He worried if we were ten minutes early.

'It was never big gambling, though, and there was always a point, about two miles out from the ground, when the call would come from the coach: "Cards away". That meant it was time to stop playing and switch on.

'Then it was time to get off the coach and you know you have got a run going when the doorman at Wembley knows you. He used to say, "Hello, how are you gents? Nice to see you again," and he really did know quite a few of us by name. I used to love Wembley, it was a fantastic place.'

It was also a venue which by now really did feel like a home from home to many of the players, although that year, when Wigan were pushed close to the edge by St Helens, it belonged to one in particular: Denis Betts.

The second-rower made 39 appearances that season, more than any other Wigan player. He also scored 12 tries, the most by any Wigan forward apart from Hanley.

In many ways it was the season when the youngster who signed professional forms as a 16-year-old came of age, somewhat appropriately at 21.

Actually, the circumstances surrounding that signing in the Wigan boardroom have become common knowledge on the after-dinner speaking circuit where Betts is in demand.

Not the story about reporters choking on their coffee when Maurice Lindsay informed them that Betts was already a father to his first daughter. That is a myth. The choking, that is.

What was true is that Betts, who was brought up in a rough, tough area of Salford, around a mile and a half from Old Trafford, arrived at that signing with his mum, and a dad who he hadn't seen for years, and was presented with a cheque for £5,000.

Let Betts himself tell the tale:

'My dad was pretty rough. He was a man of his time, knocked my mum about and it wasn't a nice family environment for me and my brother. It happened that just as I was 16 he reappeared and was seeing my mum again and living with us for six or seven months. He was full of bravado and bullshit.

'He took the cheque and said, "I'll look after this for you." I tried to get it off him but I didn't see him for a number of years. It won't surprise you to learn that my dad is called...Denis Betts.'

Thus Betts never saw a penny of his signing-on fee, although his rapid success at Central Park meant that his appearance-driven contract delivered time and time again.

He received £1,000 for playing for Great Britain colts, £2,000 for playing for Lancashire, £3,500 for Great Britain, £5,000 for touring with Great Britain and another £5,000 after his first ten first-team games.

'I was very fortunate I hit all those marks in the first two or three years,' said Betts, who was a natural athlete as a youngster and was on Manchester United's books for a while as a schoolboy.

All of that was on top of the appearance fees at the club, which saw Betts earning £25 to play for the under-19s, £50 for the second team and £250 for the first team. Not a bad week's wage in 1986.

'By the second year I was doing all right because I was playing Thursday night for the second team, training with the first team, playing Saturday morning for the colts and then turning out as substitute for the first team on the Sunday. That's why when I hear talk about overplaying these days I tell people, in those days I wanted to play in every game.'

Betts was pretty soon a fixture-and-fitting in the Wigan side, one who was to feature in seven of the eight-in-a-row finals. He also went on to coach Wigan for a season and then enjoy success in a prolonged stay at Widnes as he endeavoured to restore the club to former glories. At the age of 43 and while head coach at Widnes he even went back to school with the young students at the University of Central Lancashire where over a span of two years he gained a post-graduate diploma in sports coaching.

There is a school of thought that says sportsmen are not always the brightest, illustrated by the Wigan substitute in a mud-caked shirt who was said once to have been pulled over by the referee after a melee during a match, given a talking to, and as the official spun him round to confirm his identiy, asked, 'Are you 17?'

'No, I'm 28,' he replied.

Betts belies that image and admits the lessons learned in a lifetime of brutal physicality were crucial in overcoming the more cerebral challenges in the classroom and the changing room in his new life as a coach.

'I used the disciplines I had as a player not to be distracted by reputation,' said Betts. 'What I got from being a decent player was a foot in the door which a lot of people don't get. What I didn't want was to be put out of the room because I wasn't able to do the job.

'Getting myself some qualifications and having a willingness to work, not just at the elite end, gave me an understanding of how a club functions.

'I've seen plenty of players who think the game owes them a living because they were decent players, but reputation doesn't mean a lot to me. It's about character, about my understanding of myself.

'I don't need a moment in the sun because I have had plenty of those, so I am not chasing anything. From education and reading, what I wanted as a coach was to improve people, not to win things. The rugby playing side is easy. It is how do I make people better.'

Few coaches speak with more eloquence, passion or wisdom, derived from decades of hard-fought battles. Down the years Betts has thought long and hard about what was the most important ingredient underpinning the halcyon days at Central Park and he sums it up in one word: humility.

'It is one thing we had more than any other team,' said Betts. 'We understood that we were pretty good and that for us to stay where we wanted to stay we had to work twice as hard as everyone else. There was never any bravado in the team, never any singing and dancing. We won, shook hands and walked off the field. When we lost we shook hands, walked off the field and worked out why it happened.

'Those qualities of humility and hard work came through Graham Lowe and John Monie and Ellery Hanley and Andy Goodway.

'They came through Andy Platt when he joined and Joe Lydon, who was a free spirit but with a desire to win. They came through Shaun Edwards and Andy Gregory. I'd like to think it was ingrained in me from where I had come from and then got passed on to your Phil Clarkes and your Andy Farrells.

'For those kind of people to stay in that team they had to have humility to work hard and understand what it was to play for the Wigan club. The sacrifices you needed to make as an individual for the good of the team.'

Yet Betts would not have been surprised by the outcome of Hanley's fitness test that Friday morning at Wembley in 1991 when the captain's ambition to lift the cup once more superseded any concerns for his physical wellbeing.

'He is what great players are,' said Betts. 'He is an enigma, an iconic figure of his time. Whatever went on in his personal life or with everything else, he gave everything he had to be a winner. That meant crawling over people sometimes, even his own team.

'If you wanted to get there you had to appreciate the desire he showed to win. I didn't know him that well personally, I don't think a lot of people did, but what you saw was the determination he had and the tenacity and the relentless drive to win.'

The match against St Helens, however, was not one of Hanley's finest. The work rate and tackling, as ever, were there, but the inspirational running, which had devastated Halifax in 1988, demolished St Helens in 1989 and torn apart Warrington in 1990, was missing.

The same could be said for much of the Wigan team, many of whom were carrying knocks and niggles after the exertions of previous weeks.

It was a cagey, tactical match with Wigan taking an early lead via a Frano Botica penalty when George Mann was caught offside.

A raking kick by Shaun Edwards was then picked up by Saints' Australian full back Phil Veivers, who attempted to run the ball back. As if to demonstrate that sporting contests are sometimes swayed by quirks of fortune, Veivers's chin appeared to clash accidentally and freakishly with Edwards's head in the resulting attempted tackle, leaving the St Helens player flat out and the ball loose.

Kevin Iro gratefully gathered it up and passed to David Myers whose right-footed sidestep took him over the line for the touchdown. Botica failed to add the conversion from wide out.

Wigan's second try followed soon after, this time Dean Bell providing the break with a sidestep to send Betts galloping 40 yards before passing to Botica on the left wing who dived in at the corner despite a last-ditch tackle from Gary Connolly. Botica this time supplied the conversion from the touchline, a kick which put Wigan 12-0 ahead.

An intelligent Andy Gregory drop goal extended the lead to 13 after an hour before the tiredness and mental fatigue associated with 'Mission Impossible' began to fray the edges of Wigan's resolve.

Alan Hunte went in for a touchdown as Wigan scrambled, Paul Bishop adding the left-footed conversion. And when Edwards, who carried on despite having broken his nose and strained knee ligaments in the first half, gave away a cynical penalty for holding down and Bishop kicked the penalty, Wigan's cup run looked in serious danger of coming to an end.

At times such as that champions cling on. They scurry, they battle, they ignore the pain, they tackle for their lives, they find a way to win. They rely on characters such as Andy Goodway and Andy Platt and Dean Bell and unheralded prop Ian Lucas, the latter not realising that when the final hooter heralded Wigan's 13-8 victory, he would never again experience the addictive rush of excitement and energy that accompanied a Wembley adventure.

As if to illustrate the perilous fragility of a sporting career, little more than 12 months later Lucas, despite being in his physical prime, was contemplating how to spend the rest of his life after a random neck injury, sustained in a high tackle while playing for Great Britain on a tour of Australia, ended his rugby league days at the age of just 24.

'It was like having my legs cut off,' said Lucas, who was left with a compressed disc and deep root nerve damage. 'Being put on the scrapheap physically at 24 was a massive blow. In the front row you are constantly trying to prove yourself against the older, more established players. I never got to that level as an established player where I could start dishing it out to the younger ones.

'Did I have any regrets when I got injured? Yes, because I wondered what I would do with my life. But there were no regrets about playing the game. Rugby league was a great learning curve for life. It gave me the drive and the passion I wanted to take into my life out of the game.'

And while the first thing he did following his forced retirement was to buy a Suzuki 750 racing bike 'to get the adrenaline flowing again', the memories of his short playing career remain precious.

Such as celebrating his 40th birthday on the 1990 Great Britain tour to Papua New Guinea. Yes, that's right, his 40th.

So dedicated was Lucas to his rugby and his fitness that he rarely went out for a drink with his team-mates on that tour, so they decided he was acting more like a 40-year-old than a young gun of 22 and secretly had a birthday cake baked, complete with 40 candles, and proceeded to sing 'Happy Birthday' to him.

Lucas joined in with the joke, but there was a shrewd business brain developing in those formative years and he had the last laugh on one of his Wigan team-mates, as recalled by Martin Dermott.

Lucas was running an antiques shop at the time and had just cleared out an old person's home of furniture, complete with four-poster bed, all for the grand total of £50. By coincidence, the next day Andy Goodway just happened to mention he was looking for a four-poster.

'Ian said, "Leave it with me," recalled Dermott. 'And the next day he sold the four-poster to Andy for £400. When Andy found out he christened Ian "The Fat Robber" and it was a nickname which stuck with the lads.'

Following a short coaching stint with Leigh, that eye for a deal saw Lucas become a successful businessman and he is now managing director of his own construction company, Truline, in Wigan, within half a mile of the DW Stadium, where he employs 58 people.

There is a cartoon drawing of Billy Boston in try-scoring mode on the wall of his office, a gift after his company made a donation to help pay for the construction of Boston's statue in Believe Square.

Lucas, gently courteous and measured in his delivery, also extended a helping hand to a fellow member of the rugby league props' club after Wigan's Ben Flower was sent off and suspended for six months following his savage and infamous attack on St Helens stand off Lance Hohaia in the 2014 Grand Final at Old Trafford.

For those who might have forgotten, Flower's first punch knocked out Hohaia. The real damage was done, however, when Flower crouched low over his stricken opponent and landed a devastating second blow which rocked Hohaia's head and shocked the 76,000 crowd and millions watching on television.

Lucas, who missed the 1990 Challenge Cup Final because he had been banned for six weeks for a high tackle, does not condone the brutality but when Flower returned following his suspension Lucas stepped in to sponsor him as part of the club's individual sponsorship package.

'I know it is not in Ben Flower's nature to be like that,' explained Lucas. 'I wanted to show him, "Yeah, I've been in that position. I know what you are going through emotionally. I know it's not going to be easy. I will sponsor you this year because it might give you the arm on the shoulder you might need."'

For Lucas, kissing the cup in 1991, after it had been presented to Hanley by education secretary Kenneth Clarke, is a treasured memory.

For Betts, who had been so desperate for a taste of Wembley glory as a substitute in 1989 that he concealed the fact that he had broken a hand the weekend before, the 1991 cup win is also treasured for two reasons.

One is that he played for ten minutes on the wing, standing in for David Myers who had been sin-binned.

'It was like having a rest,' said Betts.

The other is that his all-action performance earned him the Lance Todd Trophy, although the way he discovered that fact was not exactly conventional, the news coming with an accompanying curmudgeonly sneer from his mate and mentor Andy Goodway, the sort which had become Goodway's stock-in-trade around Central Park.

After the raucous celebrations at the final whistle and the hoopla surrounding collecting the cup from the royal box, plus the inevitable renditions of 'We are the Champions' by Queen and Tina Turner's 'Simply the Best', the team were standing and kneeling side by side for the traditional celebration photo.

'I hadn't realised I had won the Lance Todd until then,' admitted Betts. 'Andy Goodway looked across at me and said, "How on earth did you win the Lance Todd?" That's how I found out. To be fair he did then grab hold of my shoulder and it was nice.'

There was also a member of the board who could have been excused a 'Told you so' smile in the direction of John Monie at that moment, Jack Robinson.

Wigan had lifted their fourth consecutive Challenge Cup with eight of their 13 points, a try and two goals, coming from Frano Botica, the player Monie never wanted. The player who had enthralled Robinson on celluloid and who was to go on to add so much value to Wigan's cup exploits in his five Challenge Cup finals, during which he slotted over kick after kick from seemingly impossible angles. On one occasion he was also required to deal with another irritant, other than the usual intensity and pressure of a big game, when he lined up a conversion on the touchline.

It is one of Wigan's best least-known stories and involves Joe Lydon, a pink porcelain pig and a Kiwi tradition.

It involved a 'select bunch', the phrase is used advisedly, of around half-a-dozen Wigan players, including all the New Zealanders, who had formed a group, membership of which entailed carrying about their person small porcelain pigs roughly the size of the top of a thumb joint. Botica apparently was known occasionally to place his pig on top of the ball when he lined up goal kicks in training to see where the pig would land.

The main purpose of the pig, however, was that it could be brought out of a pocket or wallet by any one of the 'select bunch' at any time and shown to another member. If that member of the 'select bunch' had forgotten to pack his own pig and failed to show it at the same time then he would be fined, £50 being the going rate.

Martin Dermott was a member of the group. 'You could be in the shower and somebody could come in and suddenly show you a porcelain pig,' he recalled. 'So it got to the stage where people were having showers with porcelain pigs stuck up their arses or down their trunks. Wherever you went, naked or fully clothed, you always had to have your porcelain pig or risk the fine.'

On the occasion in question, Lydon was not playing but had been given the job of carrying on to the pitch the bucket of wet sand, which was used in the days before plastic kicking tees to fashion a mound on the turf to keep the ball in position for the place kicker.

'Frano was going for goal and Joe ran on with the sand and while Frano is making the mound of sand Joe reaches over and in front of 75,000 people says, "Hey Frano", and shows him his porcelain pig,' said Dermott, barely able to contain his merriment as he re-enacted the 'historic' moment with imaginary sand and fantasy ball on a rug in the middle of his lounge at his Wigan home.

Lydon thought it was the easiest £50 he would ever make. Not so.

'Frano placed the ball on the sand and, this is true, went inside his shorts and pulled out a porcelain pig and, without looking at Joe, said, "Now get lost."

'That was the good thing with Joe and Frano. They could be playing a game of such massive intensity but could also still have a laugh.'

Some might view the story as direct from the 'pigs might fly' spectrum of sporting yarns, but Dermott insists it happened and there is no doubt Wigan in their pomp were expert at marrying the serious and the surreal.

The laughs certainly extended to the post-Wembley party, a sumptuous affair with wives and sponsors and champagne speeches plus the highlight of the night, the crucial announcement of how much the main sponsor, which at the time and for the best part of a decade was energy company Norweb, was going to deposit in the players' bonus pool.

It was always a lucrative and generous sum involving tens of thousands of pounds and as the triumphant years stacked up the players became wise to a little ruse which, with the drink and euphoria flowing, squeezed just a little extra into their pockets.

It became obvious that whatever sum the Norweb representative announced, another sponsor, namely mega-wealthy businessman Dave Whelan, who went on to own both Wigan RLFC and Wigan Athletic FC, would always go one better.

Joe Lydon explained what happened next.

'A few of us would go to the Norweb guy before the speeches and ask how much they were going to give us. I don't want to use the real figures but assume, for instance, it was £20. We used to tell him to announce it was £30 but assured him we would only take £20. So he would stand up and say, "This year we're going to give you £30," and everyone would cheer wildly. Then Dave Whelan would get up and say, "Right then, this year I'm going to give you £40." We used to get a bit extra out of Dave Whelan for the fun of it and he never knew.'

16

The King Is Dead, Long Live The King

THERE are few things more unsettling for a sporting team than losing a player who has been the life and the soul of the side.

In September 1991, Ellery Hanley, the captain, the leader, the inspiration, the supreme try-scorer, the world's best player, the Black Pearl, the talisman in cherry and white, the reporter's nightmare, was sold to Leeds for £250,000.

Wigan needed a replacement. They needed a superstar. True, the following month they signed Gene Miles, a cultured Australian centre from Brisbane Broncos, who at 6ft 4in and more than 16st went by the soubriquet 'Big Unit'. Miles was adept at offloading the ball unselfishly and basketball-style in the tackle and although at 32 he was in the autumn of his career and had been playing second row for the previous two seasons, he became a firm favourite with the fans.

But he was not Hanley. Even though his timing and positional sense were still sharp and his formidable presence intimidating for opponents, he was not guaranteed to swell the crowd or bring spectators to the edge of their seats. He was never going to score 63 tries in a single season as Hanley had done in his second campaign at Central Park.

Wigan wanted a replacement to inject excitement and do what England cricketer Ian Botham once guaranteed when he loosened his arms with a windmill motion and twirled his bat as he walked to the crease at Lord's. Empty the bars.

In Wigan's case down the town's Wigan Lane at pubs such as the Bowling Green, the Millstone and the Fox and Goose and around the ground at the Griffin and the Royal Oak, sending anticipation coursing through the veins of every supporter before scoring heavily and in spectacular fashion.

There was only one man at that time in rugby league who fitted the bill. Martin Offiah. But there was a problem.

Offiah was in a contract dispute with Widnes, which was becoming more acrimonious as each week passed. It had reached a stage where Offiah was refusing to play for the club and Widnes had slapped a £750,000 asking price on him, a price no rugby club at the time could or would have considered paying, even though Offiah's try-scoring feats over the past four years had silenced the doubters and justified the gamble of Widnes coach Doug Laughton in signing him in 1987.

Why was it a gamble? Lots of reasons.

For a start, Offiah was a London boy of Nigerian heritage who really was born within the sound of the chimes of Bow Bells.

He had played a few rugby union matches for Rosslyn Park and his speed had caught the eye on the Sevens circuit, but his main claim to fame at that point had come while playing for Essex second XI when he bowled England cricket captain Graham Gooch in a practice match.

Cricket, badminton and fencing had been his preferred sports at the Woolverstone Hall private boarding school he attended on the banks of the River Orwell near Ipswich and he had barely ventured further north than Watford Gap services when Laughton telephoned him at his London home.

That call was a leap of faith considering Offiah had not yet played representative rugby at any level. He did not have a proven record or international caps to his name like rugby union Welshmen Jonathan Davies, Paul Moriarty and John Devereux who all signed for the club in subsequent seasons.

On top of that the board of directors at St Helens had referred to Offiah as an 'uncoordinated clown' when their coach Alex Murphy had expressed an interest in him, a comment which perhaps only proves businessmen should mind their own business and not stray into other people's areas of expertise.

Some clown. For although Offiah arrived at Widnes so naïve in the history of rugby league that he thought they played in red and white, he scored 42 tries in his debut season, making him the league's top try scorer, also breaking Frank Myler's record for most Widnes tries in a season.

He also received the Man of Steel award, the ultimate individual accolade, and went on to score 58 tries in 41 matches in his second season as the club won back-to-back Championship and Premiership titles and then garnered ultimate prestige by beating Canberra Raiders in 1989 to become world club champions.

In four gloriously satisfying years with Widnes, Offiah racked up a breathtaking 181 tries in 145 matches. Then it turned sour. Burning, smarting, nasty, spitefully, 'I want a divorce' sour.

Offiah had agreed a ten-year contract in haste and with little considered thought when he surrendered his amateur status. As he puts it, 'A guy came down south, offered me a load of money and it just felt right to be a professional sportsman.'

He then signed a new three-year contract following his first try-topping, Man of Steel season.

At the end of those four years, in every one of which he had topped the try charts, Offiah unsurprisingly wanted a new enhanced deal or to be able to go to another club. Widnes, however, claimed under the terms of the original ten-year contract he was not a free agent.

Small print was studied meticulously, legal arguments were tendered, but neither party was prepared to budge and a stubborn stand-off ensued with Offiah refusing to play and the club refusing to let him leave.

'I said my contract's up. I want to leave or pay me what I want,' explained Offiah, his face grimacing in angst as he relived the perceived injustice when I met him at the semi-detached Ealing home he shares with partner Virginia Shaw and their two children.

'I wasn't the highest paid. Jonathan Davies was probably on more than me. I had been the top try-scorer for four years on the trot. If they had said they would give me £200,000 then I would have stayed but they offered me something like £75,000 a year. Maybe that was all they could afford but I was the goose that laid the golden egg. They weren't going to let me out of the door free.'

The bitter impasse dragged on through an exasperating September and October and on into an intolerable November and December with no end in sight and that initial price tag of £750,000 putting off would-be buyers.

'Widnes were basically saying no one else can have you, you can rot,' said Offiah.

'No one was going to pay £750,000. Ellery Hanley was the best player in the world and Wigan had let him go to Leeds for £250,000. I wasn't far short of going back south. I had made a few quid on the house.

'I was adamant I was not going to be bullied and there was a lot of animosity. They tried lots of carrot and stick methods to bring me in line. They had been paying my mortgage and my car and they stopped all that. A lot of the money I had saved up I had to spend in those four months to keep myself in order.

'But they had bought me for nothing. No one in the history of any club had done what I had done for that club.'

Offiah and his agent Alan McColm started putting out feelers and there was contact with Maurice Lindsay at Wigan and with Doug Laughton, the man who took him north, who by then had moved on to coach Leeds.

In fact, Offiah met Laughton at a service station off the M62 to discuss personal terms and says he came away with the offer of a £115,000 basic salary.

The truth, however, was that, at 26, at the peak of his athletic prowess, Offiah wanted to join Wigan. He craved the big stage, entranced by the prospect of playing at Wembley, just a few miles from his own home manor and where so many dreams had been realised by so many illustrious sportsmen in the past.

The hallowed green grass of home was a powerful lure. But mostly he was envious of Wigan's record, now four wins in a row and counting, at the famous old stadium.

'I had memories of watching Wigan win the Challenge Cup in 1985 and I wanted to go to Wembley and score a length-of-the-field try,' said Offiah. 'I wanted to do what Henderson Gill did and what Joe Lydon did. I wanted to have that moment of creating a bit of history.

'I didn't resent Mark Preston and his length-of-the-field try in 1990, but when I watched it I felt he was where I wanted to be and he was not as good as me.

'That is why I resisted the temptation of going to Australia. I knew I wanted to go to Wigan because Wigan meant Wembley.'

It also meant the opportunity to play alongside some of the game's biggest names and most accomplished stars, who he had looked upon with a mixture of respect and awe and watched on television and dreamed of emulating as a schoolboy, such as Shaun Edwards.

'Shaun is younger than me by a year even though he looks older,' said Offiah. 'And I always see him as older because I was literally watching him on TV when I was at school.

'I didn't leave school until I was 19 because I wasn't that great and had to retake my O Levels. I was watching him as a schoolboy not knowing that he was younger than me.

'The first time I actually saw him in person I was playing against him on a Wednesday night for Widnes. Wigan used to get off the bus and they didn't look at anyone. They walked with heads down into the changing room. I was in the corridor and Shaun and Ellery Hanley walked straight past me, so professional, not even an eye in my direction.'

That cold walk of intent had made a lasting impression.

After four testing months Widnes finally accepted Wigan's offer of a more manageable, if still hefty, transfer fee of £440,000, a world record at the time for the sport and one which owed much to the deep and generous pockets of directors Jack Robinson and Tom Rathbone, as well as club sponsor Norweb.

An initial basic salary of around £100,000 left Offiah considerably short of what he claims he could have earned at Leeds. To lend perspective, however, it was still a good deal more than the £77,083 average basic wage of a footballer in the first Premier League season of 1992/93.

'I probably wasn't worth the money they were prepared to pay but they knew they had to pay that to get me. I was in close consultation with Maurice Lindsay throughout. He understood business,' said Offiah.

'Ellery had gone, the king is dead, long live the king. Maurice and John Monie were confident I could do it for them. At the time if you weren't a Wigan junior, to get to Wigan you had to beat Wigan or hurt Wigan. If you could hurt Wigan then they wanted to sign you. That is why it was the ultimate professional place.

'I had scored three tries for Widnes to beat Wigan 32-16 in 1989 and another to defeat them in the Charity Shield at Anfield in August of that year and from that day Maurice told me he was convinced that he wanted me. I had been trying to get there even before I knew I wanted to get there. I didn't want to go to Leeds. That's not where I was destined.'

The manner in which he left the old Naughton Park, however, left Offiah facing a litany of abuse, which endured for more than 20 years.

I had occasion to gauge the extent of that animosity when I visited him to write a series of newspaper articles shortly after his move when he still lived in the Widnes area, although the 'For Sale' sign was flying outside his sparsely-furnished house and he was desperate to leave a chemical town which back then contained its fair share of chimneys spewing toxic fumes.

There was a cloud of poison drifting Offiah's way too. Hate mail, rubbish through the letter box, coins dragged down the side of his Mercedes sports car, forcing him to change its personalised number plate 'OFF 1A'. Posters with his face on them were also torn down and shredded or grotesquely disfigured. Abuse was hurled wherever he walked.

'OFFIAH ON THE RUN' was the headline on the main piece I wrote for the *Daily Express* with a strapline explaining 'Martin is being hounded out by his former fans'.

It can be a lonely and bleak existence being perceived as a traitor in the world of sport, although the backlash of perceived betrayal did not come as too much of a shock to Offiah.

'If a woman that you love leaves you, you are going to hate her,' is his philosophical view on it these days, having returned socially to the Widnes club just once on the 25th anniversary of the 1989 World Club Challenge triumph.

'I understood and accepted that at Widnes. It was tough. I got that, but I don't think the people who were abusing me got it.

'There are people who are always going to hate me at Widnes, that's a fact of life, but the feedback I get from the fans these days on Twitter is a lot better.'

17

Life as a Hooker

IF the signing of Martin Offiah supplied a tasty sprinkling of spice then the wisdom of Wigan throughout the golden era of the 1980s and 1990s was that they always gauged to perfection just how much to shake.

Invariably it seemed they knew the perfect blend of ingredients for success. In 1992, for instance, there were international stars such as New Zealand's Dean Bell and Frano Botica, plus Australia's Gene Miles, a superstar such as Offiah, and a chunky core of hometown players, such as Joe Lydon, Shaun Edwards, Andy Gregory, Martin Dermott, Andy Platt and Phil Clarke, who were all steeped in the traditions of the club and the town.

So many of them learned their trade from an early age at schools such as St John Fisher Catholic state school in the town's Beech Hill district, which down the years has become an unrivalled conveyor belt of northern talent in both rugby codes.

In fact, on one afternoon in 2013 Chris Ashton, Joel Tomkins and Owen Farrell were helping England's rugby union side defeat Argentina in the autumn internationals at Twickenham while Sam Tomkins, Sean O'Loughlin and Liam Farrell were playing for England in the rugby league World Cup. All of them Fisher old boys.

There is a wall of fame at the school with row upon row of familiar faces, including Shaun Edwards and the former Great Britain captain Mike Gregory, stretching back decades and recording the exploits of past pupils who have reached the upper echelons in the world of sport.

Then, of course, there is the renowned amateur club, Wigan St Patrick's, which was founded in 1910 and has churned out stars such as Gregory and Lydon. It continues to do so with current players, such as 'Fisher boys' Sam Tomkins, Liam Farrell, Sean O'Loughlin and Josh

Charnley, the latter having joined Sale Sharks in 2016, all having come through the St Pat's institute of how to succeed as a master rugby league player.

That home-cooked feel was no accident. It was promoted by a board of directors who recognised that there was no other place on the planet, other than perhaps Sydney, which had the knack for churning out top class rugby players almost by the dozen, year on year.

The exact moment the great Wigan rugby epoch of the 1980s and 1990s began is elusive to pinpoint but the 1981 signing, as part of a local recruitment initiative, of hometown lad Shaun Wane was significant.

As a mischievous 11-year-old schoolboy in the town's Worsley Hall district, Wane had always dreamed of playing for Wigan. One day, however, he fell down a manhole and suffered a horrific wound to a leg which required 60 stitches.

Doctors considered amputation so serious was the injury and Wane, fearing his dream of becoming a rugby player was gone, spent several worrying days confined to bed.

What happened next shines a light on the special 'we're all in it together' relationship which the club and its supporters have so often enjoyed.

'One day my dad said, "There's someone special coming to see you today,"' recalled Wane. 'And in walked Billy Boston, the biggest name in Wigan. I was in awe. I must add that my dad was scared of nobody and that day was the first time I saw my dad frightened to death. He was so in awe of Billy.' That meeting inspired Wane, once his injury had healed, to chase his dream with even greater zeal.

The day eventually he signed for Wigan was probably the moment the board put their trust in homebred players and encouraged them to have a say in the way the team was run.

True, Wane was not a superstar, but he played 149 times for Wigan, mainly at prop and second row. The coaching credentials he utilised so astutely later in his career owe much to the time in the 1980s when he was the friendliest of faces in the changing room, helping to bring through more talented local youngsters while also earning his coaching badges.

'When I left Wigan in 1990 Maurice Lindsay said I was the first player to be signed after the decision was taken to concentrate on signing local Wigan talent,' said Wane.

'He said he was sorry to let me go and he had tears in his eyes. It really hurt him. Maurice and Tom Rathbone felt that I was the start of the new era. That is something that I will keep hold of forever. Even though they let me go it was nice of them to say that I was part of building the Wigan name of the 1980s and 1990s. I got the coaching bug during that time.

'The backbone of that team was born and bred in Wigan and they controlled everything. We had the big say and that is what I tried to do when I was made coach with the likes of Sean O'Loughlin, Sam Tomkins and Liam Farrell. That hopefully is the way to get the good times back again.'

In the town's eight-in-a-row Wembley triumphs the surge of Wigan blood was plain to see in the team sheets, including substitutes.

There were five Wigan-born players in the first two of those finals, six in each of the next four, seven in 1994 and five in 1995. There was a 'Band of Brothers' feel to those teams, a sense of togetherness. That does not mean they all socialised together. They didn't. There were cliques and disagreements and squabbles, just as there are in any office or factory or school or family.

But once they crossed the whitewash they became a tight and formidable platoon where loyalty was prized above everything.

It helped that the Great Britain Lions tours during that time were also packed with players from the Wigan club. Six Wigan players were in the team which beat New Zealand 11-10 on the 1990 tour of Papua New Guinea and New Zealand with the captain being another Wigan-born player, Mike Gregory, who played for Warrington. The Cherry and Whites could have been represented even more fulsomely if Ellery Hanley, Shaun Edwards and Andy Platt had not been forced to withdraw from the squad for various reasons.

In 1992 when Great Britain beat Australia 33-10 in the second Test at the Princes Park Australian Rules ground in Melbourne the entire pack was from Wigan: Kelvin Skerrett, Martin Dermott, Andy Platt, Denis Betts, Billy McGinty and Phil Clarke. With Shaun Edwards at scrum half and Martin Offiah on the left wing it meant eight of the starting 13 were from Wigan. Just for good measure Joe Lydon was on the replacements' bench.

As Ian Lucas, a member of the 1990 squad, succinctly put it, 'Wigan is a rugby town, it will never be a football town. Kids are brought up wanting to play rugby and playing for Wigan is a huge accolade.'

Betts was not born in Wigan. He had no affiliation with the area but he swiftly realised that success was rooted in the core values of a system designed to churn out sharp rugby brains.

'There was a yardstick to measure yourself by at Wigan,' said Betts. 'A lot of good players failed to get into that team and players who had gone away wanted to come back. What was created was a centre of excellence. There are two places in this country where rugby league players are made more than anywhere else. One is Castleford and the other one is Wigan. So you are going to get a lot of homegrown players. The numbers game works and it fell into line at that time.

'Andy Gregory and Joe Lydon came back from Widnes, Shaun Edwards was a big iconic home signing. That group of really good kids who had drifted off got back into line.

'I came through a system which was pretty ruthless. Andy Platt, another Wigan lad, came back from St Helens, so there was a pulling together which drove us on.

'It was also a team of leaders. Dean Bell was a pretty inspirational leader, more a doer than a talker but he knew how to raise everyone's level of performance. Platt was a fantastic leader of men who also understood his role within the team. It's no good having one bloke out there who everybody listens to and nobody else. If you lose that bloke it falls to pieces.

'Shaun's biggest asset is he knows how to make other people better. Shaun and Andy Gregory made me a better player because they knew how to put me in position.

'Greg told me to run as hard as I could into spaces and he would find me, although sometimes he would walk past when I was lying on the floor with blood pouring out of my face and say, "Sometimes it doesn't work then, Denis."'

There is no doubt the Gregory and Edwards factors were crucial in keeping the core values to the fore. One sharp-tongued and charismatically critical, the other driven and intense.

Lydon believes team unity owed much to both.

'Greg was probably our glue,' said Lydon. 'He had such a presence about him on the field. Well balanced, the scrum half chip on both shoulders. Shaun was the constant, a great poacher. The best performance stimulus is peer pressure. A group of people who get together and own each other's reputations, who train together and would back each other up in any situation.

'We weren't all the greatest of friends. There was a core group who would socialise but when we came together we played. It just gelled. It wasn't that we were frightened of losing, we just didn't want to let anyone down. We wanted to keep winning.'

Perhaps the player who epitomised the tribal, parochial element of the Wigan professionalism was Martin Dermott, who played in five of those eight-in-a-row Wembley finals.

Dermott did not catch the eye on the pitch in quite the thrilling fashion of Gregory or Edwards or Offiah, but his team-mates always knew he was there. One, because he was a member of the wisecracking, up-for-a-laugh, pre-match club who warmed up with Millsy and Taffy.

'Derms', as he was known, succeeded Nicky Kiss as hooker. He recalls Kiss greeting him for the first time with the words, 'Welcome to the hookers' union. Once a hooker, always a hooker.'

In those days, hookers in rugby league had a reputation, probably still do, for being a bit mad. Rather like goalkeepers in football, hockey and ice hockey. With goalkeepers it is all to do with being prepared voluntarily to put themselves in the way of having balls and boots kicked, hit or smacked directly at their heads, bodies and tenderest places.

With hookers, usually the smallest of the forwards by some distance, it is a willingness to be constantly at the centre of the action. Where the hard yards are hardest. Where the big men roam. Where it kicks off on a regular basis.

'It is a rare breed, there is no doubt about that,' said Dermott. 'At the time, not like today, you actually had to hook for the ball. You had to make 40 tackles a game and be there for every play-the-ball. You had to be on top of your game in that position. You were tackling, scrummaging, at the play-the-ball, organising forwards. You had so many tasks.

'I couldn't have played anywhere else. I had to be in the thick of the action. I tried playing scrum half and it was boring. I enjoyed being in the centre of attention and being busy all game. If it kicked off it kicked off. I loved the aggression side of the game.'

Dermott came from Ince-in-Makerfield, the same stomping ground as Gregory. He represented the town in the different age groups from the age of eight.

'At one time we had 13 born-and-bred Wiganers playing at Wigan in and out of the first team, about eight of them were first team regulars,' said Dermott. 'We all had an in-bred passion to play for Wigan. All those lads would have played for Wigan for nothing. To play for Wigan was the biggest thing in a kid's life and when you sign up it is your dream come true just to run out at Central Park.

'I used to talk to the crowd. The ball would go into touch and as I was retrieving it someone would say, "Are you going out tonight Derms?" I would shout back, "Yeah, I'll see you at eight o'clock," and then throw the ball to someone. It had that buzz to it. No better stadium, no better feeling in the world than to play St Helens on Boxing Day at Central Park.

'Prima donnas wouldn't have lasted two minutes in the changing rooms at Wigan. We had big stars but they were very humble, very low key. In the 14 years I was at Wigan we never had one player that wouldn't put their head above the parapet. Everyone worked for the team. That is the key to success.'

A vital part of Dermott's work as hooker was passing or running from the play-the-ball. Passing, in particular, was a challenge because it had to be precise. Not just precise as in accurate and regular and uniform.

Precise as in lunar-module-returning-to-Earth precise, with angle of entry calculated to six decimal places and heat shield deployed.

Any minor deviation and there was hell to pay.

'I was playing with players who wanted it just right,' said Dermott, who has utilised the quick wits and people skills he learned keeping his team-mates happy in a post-rugby career, first as a prison officer and then working for a funeral director. 'If they had to turn or stoop, it was slowing them down.'

So Dermott practised and practised, with a leather ball filled with sand, spending hours passing to trees with a precise target carved on them. Off the ground. From the hip and from the left and from the right, always hitting the same spot.

'Andy Gregory was a bastard to pass to, the most awkward one,' said Dermott. 'He would be 15 yards away but instead of just passing to him, he would be running away from me at an angle so I had to curl it around so the ball would arrive perfectly in front of him just as he wanted it.

'If I did just one bad pass he'd give me that look and say, "That's not happening again, is it?" And I'd say, "No, no, Greg."

'Every player had their own preference. They wanted it softer, they wanted it into their body. Va'aiga Tuigamala, all 17st of him, used to bollock me and say, "Why are you throwing it so hard?" So I always had to slow it down for him.

'But if Shaun said it was a shit pass you knew it really was a shit pass and you wouldn't do it again. People used to say about Shaun when he was training that he was a bit ignorant because he didn't talk to you. But he isn't. He was thinking. He would have his head down and walk around angry. Very focused. He knew more about rugby league than all the coaches put together. He would be watching a team, say like Leeds, all week, every night, memorising players and their strengths and weaknesses. He was doing the coaching job when he was playing.

'I would run the forwards and Shaun and Greg would run the backs. John Monie was very good. He'd say, "Let's try doing it like this." And Shaun would say, "Why are we doing that because I don't think it will work?" And John often would reply, "Fine, you lads are playing, we'll leave it like that." He had that humility.'

If you have noticed that Greg, Giz and Derms – Gregory, Edwards and Dermott – crop up quite often then it is because their influence at the Wigan rugby coal face was inversely proportional to their diminutive size.

Thereby hangs Dermott's favourite story of the Wigan trio.

Picture the scene as the three of them walk down the tunnel one behind the other for a Great Britain Test match in Australia. They stop at the mouth of the tunnel to wait for the Australian team to take their places beside them. Fireworks are crackling in the night sky, the pre-match music is blaring, the tension is tingling.

'Greg was in front of me and he's about 4ft 1in,' said Dermott with slight exaggeration for effect. 'Then there was Shaun, about 5ft, then there was me, not much bigger. We were a team of midgets.

'Suddenly the Australian team come out of the changing room and walk alongside us and we gawp up at Paul Sironen at 6ft 5in, Bobby Linder, six feet something and Bradley Clyde, another six-footer, as they go past.

'Greg turned round to me and said, "Are we the fucking curtain raiser here?" I cracked up laughing. It was like being at school again. I couldn't play for about five minutes after that because I was crying laughing.'

18

Tunnel Vision

ONE man benefited more than most from the exit of Ellery Hanley, namely Phil Clarke, who was young, quick, an avid trainer and a natural fit for the great man's loose forward position.

Clarke was the son of former Wigan hooker and head coach Colin Clarke. He was a hometown boy who had been watching Wigan since he was a toddler and had played for the Wigan under-11 team at Wembley in 1982.

In 1990, while at Liverpool University studying for a degree in sports science, he had travelled down to Wembley with the team as a reserve.

He had seen Shaun Edwards return to the changing room that day with his shattered cheekbone and admits the sight of his disfigured face had a profound impact.

'This is serious stuff,' he thought. 'This is not schoolboy rugby any more. This game involves pain and sacrifice.'

On the coach back to Wigan on the Sunday morning he was introduced to another aspect of the big man's game.

He had taken his study notes from his bag to revise for a university exam next morning while all the players around him were laying siege to crates of celebratory beer.

Big mistake.

'I don't think we had got as far as Tottenham Court Road on the trip back when Dean Bell and a few of the others pinched my notes, ripped them up in front of me and then set fire to them with a match,' recalled Clarke.

'I didn't know it was like that on the bus. It was like Dante's Inferno at times, it was just mad, but I quickly realised my naivety.'

In 1991 that naivety returned, this time on the pitch when he played in front of Hanley at second row in his first senior Wembley final in the victory against St Helens.

Actually, 'played' is not entirely accurate.

True, he did run around in a Wigan rugby jersey that day and expended lots of energy, but much of it was of the 'headless chicken' variety before he was replaced by Andy Goodway after just 22 minutes.

Wembley can do that to the best of players, especially young and naïve ones. The enormity of the occasion, the weight of history and the bombardment of the senses seem to suck strength from muscles and common sense from minds, as Clarke admits.

'I had an absolute shocker in 1991. It was embarrassing. I played so poorly. I was lost. I was a supporter running around on the pitch with a kit on. The occasion was all too much for me. I think a lot of teams lost against Wigan because at Wembley it is easy to run around in a daze. It is about 25 minutes before you realise the match has started. Wigan usually had a lead by that point. Knowing how to handle the Wembley occasion was about an eight-point advantage.'

Clarke's own 'daze' began during the walk up the tunnel, an experience that was described earlier by Nicky Kiss as a 'marvellous, elating sensation'.

For Clarke it was 'marvellous', too, but also draining and intimidating, although he believes the architects of the £800m new stadium, with its impressive arch, missed a trick by not emulating the long walk from the changing room to the pitch.

'The Romans were geniuses,' said Clarke. 'In the coliseum the gladiators could hear the sound but couldn't see the people as they prepared and it was the same at the old Wembley.

'You had to walk up a steep incline so all you could see was the sky at the mouth of the tunnel and hear the noise. It was fantastic how it played with your senses. You couldn't see what was going to happen. It was a slow reveal. You cannot underestimate how powerful it is for a sportsman to hear the roar before you see the playing surface.

'Walking up the tunnel at the old Wembley was the greatest experience. Even though they have spent a lot of money on the new Wembley I think they have got it sadly wrong.

'The old Wembley played with your nerves and by the time you got to the top of the incline in that tunnel your legs felt like jelly.

'Handling that experience was an advantage that Wigan had over the rest for eight years.'

It was an advantage not dissimilar from the edge the sublime players at Wimbledon have always enjoyed, such as Pete Sampras, Novak Djokovic, Roger Federer, Rafael Nadal and Andy Murray, all of whom invariably have played the majority of their matches on Centre Court with its history, tradition and intimidating atmosphere.

Of course such a venue can be inspiring for lesser players, too, but over five sets and when the pressure is at its most intense and the big points most crucial, almost always those for whom the great amphitheatres and clutch situations are familiar perform at their best while the rest are prone to wilting in the heat of battle.

It perhaps explains why there are so few real upsets in the final stages of modern grand slam tennis.

In May 1992, a bizarre rugby league year which, among other curiosities, saw Sky Sports launch its *Boots n' All* programme, British heavyweight boxer Gary Mason score in a reserve match trial for London Crusaders against Sheffield and Great Britain legend Paul Charlton turn out for Carlisle Border Raiders' Alliance team at the age of 50, Clarke was still two weeks away from his 21st birthday.

But he was more mature, more capable of dealing with the paralysing effect of the Wembley tunnel and the blurring of the senses. Hanley's departure meant he had made 26 appearances during the season. He was coming of age as a professional rugby player.

The cup run started in clinical fashion with a 22-6 win at Salford in the first round, after which a Wigan squad flew out to Sydney for the World Sevens. It was hardly perfect timing. It was the middle of the domestic season with crucial league and cup games approaching.

It was, however, a lucrative assignment for the middle of February and the prospect of swapping frozen pitches and shivering training sessions for the warmth of an Australian summer was also a powerful lure.

So was the chance to showcase the skills on view at Central Park and test them against the best Down Under.

In reality it turned into the tournament that vindicated the record fee paid for Offiah a month earlier.

Offiah ran in ten tries in Wigan's five matches, including four in the 18-6 victory against Brisbane in the final, a game played in monsoon conditions but which contained one particular touchdown from Offiah, setting up Denis Betts on the right, then looping around to turn up on Betts's left to take the killer pass and squirm over at the corner with a spectacular dive and splash, which only confirmed his credentials as a ruthless finisher and as a showman.

The significance of that Sevens victory cannot be underestimated. Yes, it was in a form of rugby deemed to be fun and more frivolous than the 13-man game.

But the opponents were Cronulla Sutherland, Gold Coast, Penrith, Manly-Warringah and Brisbane, teams and names lauded in rugby league.

The trophy did not carry the kudos of a Wembley medal but it placed Wigan on the world stage, enhancing their reputation, demonstrating the excellence that was being witnessed week in and week out in a little north-west town. Reinforcing their claims as arguably the finest rugby club side in the world.

Then it was back home to beat Warrington 14-0 in the second round of the Challenge Cup, a fixture which had been postponed for a week to enable their trip Down Under. Offiah was again on the scoresheet, along with Kelvin Skerrett.

A 13-6 victory at St Helens set up Wigan for a semi-final against Bradford at Bolton that turned into one of those annihilations which does the game no favours. It started with a drop goal from Andy Gregory and quickly developed into a 71-10, 13-try, no-contest exhibition with Offiah scoring five of them.

Wigan were back at Wembley for the fifth time in a row and 12 days later, as if to prove this was the age of dominating powers, the Conservative Party were re-elected for a fourth consecutive term in their first election under the leadership of John Major.

Perhaps the defining newspaper image of that time was *The Sun*'s front page on the day of the election which superimposed Labour leader Neil Kinnock's face on the picture of a light bulb with the headline, 'If Kinnock wins today will the last person to leave Britain please turn out the lights'.

The biggest-selling British daily newspaper followed that up a couple of days later with the blatantly self-congratulatory, 'It's *The Sun* Wot Won It'.

Brash. Showy. Flamboyant. Direct. Controversial. Not that dissimilar from the way Offiah was beginning to prove himself as the most accomplished finisher in world rugby.

Two more tries in the 42-16 Premiership Trophy quarter-final victory against his old club Widnes the week before Wembley only amplified that point.

So it was to Wembley, with the title already won by an eight-point margin from St Helens, and the chance for Offiah to realise his dream. To try to do what fellow wingers Henderson Gill had done in 1988 and Mark Preston in 1990.

It took Offiah just five minutes to set the scoreboard ticking. It was not the length-of-the-field try of which he had dreamed. It was by no means a thing of beauty.

But as an example of the finisher's art, it was a masterpiece. An example of quick wits and quick-twitch muscle fibres.

When Offiah took a pass from Andy Gregory, 25 metres out on the fifth tackle, there were few options open to him and little space to work in.

So he kicked the ball along the ground, nutmegging opposing winger Jon Wray in the process, and gave chase. Castleford full back Graham Steadman reached it first but made a three-course meal of fielding the ball and while the full back lay on the turf trying to reel the ball into his chest, Offiah dislodged it from his grasp with his foot.

The ball was now loose and over the try line but Offiah had overrun it and many players might have given up. Not Offiah, which was where the quick wits came in. He swiftly flipped around while at the same time flopping to the floor and slapping down his left hand on the ball to complete the touchdown for the try before Steadman could recover.

Offiah is not always credited with a smart footballing brain. People often concentrate purely on his searing speed and elegant running style. But Offiah was a predator when it came to tries. True, he loved the long-distance variety, but he would devour them however they were served. That self-created, opportunistic opener against Castleford, to which Frano Botica added the conversion, is a perfect example.

It set the tone for a final that arguably lacked the drama of 1990 and the tension of 1991 but instead conveyed the inevitability of sport when one team is near its peak, confident in its game plan, familiar with the surroundings and entirely at ease with producing its best despite the distractions of the occasion. And the other is not.

It looked that way when Martin Dermott darted through from dummy half before feeding the ever-available Shaun Edwards for the second touchdown after 21 minutes, a try which again was converted by Botica and confirmed two things.

One was the talent of Edwards as the supreme support player, even if that was a label he came to despise in that he saw himself as a playmaker, a creator, a conductor, rather than a man who benefited from the imagination and talent of others.

The other was the influence of coach John Monie on someone such as Dermott. The Wigan hooker, as we have established, was one of the fun-loving members of the squad, who liked a drink and a joke, but there was serious intent when it came to improving his game and the manner in which he spied the gap and seized the moment against Castleford owed much to what he had learned from Monie and in particular his emphasis on preparation and visualisation.

'John always used to say, "When you are in bed the night before the game think what you are going to do. How many tackles you are going to make. If you are going for a try think how it might happen,"' said Dermott.

'I did that before one game for Great Britain against France and got man of the match, made the most tackles and scored two tries. I always did it from then on.'

It was not dissimilar from the methods used at the time by television hypnotist Paul McKenna who was enlisted by England cricketer Robin Smith to improve his batting by playing an innings in his head before going out into the middle and by Olympic swimmer Adrian Moorhouse who claimed to have clipped two seconds off a world record in a training session after one visualisation workout.

Okay, there were others who, after a session with McKenna, were probably just as likely to walk into a police station claiming to be Napoleon, but in a way that would only prove the power of mind over matter.

It is why, in recent times, the psychology of sport has become ever more important. In fact, Dermott earned a diploma in the subject, studying such techniques as how racing drivers visualised the safest and quickest lines to take a chicane in the comfort of their armchair, how cricketers contemplated the angle of delivery and likely bounce of the ball in the changing room and how tennis players used similar routines to familiarise their mind with the angle of the serve.

That day against Castleford it was about Dermott arriving behind Gene Miles as the big centre was tackled and, as he explains, clicking into his visualised thoughts of the night before.

'At the play-the-ball I would take a snapshot in my head for a split second of what was in front of me. Three on this side, two on that side. I took a picture of the scene and immediately knew what I was going to do. I made a mathematical choice. I need to go that way because he is faster.

'That sort of thing. I would weigh up around five different solutions in a split second and that time I just spotted the sort of gap I had been visualising and went for it.'

He still needed to evade two tackles before a perfectly-delivered pass sent in Edwards for the touchdown.

A drop goal from Joe Lydon followed after 37 minutes. A typical Lydon effort. Around 40 yards. Only one point, but taking Wigan 13 points and three scores in front, effectively dealing a hammer blow to the psyche of the opposition.

What came two minutes later, just before half-time, must have felt like a wrecking ball if you were a Castleford supporter.

As Wigan broke forward Steve Hampson passed to Edwards on the halfway line. The defence was set. There appeared to be no imminent danger but Edwards, sensing Offiah to his left, spotted space beyond the Castleford defensive line and kicked the ball forward with the perfect weight to roll and stop within the generous Wembley dead-ball area.

Two Castleford players raced back and appeared to have the situation under control until, that is, Offiah engaged what NASA would call the after-burners and somehow squeezed, barged and wriggled his way between the defenders before diving to claim the try.

It was a try down not just to speed, although Olympic pace was an essential ingredient to run down Edwards's kick. It also required strength, athleticism, hunger, courage and determination. The determination of a player who does not give up on seemingly hopeless causes, one who sees opportunities where others see only obstacles.

Botica added the conversion and Wigan went in for their half-time refreshment with a 19-0 lead.

Fair play to Castleford, they could have accepted their lot as another victim, just one more notch on the Wigan cup victory post. They didn't.

In fact, they made the second half a much more competitive affair, Ritchie Blackmore scoring an early try to which Martin Ketteridge added the conversion. The fightback was on and there were 15 minutes of distinctly uncomfortable defending for Wigan as Castleford wound up the pressure before Hampson took a reverse pass from Botica to go over in the corner. Inevitably, the dependable Botica added the conversion from the touchline and while Keith England scored a try after 68 minutes, which Ketteridge converted, a penalty kick from Botica and another long drop goal from Lydon with two minutes remaining gave Wigan a comfortable 28-12 triumph.

There were no wild celebrations or overt proclamations of joy even though it was Wigan's fifth Challenge Cup win in a row. The fans had come to expect trophies and Wigan had delivered. It was business as usual and the obligatory roars reverberated around Wembley as captain Dean Bell received the cup from the Earl of Derby.

But as the trophy was passed down the line, from Bell to Lydon to Hampson and the rest, the ecstasy of 1988 when Henderson Gill disco-danced in celebration was notable by its absence.

Phil Clarke played in the last five of Wigan's eight-in-a-row finals. He has studied those triumphs and while each player necessarily will view their time in the sun differently, this is his explanation why the joy of winning seemed to wane as the years went by.

'My enjoyment of Wembley went down during those years because we were expected to win. It was relief rather than joy at the end of the match. That's my perception. Look at the celebrations at the end of the matches and as time goes on players no longer jump in the air, they drop to their knees relieved. It was because of all the people saying, "You are going to win again."

'I admit my strongest memories from playing, and maybe I should see a psychologist, are negative ones. Missed tackles and dropped chances, rather than success.

'I don't like to spend too much of my life looking back. I would rather look forward, so perhaps that is why I don't have a great memory of the past.

'But I remember one of my highlights of going to Wembley was sitting in the front of the coach because I loved seeing the power of the police motorcycles stopping the traffic for us.

'At times at the end of it all there was a sense of anticlimax. You spend all your life thinking what it would be like to play at Wembley and then you win and there is a bit of an empty feeling. Like, "I thought it was going to feel better than this."'

It is not an uncommon experience in the world of sport.

In tennis Andy Murray admitted to being in a state of shock after he won Wimbledon for the first time, unable to savour the experience because of the strain, pressure and expectation that went before.

Serena Williams, arguably the greatest sportswoman of modern times, has always admitted being driven by the fact that the pain of losing far outweighed and endured much longer than the joy of winning.

For Offiah, however, the 1992 final was a defining moment in his career. Not only had he accomplished a lifetime ambition by scoring two tries at Wembley, two brilliantly individualistic touchdowns at that, he had also used his pace and awareness to prevent Castleford centre St John Ellis from scoring what seemed a certain try which could have altered the whole tone of the afternoon.

That is why he was worth his world record transfer fee. That is why he was awarded his first Lance Todd Trophy. That is why, after the events of Wembley 1992, he knew he had taken a lengthy stride on his journey to greatness, especially when he followed up his achievements against Castleford by scoring ten tries in a 74-6 victory against Leeds eight days later in the Premiership Trophy semi-final and another two in a 48-16 dismissal of St Helens in the final.

'I didn't quite nail it that year,' is how Offiah puts it in reflection.

'I got close with the Lance Todd and those two tries but for me there was always more to come. The Lance Todd was affirmation that I was in the right place. For a winger to win the Lance Todd you have to do great things. If you win the Lance Todd Trophy you know you have had a great game. A lot of half backs win it and you remember they won it but not what they did. If a winger wins the Lance Todd Trophy you will always remember what he did.'

Prime Minister John Major, one of the Wembley dignitaries that day, famously described Offiah as 'faster than a camera shutter'.

So impressed was the Prime Minister with Wigan's performance that he accepted an invitation to visit the players in the Wembley dressing room immediately after the match, which is why to this day he regards second-rower Billy McGinty as one of rugby league's more colourful characters.

McGinty made 75 appearances for Wigan, four for Great Britain and five for Scotland. He was born in Glasgow, went on to coach the Scotland team and apparently has a tattoo of a thistle on his behind to illustrate his patriotism.

He was not one of Wigan's superstars, but more of a foot soldier, signed from Warrington as cover after Andy Goodway had broken an arm. He was one of the head-down battering rams, deployed to make hard yards and drain energy and resolve from the opposition defence.

He had played for Warrington as a second-half replacement against Wigan at Wembley in 1990 and had dreamed of lifting the Challenge Cup since marvelling at his rugby heroes, Widnes stars Reggie Bowden and Jim Mills, as a child.

In 1992 he sat in the toilets at Wembley prior to kick-off in his Wigan rugby kit because it was the only place in the changing room area where the crowd could be heard clearly. He was determined to drink in the occasion. In truth, he was waiting to hear 'Abide with Me' and soak in the emotion.

The timeline of his match personified the role of the utility forward in rugby league at the time, a role that does not always receive the credit it deserves.

McGinty was replaced by Steve Hampson after 27 minutes, returned to replace Andy Gregory after 48 and then was replaced once more by Neil Cowie after 64. It was the sort of stop-start, staccato performance, which is rarely fully satisfying for the individual but frequently crucial in supplying impact and energy for the team.

McGinty's selfless contribution on that steamy day at Wembley has long been forgotten.

But he will always be remembered for what happened afterwards when, 'for a laugh', he emerged naked from the shower with a circular knee protector made of yellow sponge with a hole in the middle strategically placed on what a rugby player might well describe as his personal tackle.

In front of him, no more than a yard away and quite unexpectedly, was the Prime Minister.

A dripping McGinty spotted the quizzical look on Major's face and said, 'It's a pineapple ring.'

Major looked down and then back up at McGinty and, with a bewildered chuckle, replied, 'That's the last time I will eat pineapple.'

The incident was captured by a TV film crew and the recording surfaced two weeks later to cost McGinty sleep when it was screened on the northern TV show *Up and Under* while he was in Papua New Guinea on tour with Great Britain.

He ended up taking several middle-of-the-night phone calls from national newspapers wanting to verify the details of his chance encounter with Major and, as if to underline the power of trivia in the modern world, it is by far the most recalled event of his rugby career.

Major, perhaps in tongue-in-cheek fashion to illustrate he wasn't quite as 'grey' as he was perceived, even included McGinty in a Sunday newspaper article some years later compiling the ten most important and colourful people he had met in office.

McGinty and the 'pineapple' incident came in at number seven, amid kings and queens and characters such as the Sultan of Brunei.

These days McGinty, who had spells at Sale Sharks, Worcester Warriors and Edinburgh Rugby, revels in relative anonymity as head rugby coach at Malvern College, an independent school in Worcestershire where rugby league is not on the curriculum.

His pupils occasionally remind him of his former days when they stumble across his name on the internet and say, 'Sir, you have a Wikipedia page,' or, 'Sir, did you really play for Great Britain?'

Only then does McGinty reveal the pride he still feels as a former Wigan player, describing himself as a 'little cog in a magnificent engine'.

'It is great to have been part of a fantastic club with so much history, probably the most famous rugby league team ever,' said McGinty.

'The year 1992 was a crazy time for me. I had a bucket list of things I wanted to achieve when I started playing rugby, one was to play for Great Britain, one was to go on tour and the other was to win a Challenge Cup Final at Wembley and it all happened. I loved my time at Wigan.

'The fans were so friendly. They were passionate about rugby and not once did I ever think I was better than them. I always respected them and understood I was lucky to be there.'

The fans remember McGinty, too, as evidenced when he was walking with his wife and daughter on a Mexico beach a couple of years ago, thick dark hair of yesteryear now grey and much of it having fled the roost, when a man, around 60, wearing a Wigan rugby cap, sauntered by idly watching the surf.

The man suddenly turned and, in an unmistakable Wigan accent, said, 'You're Billy McGinty, aren't you?'

McGinty nodded and stopped for a prolonged and nostalgic chat recalling the most impressionable and enjoyable years of his career, including 1992 and all that. Happily, the 'pineapple ring' wasn't mentioned.

19

Who Wants to be an Astronaut?

A FTER a concert in Nashville, a young Elvis Presley was advised by the concert hall manager that he would be better off returning to Memphis and his former job of driving trucks.

Steven Spielberg was rejected from the University of Southern California School of Theatre, Film and Television three times.

Rudyard Kipling, meanwhile, was sacked as contributor to the *San Francisco Examiner* in 1889 with an editor telling him, 'I'm sorry Mr Kipling, but you just don't know how to use the English language.'

Careers in all walks of life rise and fall on other people's opinions. Sometimes after studied analysis and sometimes merely on a whim. Some people are crushed by their first taste of negativity. Others, the brave, the stubborn, the successful, those convinced of their burgeoning talent, look rejection squarely in the eye and refuse to accept it.

None more spectacularly than J.K. Rowling whose first Harry Potter book, *Harry Potter and the Philosopher's Stone*, written on an old manual typewriter, was rejected by 12 publishers. A year later Bloomsbury took her on board but only if she promised to take a day job because there was no money in children's books. At the last count Ms Rowling was richer than the Queen.

The point is publishers, promoters, editors, people in positions of influence and authority, even sports coaches, get it wrong. Sometimes spectacularly wrong.

In the case of Jason Robinson, it could be said Leeds were wrong when they decided not to sign the teenager from Beeston, a distinctly underprivileged suburb of the city.

Robinson had started playing the game at Hunslet Boys' Club and Hunslet Parkside before launching his rugby league career at semi-professional side Hunslet Hawks.

When it came to Leeds it was a straight choice between Robinson and Gareth Stephens, both precocious and promising 16-year-old scrum halves at the time. Leeds chose to hand a contract to the talented Stephens, who went on to enjoy a workmanlike career with Leeds, Castleford, Hull, Sheffield Eagles, Halifax and York Wasps as well as playing four times for Wales.

It was not quite a mistake of Harry Potter proportions, but Robinson did go on to beguile the rugby world in both codes like no other player before or since with his mesmerising running. After, that is, being picked up by Eric Hall, a talent scout for Wigan who was based in Leeds.

Robinson was full of apologies when we met in Milton Keynes. His business meeting had overrun by half an hour and even though he had kept me informed by text, he takes pride in his punctuality.

'I really wanted to play for Leeds,' he explained. 'When you grow up playing rugby league you want to play for your hometown. But looking back now it was a blessing in disguise.

'It is only when you get to Wigan you realise how big rugby is there. The environment was so competitive. If we were doing weights, there would be a competition for who could lift the heaviest and Andy Platt was always up there.

'If we were sprinting everyone wanted to beat Martin Offiah, although I don't think anybody ever did. It created a real healthy competition within the group and you knew if you did not perform in training or in a game there were so many people waiting to take your position.

'For a young lad it was just great to be part of that environment. I had watched them and now I was training with them. You had to earn respect. At first you were never sure where to look or sit in the changing room and I found my clothes slung on the floor a few times when I had sat in the wrong place.

'But there was huge excitement because I was playing for the best team in the UK, if not the world.'

Robinson made his Wigan debut as a substitute against Sheffield Eagles on 28 August 1992, replacing Sam Panapa after 28 minutes during a 46-6 victory in front of 5,987 spectators at the Don Valley Stadium.

Earlier that same day Wigan had sold Andy Goodway to Leeds and Australian Andrew Farrar had been signed from Western Suburbs to replace Gene Miles, while Andy Gregory had left for Leeds during the summer. Change was in the air, the sort of subtle improvement Wigan managed effectively, at times ruthlessly, during their halcyon years.

Robinson, however, was there to stay and immediately was struck by the warmth and knowledge and the demands of the Wigan fans.

A smile plays on his lips and his eyes light up as he winds back the years to recall the special ambience of Central Park, a ground which was built on the banks of the town's River Douglas in 1902 and first saw action when around 9,000 spectators watched Wigan beat Batley 14-8 and which went on to witness so many of the most dramatic moments in rugby league.

The memories have stayed with Robinson ever since. Memories he has relayed to his eldest son Lewis Tierney who signed as a full back for Wigan in 2013 and made his Super League debut in a 33-32 win against Widnes Vikings.

'Wigan fans were expectant. They expected to win at Wembley. They expected to win the league,' Robinson said.

'I remember days at Central Park with nearly 30,000 people, just a great atmosphere. The stadium was falling down but a packed-out Wigan crowd was just amazing. That is why Central Park has so many great memories for all the players. The DW Stadium today doesn't come anywhere close.

'There were lots of fans standing up and they were there hours before a big match just to get a good position. It was like a religion to everybody. You would do your warm-up and you could guarantee to see the same people in the same places week after week. And if they weren't there they had probably died.

'The Wigan fans meant a lot to the players. They appreciated good rugby and great players no matter where they came from and there have been some great players over the years.

'I will never forget the noise, the songs, the atmosphere, the fact that Central Park was in the heart of the town.

'On matchday it was like everybody just came out of the woodwork and descended, as if Wigan just shut down when a game was on.

'There was a very healthy youth system. Mick Cassidy, Mike Forshaw, Steve Blakeley, Andy Farrell, B.J. Mather, all Wigan lads and proud to have come through the system. As a young Wigan lad, who would want to be an astronaut when you could play for Wigan rugby? It was the greatest thing you could do as a young man in Wigan.

'The difference with Wigan back then was that they produced good players who went on to become great players. You cannot say that about every club. You can bring good players through the system and they can play first team rugby but do they become great players? Look at players at Wigan who came through, like Shaun Edwards and Andy Farrell, they became great and made it through to the top echelon.

'Without sounding like an old has-been player there are not, and I could be wrong, players like that around any more. There are very few players like that.'

Listening to Robinson the mature man, talking intelligently, effusively and eloquently, romantically even, about those distant days it is difficult to equate him with the hard-drinking, impetuous, wild youngster who almost threw it all away.

The Robinson story has been well chronicled. His autobiography, *Finding My Feet*, was published to coincide with the rugby union World Cup in 2003 and scores of newspaper articles and a handful of TV documentaries have recorded the challenges and low points in his personal life.

It does not make easy reading or viewing.

There are the harrowing tales of a stepfather who beat his mother. Episodes of plate-throwing violence and unremitting alcohol-fuelled rage in the family home in Beeston, which he witnessed as a cowering kid in the corner.

There are his own hard-drinking days at Wigan when at one stage he was drinking six nights a week.

'Monday it was Wakefield, 10p a pint night. Tuesday I would be over to Liverpool, Wednesday it would be Oldham, Thursday it would be Wigan. And after the game we would go out wherever,' he told an ITV4 documentary.

He even admits considering committing suicide when he was arrested for affray, assault and criminal damage, revealing that he sat in his bedroom with an old meat cleaver one night and 'wept like a baby'. Tormented by a troubled past. Tortured at times by loneliness and depression despite a burgeoning career.

His salvation is equally well documented and owed much to his relationship with Samoa star Va'aiga Tuigamala, who joined Wigan in 1993 and would read his Bible in the Central Park treatment room. Tuigamala did not drink, did not swear, did not drive flashy cars, yet he was happy. Robinson's conversion as a born-again Christian subsequently followed.

In Robinson's autobiography, hooker Martin Hall, one of his closest friends at Central Park, pinpoints the day of the transformation.

It was a Bank Holiday Monday in 1995 after a match against St Helens and Robinson as usual went out in Leeds and Wakefield, only this time he revealed that it was the last time. He would not be drinking in pubs with his team-mates again.

There was the usual dressing room mickey-taking banter and most of his team-mates did not believe Robinson would stick to his pledge. He did.

Fifteen years later he would also go on to search out and reconcile with his real dad, who abandoned him before he was born, a Jamaican living in Leeds called William Thorpe.

The purpose of this book, however, is not to dwell on the peccadilloes of Robinson's colourful past. I mention them only to put into context the personal obstacles and self-induced problems Robinson had to overcome in his fledgling years as Wigan consolidated their position as the most successful rugby league team of the time.

If Tuigamala was Robinson's ultimate saviour in life, then he also owed a debt to Wigan head coach John Monie and his wife Julie, with whom he lived for a period when he first made the first team at Wigan.

'He took me under his wing and it was good because I got to spend some time with him and go through some training videos,' said Robinson.

'It was good to see the other side of him. Looking back now, for him to take in a young lad was not an easy thing to do. I am sure I was hard work. But John Monie was an amazing coach, he was phenomenal.'

Robinson had signed as a scrum half, but Monie soon worked out that here was a lad whose talents did not surround constantly giving the ball to someone else. This was a player who needed the ball in his own hands as much as possible. He was put on the wing for a Sevens competition and largely that is where he stayed, apart from the occasional match at stand off or full back and one intriguingly at loose forward, the latter coming on 29 September 1992 in a Lancashire Cup second-round mismatch against Swinton at Gigg Lane, Bury, a game Wigan won 78-0 and which was remarkable mainly for the fact that Shaun Edwards scored ten tries. For the record Robinson was also one of the try scorers, along with Offiah, Sam Panapa and Dean Bell.

'John Monie said to me, "Just go and play." I didn't have any restrictions which was the best thing that could have happened to me,' said Robinson.

'I would get in at the play-the-ball and try to make some yards early doors, which was quite different from some other wingers. He gave me a licence to do what I wanted, which brings a lot of pressure but at the same time it freed me up to just run and take people on.'

Despite the young Robinson being mentored by Monie, sharing meals and family life for a while in his Wigan home, it did not mean he was treated differently to anyone else in the changing room or on the training field.

Part of Monie's success was his even-handed approach and an ability to share a joke or an off-guard moment with individuals while retaining their respect and trust. And their undivided attention.

'He struck fear into all the players,' said Robinson. 'He was only 5ft 4in tall but somehow you didn't want to cross him. You could tell who had a bad game because they would be sat at the back and then he would pull you out.

'There was no hiding place, that's for sure. It was brutally honest. He told it how it was and sometimes it was harsh and it was the same for everybody.

'Maybe that is why I was playing some good rugby at the time. I didn't want to upset him. He was a great, great coach and as a young lad just coming into it, to play under him was a pleasure.'

I met Robinson just once outside the formal press conference gatherings during those formative early years. It was at the *Daily Express* sports awards, a lunch held in a Piccadilly hotel, with trophies in various categories given to the sporting high-achievers of the year.

It was an annual affair, which prided itself on being the original newspaper sports awards bash, dating back decades and as such a contemporary of and an inspiration for the BBC Sports Personality of the Year awards of today.

It took some detailed organisation, although inevitably its success was gauged on how many top sports stars it was able to attract. The head count as the celebrities were ticked off on arrival always heralded an anxious hour or so for the *Daily Express* sports editor, who in the early 1990s was the affable and well-connected David Emery.

One particularly nervy moment had come in 1990 when midfielder Paul Gascoigne won the main award after inspiring England's football team to the semi-finals of the World Cup in Italy and a match against Germany, which was as famous for Gascoigne's tears when a yellow card meant he would miss the final through suspension as for missed penalties by Chris Waddle and Stuart Pearce in the inevitable shoot-out which meant England never reached the final anyway.

Would the famously erratic Gazza turn up at the hotel? Would the limousine detailed to pick him up from the Tottenham training ground in Loughton negotiate the London traffic in time?

As it turned out Gascoigne, wearing a white shellsuit and a mischievous grin, swaggered into the hotel ballroom bang on time. He was gracious and fun in his acceptance speech and then made his excuses and apologised for leaving early.

A few hours later, however, the sports editor received a phone call from the limousine driver to say he was in Newcastle and would there be any objections to picking up Mr Gascoigne's friends for a night on the town.

Effectively, Gazza, already labelled 'daft as a brush' by England manager Bobby Robson, had 'hijacked' the car and driver to take an 800-mile detour at the *Express*'s expense. Typical Gazza.

However, what was also typical of the warm-hearted if wayward footballer was that a few days later he wrote a letter of apology which included a cheque covering the cost of the limousine, plus a chunk more which he suggested be donated to a charity of the sports editor's choice.

Gascoigne had his problems but he also possessed a generosity of spirit which was difficult not to admire.

The same could be said of Maurice Lindsay, who is the man Jason Robinson had to thank a couple of years later for the *Daily Express* Newcomer of the Year trophy, which probably resides somewhere in the recesses of Robinson's attic these days.

Robinson had been nominated for the award along with England rugby union scrum half Kyran Bracken and several other budding stars.

Unfortunately, when Robinson awoke in Wigan that morning a heavy December snowfall meant his train had been cancelled. Enter Lindsay, who as RFL chief executive at the time had been invited to the awards lunch and was anxious that a rugby league youngster should be part of the proceedings to promote the sport, especially as recorded highlights of the ceremony were being shown that night on Sky television.

Lindsay telephoned Robinson and arranged a flight from Manchester to Heathrow, where a car was waiting to ferry him into the capital. Robinson duly arrived in shiny purple suit and on time.

What neither Lindsay nor Robinson knew was that the southern-based, rugby union-leaning *Daily Express* sports committee, who chose the winner, had already voted for Bracken.

Sometimes, however, fate gives life a nudge in the right direction and shortly before lunch was due Bracken telephoned to offer his apologies and explain something urgent had cropped up and he could no longer make it. Lindsay's persistence and ingenuity was rewarded when an hour or so later, and, after a speedy and secretive recalibration by the committee, Robinson was accepting his trophy alongside a hastily-gathered video clip of himself in action.

It was the first national recognition that here was a superstar in the making.

20

'Heaven's There!'

I F Jason Robinson was a young man in a hurry to prove the sporting maxim that decrees if a player is good enough he is old enough, then he was not alone.

This was rugby league's age of precocious superstars, none more precocious or more prodigiously talented than Andy Farrell, who walked on to the Wembley pitch for the first time wearing a cherry and white jersey, like Shaun Edwards a decade before him, when still a boy of 17.

He did not look like a boy. His shoulders were wide, his 6ft 4in, 17st frame developed with bulges in all the right places, a product of hours of one-to-one training in the gym with Bob Lanigan, the renowned strength and conditioning coach John Monie had brought to Wigan from Australia.

It was 1 May 1993 and Farrell had been named, along with Sam Panapa, as a substitute for Wigan's Challenge Cup Final against Widnes.

For so many of the Wigan team, Widnes at that time held a special resonance. Joe Lydon and Martin Offiah had played for them, the latter famously falling out with the club during the feud which resulted in his world record transfer to Central Park. Edwards had turned down their offer as a schoolboy when they were in their pomp.

The resonance for Farrell, however, struck home as he emerged from the Wembley tunnel and looked up to the spot at Wembley where he had sat with his mum and dad as an eight-year-old in 1984.

That day he had waved his cherry and white scarf, sung his heart out and soaked in the electric atmosphere which radiates around Wembley on Challenge Cup Final day.

It had been Farrell's first experience of a live rugby league match. Widnes v Wigan. The match which had seen Edwards become the youngest Challenge Cup finalist and Joe Lydon score those two outstanding long-range tries to give Widnes a winning edge. The match, too, which had seen Widnes stand off Keiron O'Loughlin score a third Widnes try.

Little was Farrell to know then that, as the 1990s dawned, Edwards and Lydon would become his team-mates and O'Loughlin his father-in-law when he married childhood sweetheart Colleen, after the couple had a son, Owen, at the age of 16.

Nor was the football-mad schoolboy that Farrell was then to know that the inspiration provided by that Wembley day in 1984 would transform his passion almost overnight from the round ball to the oval one. A passion which in time was to see him captain Wigan and Great Britain, become Man of Steel twice and win the Golden Boot as the best player in the world.

The thoughts coursing through his mind as he walked out in 1993 were not yet so grand and more to do with the remarkable journey which had taken him from a seat in the stand to one at rugby's top table in a whirlwind nine years.

'That match in 1984 ignited something inside me,' said Farrell.

'I hadn't played rugby until then and straight after that final I went to a Graeme West summer school because of the euphoria I had experienced at Wembley even though Wigan lost. I never looked back after that really.

'I used to love Wembley week coming around. I used to go into Wigan town centre and soak up the build-up with the town dressed in red and white and then go down to Wembley, either by coach from the Gas Showrooms, or by car or train. We did them all.

'I signed at Wigan at 14 and at 15 I was going down to Wembley with the second team, which was a bit spooky. When you go down as a reserve grade player while still a kid at 15 that really ignites your fire.'

The precocious Farrell was on a fast-track to sporting stardom, still playing with his amateur club, Orrell St James, at the weekend but training with superstars of the sport, such as Ellery Hanley, Shaun Edwards, Andy Platt and Andy Gregory, during the week.

'It was unbelievable for me,' said Farrell. 'I felt bulletproof, training with guys like that and then going back to play with my own age group. It was fantastic.'

It was a career path which owed much to the professionalism and camaraderie which existed within the Wigan set-up at the time.

Respect, as decreed by the 'pecking order' rituals already mentioned, was demanded by the senior players from the youngsters on the fringes, but in return there was a generous sharing of experience and life skills.

Farrell took up an apprenticeship in joinery when he left school, so his training sessions in the gym began before work at 6am. He was not alone. Frano Botica and Sam Panapa, as well as Dean Bell and Andy Platt, invariably joined him for those instructive early-morning sessions, the sort which eased him into the disciplines and protocols of the professional environment.

'Denis Betts and Phil Clarke also used to train the house down,' said Farrell. 'Me and Mick Cassidy latched on to them and they dragged us through. At Wigan in those days it was like a conveyor belt with players from the different eras trying to pull each other through.

'My wife's father, Keiron O'Loughlin, had been a rugby player for a long time and he always said to me that time in the gym was money in the bank when it came to looking after yourself. You need to be big as a youngster because however strong you are in the gym a man's strength is always going to be a problem at that age.'

It is why, if you study the videos of Farrell's early days, he appears to be at least a stone or two heavier than in his later career.

It was not the physical excellence of those days, however, which left an indelible mark on Farrell as he traversed a career which saw him become the second-highest points scorer in the club's history behind Jim Sullivan before he turned to rugby union to play for and then help coach England in a World Cup.

The camaraderie of the senior players and the sheer competitiveness of a town which consistently punches above its size and weight compared to the big city clubs in England, Australia and New Zealand, are the themes which Farrell marvels at to this day.

Like so many before him Farrell had to earn his place in the Wigan dressing room, spending 18 months conforming to pecking order protocol and changing in the 'A' team room following his first team debut in a Regal Trophy match against Keighley in 1991. Yet always he was made to feel that he belonged.

'I always felt part of it as a kid,' he said. 'For 30-year-old blokes with probably 20 international caps under their belt to look after the 16-, 17- and 18-year-olds and take them under their wings and make them team-mates as soon as possible was pretty special.

'It has stuck with me forever and even now in my coaching days I always try to help people through.'

That duty of care for the next generation is a recurring theme in Wigan's glorious Wembley years, but Farrell's pride in his hometown success goes deeper. It goes to the heart of what has made Wigan a rugby league phenomenon.

'I remember as a kid the Wigan town team trials were harder than the Lancashire trials,' said Farrell. 'I know brilliant players who didn't get in. It was fierce competition. There were lads from St James, St Pat's, St Williams, St Jude's amateur clubs. Central Park was the iconic place in town. Every day I went past in the car as a lad my dad used to point and say, "Heaven's there." He always called it heaven and every lad in the town was in awe of the stadium.

'Every lad aspired to get there and the amateur game was ruthless, absolutely ruthless.

'It was why some people didn't go to Central Park, their game was the amateur game, possibly because they didn't have the funds to go to Central Park every week. The amateur game was thriving, so much so that when Wigan went from Central Park to the JJB Stadium, as it was called then, some fans would rather go to St Pat's. The amateur game is the strength of the town and the breeding ground.

'It happens in Warrington and St Helens too, which is why they are always strong, but I think the competition is just that little bit more in Wigan.

'The strong amateur game, with kids competing against each other, is why rugby league in the working-class towns in the north of England is so tribal.

'When you are playing for Great Britain the camaraderie you have as a team has to be a given, but you always got a sense from the crowd that they were St Helens supporters, Wigan supporters, Leeds supporters and were cheering their own players on and wanting them to do well, not necessarily wanting Great Britain to be their team. Great Britain always felt like their second team. It is different in rugby union because everyone's team is the national team.'

Wigan's nucleus of players, steeped in the town's unique amateur grounding, was to the fore in their journey to Wembley in 1993. None more so than Martin Dermott and Joe Lydon at Thrum Hall, Halifax, on 28 February, a bitterly cold and windy Sunday afternoon when the frequent snow squalls turned a heavy and sloping pitch into one resembling an iced Christmas cake.

Suffice to say that Wigan were losing 18-12 in a fraught quarter-final with less than ten minutes remaining and Halifax, urged on by an intimidating and raucous crowd, increasingly were looking like deserving winners. The glorious cup run appeared to be faltering at the 29th hurdle.

Enter 'Bondy', that is Mark Preston, the winger whose two tries had clinched victory for Wigan at Wembley in 1990, but, strive as he might, had never floated John Monie's boat and had left Central Park for Thrum Hall.

Poor 'Bondy'.

Some sportsmen, it seems, are drawn to calamity and just when it seemed he was in sight of a hugely satisfying victory against his former team-mates Preston contrived to collide clumsily with Halifax full back Warren Wilson as they attempted to field a high kick.

The ball squirted into the path of Joe Lydon, who calmly picked up and completed the touchdown which, following Botica's conversion, saw the score locked at 18-18.

Preston and Lydon were good friends. They used to holiday together and it was Preston who was the first to know when Lydon decided to get married.

They were so close, yet their rugby careers could not have been more different. Preston, the nearly man who experienced a fleeting glimpse of the sun but was destined to languish in the shadows. Lydon, the special one, showered with stardust. Blessed with talent. Always the hero. Forever Hollywood.

So it proved again at Thrum Hall, 36 seconds from time, when Lydon, the world record kicker at Maine Road four years previously, dropped yet another remarkable goal from 40 yards to clinch a 19-18 victory.

This time, as a sustained snow flurry distracted the Halifax players, Dermott delivered the crucial pass to Lydon from the play-the-ball in the middle of the field.

'If any game was tight near the end, Joe was never far away,' recalled Dermott. 'He just shouted, "Derms", and that's when I knew he wanted to try a drop because usually it would be Shaun Edwards or the playmaker around that position on the field.

'I knew the pass had to be accurate, fast and be placed to Joe's right so he could just catch it and release the kick in one movement due to pressure from the Halifax players and the conditions. It was a great kick.'

And so the cup run continued.

Wigan had already beaten Hull 40-2 in the preliminary round, Dewsbury 20-4 in round one and St Helens 23-3 in round two. A 15-6 semi-final triumph against Bradford Northern at Elland Road followed the escape at Thrum Hall, paving the way for Farrell's first appearance at Wembley in a sporting year which was notable for the death of beloved England football captain Bobby Moore from cancer at the age of 52, Manchester United winning the inaugural Premier League, Aussie spinner Shane Warne bowling the so-called 'Ball of the Century' to dismiss England's Mike Gatting in the first Ashes Test match at Old Trafford and the Grand National horse race being declared void when 30 of the 39 riders failed to realise a false start had been called and set off around the racetrack.

There was no such confusion at Wembley, a venue with which Wigan by now were entirely comfortable, having perfected their routine over the past five years.

As the baby of the team Farrell was paired up in a room in the team hotel with captain Dean Bell, the reasoning being that the experienced and composed New Zealander would help soothe any anxieties the 17-year-old first-timer might have.

It did not quite work out that way.

In fact, the night before the game, Bell, a Man of Steel and already a five-time Challenge Cup winner, was throwing up in the toilet, consumed by nerves at the prospect of leading out the team next day, while it was left to Farrell, whose dressing room presence and sense of oratory were to become some of his greatest assets, to prove that not only was he young but that he was also composed and fearless.

'Don't worry,' Farrell told Bell. 'We'll batter these guys tomorrow.'

'Batter' turned out to be far from accurate, mostly because the Widnes side was full of characters with a point to prove. Players such as Welshman John Devereux and Jonathan 'Jiffy' Davies, former international rugby union stars who had switched codes and were experiencing their first taste of rugby league's showpiece occasion. Men, too, like winger David Myers, who died tragically early from a heart attack after being involved in a car crash on the M6 at the age of 37 but who had played and scored for Wigan against St Helens in the 1991 final before finding himself surplus to requirements at Central Park following the world record signing of Martin Offiah.

Widnes also possessed a playmaker in Bobbie Goulding, who had picked up two winners' medals with Wigan in 1990 and 1991 from the substitutes' bench and had moved on because the mercurial talents of Shaun Edwards and Andy Gregory blocked his way.

There was a devilment about Goulding. He was a man with a feisty temperament and a winning mentality, which he proved most memorably when he captained St Helens to the cup and league double in 1996.

In 1993 there was no doubt his fuse was fizzing long before he lined up to meet the dignitaries.

Farrell bumped into him as he walked up the tunnel to take a look at the pitch, 90 minutes before kick-off.

'I said, "Hi Bobbie, you all right?" said Farrell, glad to have spotted a familiar face. It soon became apparent Goulding was in no mood for pleasantries.

'I used to train with Bobbie at Wigan but he was not too obliging right then,' added Farrell. 'I could see the rage in his eyes. He was unbelievably fired up and he tried to put the wind up me in that tunnel. It is my most lasting memory of that occasion.'

Goulding's intimidation tactics, verbal and physical as he niggled away at the referee and the Wigan players, continued once the game began and in truth he ran around for most of that final threatening to do what comes naturally to Krakatoa once a century.

The lid finally blew in the second half, an altercation with Wigan centre Andrew Farrar provoking the inevitable explosion, which quite possibly would have led to Goulding being handed a sharp, short lesson in Australian corporal punishment if players had not rushed in to prevent Farrar taking the law into his own hands.

The sight of fighting on the verdant green of Wembley is a particularly distasteful sight. It can never be condoned but the 1993 final was a tight, closely-fought game with all the tensions and frustrations which make sport at the elite level such an enthralling spectacle.

True, it did not tick all the boxes for fans who prefer rugby league to be out of the Harlem Globetrotters school of entertainment, for those who remember the exhibition basketball team probably most famous for Meadowlark Lemon's audacious talents in the 1970s.

The 1993 final was a man's game. It was full of thunderous tackles and substance with the lead changing hands and whatever it lacked in style and free-flowing rugby being made up for in tension and drama despite the fact that the scoring dried up shortly after half-time.

It saw a player sent off at Wembley for only the second time in a Challenge Cup Final, some 22 years after Syd Hynes of Leeds had become the first sportsman to be sent off beneath the Twin Towers for that alleged headbutt on Leigh's Alex Murphy, as referred to earlier.

In 1993 the player who saw red was Richie Eyres, dismissed by referee Russell Smith in the second half for throwing an elbow into the head of Offiah. It was an out-of-character foul from Eyres which not only made Wigan's task that much easier but also ensured that Offiah, the two-try hero of 1992, was again the centre of attention and controversy even though it was by no means one of his most productive matches.

To be fair, he had supplied the basketball-style pass with a piece of quick thinking which sent in Dean Bell for an easy try after Devereux had spilled the ball near his own line, but there were no scything line breaks, no length-of-the-field runs, no balletic brilliance.

Yet, as Offiah has always argued, the Eyres incident quite possibly kept the Wigan run alive. Second row Eyres was a crucial player for Widnes, a rumbustious character. He added weight and direct running to their forward momentum and had scored the first try of the match, exploiting a darting run by Goulding and touching down, after which he formed the forefinger and thumb of his right hand into the shape of a gun and shot a kiss to the Widnes fans.

'Eyres going off probably helped us to win the game,' admitted Offiah, who had regarded Eyres as a friend and colleague when they played together at Widnes. 'I was looking to get into the game but after he elbowed me I should never have stayed on the pitch. Anyone who has seen the footage can see Richie just sticks his elbow out there. For many years after that, me and Richie didn't see eye to eye. We connected again when we went back for an anniversary dinner a few years ago and we are on friendly terms now.

'But for years there was great animosity between us. We were quite close at Widnes. Whether he felt betrayed when I went to Wigan I don't know, but he later went to Leeds.

'I know he did it on purpose but he tried to make out that I had dived. It wasn't much contact, I know, but you don't need much contact on the temple. I went straight from the changing room to the team bus. I had concussion basically. I had a headache and he walked past the bus abusing me saying, "You've just cheated, you got me sent off."

'I would never have been allowed to stay on these days with the concussion protocols, I was out when I hit the floor. It affected my game and I wasn't the same player for the rest of the game. We won, but for me it always felt like a hollow victory.'

For Farrell it was anything but. He had come off the bench in the 55th minute to replace Kelvin Skerrett after Eyres and Kurt Sorensen had scored for Widnes, with Davies adding three goals, while Wigan had scored three tries from Skerrett, Bell and Panapa, boosted by four goals from Frano Botica.

The score was 20-12 when Farrell arrived and it stayed that way, but it was the energy draining out of legs which suddenly felt like iron girders as he ran on to the pitch which he recalls most.

The weight of Wembley, something players of all ages and varying pedigrees have experienced down the years.

The point, however, was not the extent of Farrell's contribution that day, rather the fact that his trophy-laden career was under way, a career which in 370 appearances saw him score 3,135 points for Wigan, behind only Jim Sullivan on 4,483, and win 34 caps for Great Britain, scoring 134 points.

Statistics do not always tell the whole story, however, and perhaps the best judge of Farrell's enduring influence on his sport and on his hometown club is Denis Betts, the senior professional who inspired the young Farrell with his training discipline and took him under his professional care in his formative years.

'Andy Farrell is the best player I ever played with,' is the informed opinion of Betts. 'If I could choose to mould a player now and pick any player I wanted to play in my team I would pick Andy for his leadership skills, his ability to kick off both feet, his ability to pass with both hands.

'He was big, he was tough, he knew the game, he could play at different tempos, he just knew what the game needed. It's a special trait and that's what made him such a phenomenal player. In a list of my top two or three players Shaun Edwards would be around there as well, but if you could mould a rugby league player he would be 6ft 4in, 16st, and be able to run strong with a great engine. That was Andy Farrell.'

Two weeks after lifting his first Challenge Cup, however, Farrell found himself in the starting line-up for the Premiership Trophy Final against St Helens at Old Trafford. Wigan lost 10-4 and at the final hooter head coach John Monie's remarkable reign at Central Park came to a somewhat inappropriate end.

His initial resistance when Maurice Lindsay repeatedly telephoned him at his home Down Under had turned into four seasons of unrivalled achievement. Under Monie's guidance Wigan had won four consecutive Challenge Cups, a World Club Challenge and four league championships.

On the way he had set the standard for rugby league coaches in the northern hemisphere. To this day coaches throughout the sport of rugby still reference Monie in the way they prepare teams and employ tactics, such as Edwards with Wales and Farrell with England and Ireland, even if the latter's transformation from a rugby league great into a rugby union international was hampered by injury and a back problem associated with a car crash when he left Wigan in 2004 for Saracens.

Farrell did play for England eight times at union with limited success and was defence coach of the England side under head coach Stuart Lancaster, an appointment which ended in failure in 2015 when England suffered consecutive defeats against Wales and Australia to exit the World Cup at the pool stage.

I spoke to Farrell, who was appointed Ireland rugby union defence coach following his England demise, on the day he was moving his family to Dublin, driving a van himself packed with white goods, television and assorted home essentials, before the 2016 autumn internationals.

When the conversation turned to the art of coaching, the name of Monie was quick to follow.

'He had a big effect on me,' said Farrell. 'He made sure he was at every "A" team match when I was playing for them and used to select subs who had played well for the first team. He knew what he wanted and you daren't put a foot wrong. If you made mistakes you certainly knew about it on Monday morning.

'I remember one game, Steve Hampson got man of the match and scored three tries but the video next day was about all the errors Steve had made.

'Monie was a fierce competitor and had a steely way about him but he was always very fair and great at bringing one or two youngsters through to the first team each year.

'He could have harsh words. That was his strength. You had so many superstars and some of them could have run riot on other coaches but not on John. He was the boss and everyone knew that. He knew exactly what he wanted you to do and you did it to the letter.'

Monie had been fortunate to learn from the accepted master in Jack Gibson, an Australian innovator who earned the soubriquet 'Supercoach' after taking Eastern Suburbs to Premierships in 1974 and 1975 and later the Parramatta Eels to three successive titles from 1981 to 1983.

As his assistant at Parramatta, Monie had watched and learned as his mentor put emphasis on the importance of meticulous preparation, identifying mistakes and eliminating them.

It was radical thinking in a world of machismo which at that time too often saw the coach's main job as ranting and swearing at the players on matchday to pump up the passion to levels approaching mania.

Farrell has had the best part of two decades since he last played under Monie, in the coach's second short spell at Wigan in 1998/99, to reflect on the little man's biggest talent. He has no doubt that was to give his players a sense of direction.

'You soon learn as a coach that is essential when you are dealing with 40 players in rugby union and 25 players in rugby league,' said Farrell. 'John was good at giving clarity. Everyone has an opinion and an idea but it would always come down to what John had decided. That takes strength in a coach.

'He had a good way about him with the senior players and kept the rest on their toes. You learn through the years. He was there in the glory days of Parramatta with all the superstars and man-management doesn't change through the years. It comes down to how, as a coach, you make people feel. John was exactly the type of coach we needed.'

Perhaps that was epitomised by the way in which he broke the news to Joe Lydon that his playing days were numbered.

Lydon remembers struggling through a difficult match at Central Park and as he walked off the pitch at the final hooter, Monie caught up with him as they entered the players' tunnel.

'We had really good young players coming through such as Jason Robinson and Kris Radlinski and I'd had two or three knee operations,' said Lydon.

'John came close beside me and said, "Joe, come and sit next to me for a couple of years." I said okay and it was probably the nicest way anyone could have put it. I played a few more games, but I knew then it was over. It was such a nice way to tell you to stop.'

By contrast, the career of Farrell, who captained Wigan through some troubled times when the salary cap ended their domination and the move from Central Park robbed the club of its iconic home, was just beginning and he speaks of those early years with genuine affection.

They are also deep-seated in the affections of his son Owen, England rugby union's prolific goal-kicking fly half or centre, who used to visit training at Central Park and watch his dad on a regular basis from being a toddler.

Owen started playing rugby league at six years old and went through the same county and town trials as his dad before him.

'I never pushed him to do anything but he came to training with me all the time and watched all those great players,' said Farrell. 'He has been down in London now for 11 or 12 years but he still classes himself as a Wiganer. We never miss watching a Wigan match. Once a Wiganer, always a Wiganer. You are always going to support your hometown club.'

Which leaves just one question for the man who has been inducted into Wigan's hall of fame alongside a gallery of greats including Jim Sullivan, Joe Egan, Billy Boston, Eric Ashton, Shaun Edwards and Ellery Hanley.

Would he ever return to Wigan as head coach?

'You never say never to anything,' said Farrell. 'I want to be a coach for as long as I can. I want to stay within the game of rugby, rugby league or rugby union. I love doing what I do, managing players and galvanising people.

'I am unbelievably jealous of the people who stay within the game and bow out at 60 or 65, that would do me. It's not a chore, it is a passion. My only goal really is to keep getting better as a coach. There are always situations which aren't completely in your hands and that's why we move around a bit more than other professions. But, if I am coaching well enough, the players will always have a word to say about that and hopefully I can carry on getting the joy out of it that I have done since I was 14 years old.

'I consider myself unbelievably fortunate to be a Wiganer and have had the career I had there. To captain the club and go everywhere with them and win a few things along the way was a dream come true and would be for any Wiganer.

'I was fortunate to get on the back of that great era and get shown how it was done. I can't see it happening again. What sums it up for me is that lots of players over the years who were not Wiganers stayed in the town because of their love for rugby.'

Halfway through 1993, however, Monie was gone, his contract complete, his contribution immense, his reputation enhanced and his desire for a well-earned break and a spot of surfing fulfilled, but his departure an undeniable factor in destabilising the mightiest dynasty in British rugby league.

21

View from the Press Box

L ET'S face it, by the time Widnes had been dispatched there were some rugby league reporters who might have preferred to listen to Prime Minister John Major documenting the details of how he saved the United Kingdom from the Euro via the complexities of the Maastricht Treaty than report on another Challenge Cup Final involving Wigan.

Six Challenge Cups in a row. The feat was stupendous, no doubt about that.

So much so that the chief sports writers from the national newspapers, literary sporting heavyweights such as Patrick Collins of the *Mail on Sunday*, James Lawton of the *Daily Express*, Simon Barnes at *The Times*, Michael Parkinson of Yorkshire and Colin Welland of *Chariots of Fire* fame, regularly turned up at Wembley to craft their plaudits, for one afternoon only, to a game which is rich in history and culture, if also home to clichés of the 'cloth caps and whippets' variety.

Any extra publicity was welcome for a sport which had always struggled and still does to carve a niche in the national psyche.

Fleet Street's finest marvelled at 'a tackler's game'. They recognised a sport of brutal, head-on assault where nothing was hidden in feet-flailing rucks and sweaty mauls and endlessly reformed scrums.

'Rugby league is about flagrant, naked confrontation,' wrote Simon Barnes. Easy to understand. Easy to appreciate.

Yet the fear in the 1990s was that Wigan, directly because of their enduring excellence and domination, were rendering the sport dull and predictable and there are few more pernicious enemies of sport than predictability.

In the two decades that have passed since a Wigan captain lifted the Challenge Cup for an eighth time in a row, Dave Hadfield, of *The*

Independent, has weighed up the pros and cons of that golden era on many occasions.

'In the end I think the success was perceived as being bad,' said Hadfield. 'You started the season pretty well knowing that Wigan were going to win everything. Even some Wigan fans got a bit bored with it in the end. On the other hand it can be quite good for a sport to have one icon at the top that everyone is shooting at all the time. Like the St George side of the 1950s and 1960s in Sydney and Liverpool FC in their pomp.

'It did have an effect because ever since the game has been frightened of having such a powerful single entity on top of everybody and things being decided before the end of the season. The whole thing now is geared to having the big occasion at Old Trafford and the biggest game of the season, the Grand Final, being the last game of the season. That Wigan side wouldn't have been good for that because that Wigan side had a habit of winning things by Easter.

'You still get people now who don't know much about the game who think Wigan have won everything for the last 20 years. They still carry that aura with them. You always sat up and took notice when Wigan lost a game because it was a story in itself.

'I can't say that I got bored with it. There was always some drama going on. I used to say that covering Wigan built my house for me. They did me a favour on the way up and on the way down because they were newsworthy in both directions. It was never dull. It might have been predictable in that you had a damned good idea that Wigan would come out of it and win things but it was never dull.'

In fact, one could argue the personalities and big names Wigan assembled during their cup run helped rugby league keep their slender grasp on column inches in the national newspapers during a period of turbulent change for the sport and newspapers alike.

While Wigan were winning their cup finals under coach Graham Lowe in 1988 and 1989, major newspapers such as the *Daily Mail*, the *Daily Express* and the *Daily Telegraph* were closing down their autonomous operations in Manchester and running for their centralised boltholes in London on the back of the Wapping dispute in 1986 when 6,000 newspaper workers went on strike after protracted negotiations with News International, which owned *The Times*, *The Sun* and the *News of the World*.

News International immediately activated a new secretly-equipped, state-of-the-art printing factory in Wapping for all its titles, a move which saw angry picketing and violence reminiscent of the miners' strike. The dispute lasted 12 months, ending in virtual bankruptcy for the print unions and yet not one day's production lost for the newspaper proprietors. It proved to be a defining moment in the history of the trade union movement with thousands losing their jobs and yet another industry decimated. For rugby league it also had repercussions. Many of the sub-editors who lost their jobs, and the few who chose to relocate to London, were steeped in the sport and recognised its importance to communities the length of the M62 corridor.

In ensuring matches from Naughton Park to Watersheddings to Thrum Hall to Old Craven Park received coverage, often changing editions to give Yorkshire, Lancashire and Humberside clubs more space in their own areas, they had been guardians of the sport's heritage.

Suddenly, the sport had to fight its corner in the cut-throat environment of Fleet Street, with all its pressures of space and budgets at a time when the personality culture was beginning to dominate British newspapers and sport in general was swiftly growing in power and influence.

Fleet Street editors could see the mass appeal of Manchester United and Arsenal. They welcomed the breadth of interest, from Carlisle to Cornwall, in sublime footballers such as Paul Gascoigne and even headline-grabbing journeymen such as Vinnie Jones. They understood their value in selling newspapers. The same could not be said for most rugby league players, apart perhaps from Ellery Hanley, Martin Offiah and later Jason Robinson and to a lesser extent Shaun Edwards and Andy Gregory.

It was a battle but the *Daily Express* did more than most to fly the flag for northern sport on a daily basis during those times, part of which was down to an inspirational and flexible sports editor in David Emery, a former rugby union reporter but a man who respected and chose to see the best in all sports. Mostly, however, the passion came from a young and enthusiastic team of sub-editors who had relocated south to Fleet Street from the Ancoats area of Manchester where the *Express*'s famous Black Lubyanka building in the north was located.

Even so, there was a gradual and inevitable erosion of the sport's coverage with several rugby league correspondents across the industry losing their staff status.

The increasingly limited coverage given to the sport by most of the national newspapers on a Monday morning following the weekend matches, however, did prompt the birth of the *League Express*, a specialist rugby league newspaper whose first edition appeared on 10 September 1990, published in Wakefield, although production was quickly switched to Bradford.

In 2002 the *League Express* was merged with the *Rugby Leaguer* newspaper, the latter being the sport's first weekly newspaper and which is famous for the slogan which appeared in 1949 on the masthead of the first issue:

'By rugby league people – for rugby league people'.

This was doubtless supposed to express a solidarity and build an identity with its customers. Yet there is something about that phrase which goes to the heart of explaining why rugby league has refused to transcend its heartland in any meaningful fashion.

Perhaps it has been happy in its insularity and proud, sometimes stubbornly so, of its history. A history that suggests a class divide still exists between rugby league and rugby union.

The northernness of league is founded in its industrial, working-class roots. In places such as Batley and Bramley and Huddersfield and Halifax.

Union's strongholds in the north still emanate from places such as Sale and Harrogate, well-to-do market towns and middle-class suburbs with a preponderance of private schools.

I went to a down-to-earth boys' prep school and grammar school, now a sixth form college, in Orrell on the outskirts of Wigan called St John Rigby, the same one which a decade later was attended for a time, in its college reincarnation, by Joe Lydon and Shaun Edwards. Rugby league in my time had as much chance of featuring on the curriculum as synchronised swimming or rhythmic gymnastics.

Rugby union and cricket were the grammar school games of choice. To play league, or football for that matter, pupils had to attend the old secondary moderns or comprehensives in the area or join the amateur clubs.

So the divide was not all about geography. It was not merely about north and south. It was about class and perceptions of class and, by association, which classroom you happened to find yourself in during your teenaged years.

Much, of course, has changed in the last quarter of a century, not least the fact that rugby union went professional in 1995, allowing many of the old bigotries to be laid to rest.

Yet while union has flourished and grown inexorably in the national consciousness, with international matches, in particular, receiving universal coverage across all media, league has continued to struggle outside its heartland.

There is no doubt Maurice Lindsay, in his days as Wigan chairman and then chief executive of the Rugby Football League, tried to spread the word. He courted the sports editors of national newspapers and the high-ranking sports executives in television. He held lunches and briefings and talked about the sport with a missionary zeal.

He afforded the press entry to the changing rooms, especially following the Wembley finals, the sort of enlightened up-close access commonplace in American sports but virtually unheard of in major British sports.

But, despite those efforts, taking a sport to new frontiers, where there is no history or tradition, even a short train ride outside the Lancashire, Yorkshire and Humberside fence in which it is mostly contained, is not easy.

The history of the sport is well-recorded but that history is important to remember in any analysis of the journey it has taken.

British rugby league originated in 1895 from rugby union's decision to enforce the amateur principle of the sport, preventing 'broken time payments' to players who had taken time off work to play the sport.

Northern teams, comprising poorly-paid working-class miners and mill workers, had more players who could not afford to play without the broken-time compensation.

The famous meeting at the George Hotel in Huddersfield led to 22 breakaway clubs forming the 'Northern Rugby Football Union' which led in 1897 to the line-out being abolished and the following year professionalism being introduced.

It was not until 1906, however, that the schism was complete when the Northern Union changed its rules, reducing the players from 15- to 13-a-side and replacing the union ruck with the play-the-ball.

In 1907 a similar split took place in rugby in Sydney when the New South Wales Rugby Football League was founded at Bateman's Hotel in George Street. League went on to replace rugby union as the primary code in New South Wales and Queensland.

Rugby league in New Zealand was founded around the same time as in Australia with the New Zealand Rugby League governing body founded in 1910 in preparation for a tour of Great Britain later that same year.

As for the the French, they took up the game quite unexpectedly when the union bodies of England, Scotland, Ireland and Wales in 1931 decided their teams could no longer play the French because of 'professionalism' in the Gallic game.

France did not take part in rugby union's home championship again until 1947. The void was filled on the other side of the channel when international centre Jean Galia decided to try league and was successful in persuading a cohort of players to join him, so successful, in fact, that the first short French rugby league tour of Great Britain took place in 1934.

It was about this time that the sport also caught hold in Papua New Guinea, having been introduced by Australian miners during the gold rush, although it was 1949 before the Papua New Guinea Football League was founded.

The point is that rugby league's roots are deep and sparse at the same time. It is not, and never will be, a global sport and arguably it is futile to continue to pursue that aim, but the cultural identity in the places where it thrives is powerful and enduring.

Elsewhere, well, it has always proved something of a challenge, despite repeated attempts to sow seeds.

In June 1989, for example, Wigan and Warrington took the game to the biggest sporting market place on Earth, the United States, playing an exhibition match on American soil in Milwaukee on the western shore of Lake Michigan.

Why Milwaukee? Mostly because of its blue-collar, heavy industrial traditions, although given its population is made up largely of immigrants descending from Germany and Poland as well as Lithuania, Italy, France, Russia, Bohemia and Sweden, it does not appear to be steeped in rugby traditions.

The exhibition match, driven more by American rugby league evangelists than the RFL, was won 12-5 by Wigan, in front of 17,773 supporters.

In every way, other than financial and some organisational glitches, the exercise was a success with American viewers enraptured by the athletic prowess and sheer physicality of the players.

Was it worthwhile? Did it catch on? It is not easy to gauge the impact of one luminous shaft of creative thought, but a quarter of a century later the USA national rugby league team competed in the 2013 World Cup, the nation's first appearance at the tournament, and exceeded all expectations by reaching the quarter-finals before losing to Australia. That surely is progress of sorts.

Progress which in turn swiftly led to the USA and Canada being awarded the right to host the 2025 rugby league World Cup, the first time the tournament will have been hosted outside the sport's traditional heartland.

The bottom line is that rugby league, despite its problems, continues to be an honest, democratic, egalitarian sport, one that retains an evangelical zeal to expand and yet still reflects life in all its hardships and all its glories.

For all its struggles in promotion, these days it is as likely to be watched by bankers, accountants and solicitors as it is by ordinary working men and women on zero hour contracts.

Much of that is down to the Super League revolution, the satellite television coverage of which has brought to rugby league the close scrutiny, the meticulous data and the fan-friendly touch screen analysis which has made Premier League football such a watchable product.

Yet rugby league's roots remain entrenched in its working class heritage. And that has proved remarkably robust when faced with outside threats.

The fears back in the 1990s when union turned professional were that league would see mass defections or that the sports would somehow amalgamate.

Neither came to pass. True, there has been traffic between the two codes but it has been a two-way process, with the most high-profile player conversions to union including Andy Farrell, Jason Robinson, Henry Paul and Sam Burgess, the latter returning swiftly to league after his disappointment at the 2015 rugby union World Cup.

Only Robinson can legitimately claim to have been a complete success, although, on the coaching front, union is saturated with top-level coaches who all plied their trade in the league code.

For instance, Joe Lydon, Farrell, Phil Larder and Mike Ford have all held down key coaching positions with England rugby union while Shaun Edwards has gained guru status as a coach with Wasps and latterly with Wales and the British Lions.

As for league and union amalgamating, it is not going to happen. Nor should it, although esteemed rugby league writer and author Geoffrey Moorhouse put forward a persuasive case in 1990 when he wrote, 'I think the intrinsic pointlessness, not to mention the wastefulness, of two forms of rugby will become increasingly apparent to everyone. Think how daft it would seem to have two forms of soccer, with teams of 11 players and a throw-in from touch in one version, but 13 footballers in the other and a bounce-up by the referee every time the ball went out of play. The pointlessness will become apparent soonest and most of all to the best players.

'As the bigots on both sides die off, so too will the pointlessness become more obvious to the mass of watchers in the grandstands and on the terraces.'

The two cross-code matches between Wigan and Bath in 1996, the league match won 82-6 by Wigan at Maine Road and the union game seeing Bath triumph 44-19 at Twickenham, only served to highlight that Moorhouse was wrong and much more separates the two codes than a 'throw-in' or a 'bounce-up'.

There are obvious similarities but essentially they are fundamentally different disciplines that just happen to use the same shaped ball, as former Wigan coach Graham Lowe, who suffered a bout of ill health after leaving Central Park, insisted with a touch of exaggeration and a splash of bias around the time of the cross-code matches.

'I've had a brain haemorrhage and a triple bypass and I could still go out and play a reasonable game of rugby union,' said Lowe. 'But I wouldn't last 30 seconds in rugby league.'

To this day if a rugby league side opt to kick a penalty goal rather than run the ball it is likely the opposition fans will burst into a rendition of

'Swing Low Sweet Chariot', mocking the tendency of the union game in which penalties often determine the outcome of the match.

Kicking a penalty in rugby league is almost seen as cheating by some fans, which probably explains why the calibre of goal-kicking is so much higher in the union code.

One man who believes Wigan's dominance was not only good for the game but fundamental in taking the sport to new frontiers is Peter Aspinall, who as rugby league correspondent for the *Wigan Evening Post* reported on every match in their 43-game unbeaten cup run as well as covering the sport in the town for more than a quarter of a century.

Aspinall wrote columns with many of the players, some for the newspaper, others for the matchday programme, and was invited regularly into the inner sanctum of the changing rooms after victories.

'Newspapers were still in their pomp and there was a vast audience, especially in Wigan, for the rugby,' he recalls. 'You wrote stuff and it was lapped up. You had a strong audience, circulation figures were good. They were great days.

'There was always plenty going on at Wigan. There were some players at the beating heart of it throughout, determined, driven individuals such as Dean Bell, Shaun Edwards and Gary Connolly.

'And, yes, their dominance was good for the game because it set a standard others realised they had to meet and try to match, which eventually they did. It has evened out nowadays, although Wigan still retain a foothold at the top of Super League. Other clubs said, "Right, how are we going to beat Wigan?" It took them a long time to get there, but eventually they got there.

'Wigan had individual players who could turn games like Bell and Edwards. Other teams decided they had to do the same themselves.

'I don't think that it will happen again. No club will achieve what Wigan did in those years, mainly because the players are now of a similar professional and physical standard at the top six clubs in Super League.

'I used to gamble quite a bit on rugby because I used to think I knew what I was doing and I made quite a bit of money out of it but now I don't touch it because it is so unpredictable. That unpredictability, which is perhaps good for the game, is the reason why I don't think Wigan or any other club could do it again. You can watch a team play really well one week and then the next lose to somebody they shouldn't, it happens all the time now.'

Undeniably, events surrounding Wigan on the field circa 1993 could be viewed as predictable.

Off the field, however, they were about to become distinctly more volatile.

So much so, that rugby league reporters, such as Peter Aspinall and Dave Hadfield, would soon be filling their notebooks with stories you really could not have made up.

22

'I Thought I Was In *Coronation Street*'

IT was the best of years, it was the worst of years. It was the season of glorious achievement. It was the season of relentless angst.

It was the period when Wigan's long-running Wembley story threatened to implode amid the fractious forces of division and uncertainty released by the departure of John Monie and the arrival of his successor, John Dorahy.

Truly, Charles Dickens would have struggled to match the drama and intrigue from May 1993 to May 1994 as a whiff of revolution permeated Central Park.

Following in the elegant footsteps of Monie was always destined to be a tough assignment. The engaging Australian had missed out on a sabbatical surfing on the Gold Coast due to Maurice Lindsay's persistence, but he had adorned the Central Park trophy cabinet with four Challenge Cups, four Championship titles and a World Club Challenge crown.

By contrast, Dorahy, a stylish full back or centre with Wests, Manly-Warringah and Illawarra Steelers in Australia as well as Leigh, Hull KR and Halifax in England, had won precisely zilch as a head coach.

Suddenly, after just one season as player-coach with Halifax and two as assistant coach at the Newcastle Knights, he was in charge of Wigan, the Manchester United of rugby league.

He had applied for the job after telephoning Maurice Lindsay from Sydney, not realising Lindsay had already left Wigan to run the RFL. Lindsay put him in touch with Wigan chairman Jack Robinson and Dorahy, accompanied by his wife Linda, flew to Wigan for an interview as the 1992/93 season drew to a close.

It could hardly have been more informal. A tour of the ground and facilities, a convivial meeting with Robinson and the directors and an invite to that week's Friday night match against Castleford in the Premiership Trophy semi-final at Central Park.

Dorahy, aware of his inexperience, harboured few expectations, so it came as something of a surprise when on the morning of the match Robinson pulled him aside and said, 'Look John, I'm happy to tell you, if you want it you've got the job.'

There were just three stipulations made by Robinson. Beat St Helens on Boxing Day and Good Friday, retain the league title and win the Challenge Cup once more at Wembley.

'Wow,' said Dorahy. 'That was my first reaction. It really was a surprise. I had to keep it quiet for a few weeks before the news finally broke when I came back across from Sydney at the end of May.'

Dorahy was familiar with many of the personnel from his own playing days, although the majority of the squad were either playing Down Under or away on holiday when the new coach arrived.

One of those was Shaun Edwards, who had opted to use the summer break to visit training venues in Fiji and Sydney to refresh tired limbs and explore new ideas after a 20-month spell of non-stop action, which had seen him appear in close to 100 consecutive matches.

His training companion was Ellery Hanley, who was now with Leeds. They had trained twice a day, every day, on the track in the mornings and in the gym in the afternoons.

So it was that Edwards stepped off the plane from Sydney feeling mentally rejuvenated and physically fitter than he had been for years. Eager for the new season to start.

The first hint that everything might not be quite as once it was, however, came when he learned from a team-mate the time of Dorahy's next training session. Sunday morning, eight o'clock.

'I said, "Does he realise we have just been playing for nine months non-stop, two games a week most of the time?" said Edwards. 'Anyway, I turned up for training and because I was in such good shape did the running up hills pretty easily. It was stuff I was good at. But I was thinking all the time, "What the hell are we doing here so early on a Sunday morning with Kelvin Skerrett and the lads from Yorkshire having to come all the way over?"

'I just thought it was clearly, obviously wrong. He should have been giving the lads a weekend off to see their family. I think John just wanted to assert his authority.'

There is an old adage which says you never get a second chance to make a first impression and from that initial early-morning training session it was clear Dorahy was struggling to gain the full support of one of Wigan's key characters.

Actually, 'first impression' is somewhat misleading because the pair had history stretching back to a match between Wigan and Hull Kingston Rovers at Central Park in the mid-1980s.

Dorahy, playing centre for Hull KR that day, remembers in some detail being 'whacked' in a tackle by Edwards early in the match, a hit which he claims 'deserved retaliation'.

When the opportunity arose Dorahy admits he seized his opportunity.

'As Shaun ran to his left I followed, even cutting in front of my own player to effect the tackle,' said Dorahy. 'Shaun stepped off his left foot and dummied to try to make the break. At that point I made a strong tackle, knocking down Shaun's right arm with my left arm to stop the fend and hitting Shaun with a swinging right arm off the chest and ball which connected with his chin.'

Edwards recalls the incident differently, insisting Dorahy simply swung round and punched him as he tugged at his shirt as he chased upfield.

What is clear and uncontested, however, is that the punch stopped Edwards immediately in his tracks, the coppery taste of blood filling his mouth as he peered through a stunned haze only, he recalls, to see one of his top front teeth, snapped clean off on impact, arcing through the air in apparent slow motion as if in some Tom and Jerry cartoon before disappearing into the mud.

The tell-tale gap where that tooth hung has been filled now but for the remainder of Edwards's playing career, and for years afterwards, it featured on countless photographs of him celebrating triumph after triumph, a dark and empty souvenir of the occasional ruthlessness of an opponent whose soubriquet as a player, ironically, was 'Joe Cool' because of his trademark composure under pressure.

Both Edwards and Dorahy are quick to insist they bear no grudges these days over that incident and Edwards, a boxing enthusiast, even appears to hold genuine respect for what he remembers as 'a vicious and fantastic punch'.

Dorahy's considered view with 30 years of separation is contrite.

'I was not happy I inflicted such a bad injury and it was never my intention to injure an opponent in that way,' he said. 'Apologies Shaun.'

Dorahy, however, believes that incident was the catalyst for the friction evident between them from the start at Central Park and suggests, 'The old competitor in Shaun still harboured deep-seated angst.'

That may or may not have been true and if it was then it would be understandable, but what was certain was Edwards's antipathy towards

Dorahy's attempts to change the calls and the moves, which to him had personified the fabric of Wigan's enduring success over the past six years.

'If it's not broken, why fix it?' was Edwards's philosophy while Dorahy was convinced he could make improvements by bringing in cutting-edge coaching ideas in vogue in the Australian rugby league hotbed from which he had just emerged.

Today their views on that time remain as diametrically opposed as ever, but their recollections of the main events are not dissimilar.

Edwards admits he whinged. Dorahy accepts Edwards found change difficult to handle, while insisting not one other member of the squad questioned the changes in the four weeks of off-season training before Edwards arrived back from his holiday.

'Shaun was a challenge,' said Dorahy, who lives in Sydney and in recent years has worked as a sales director at a company in the gambling and casinos business.

'Shaun has a lot of confidence in himself. He has a big ego. I said to him, "Look mate, these are the calls we will be making for the year. Get your head around those. You are the incumbent half back. You are the man."

'Straightaway, he put up a brick wall. He said, "Why are we changing the calls?"

'I told him whenever there is a change of coach there is usually a change of calls. He said, "I don't think we need to." I said, "I beg to differ."

'He really fought against those changes and continued to do so going into matches. I said to him on one occasion, "You're hurting yourself and you're hurting your team-mates. The biggest thing about teams is pulling it together and right now you are the one piece in the jigsaw that is not fitting correctly." We had our differences of opinion for a while there, for longer than I would have liked as a coach. He is one of the great competitors in rugby league, as he is in the rugby union world now. He didn't like change and wanted things to be as they were.'

The impasse between them came to a head when Edwards and Martin Offiah failed to turn up at a scheduled Wigan training session the day after they had played for Great Britain against New Zealand in November 1993.

The pair had gone out for a few drinks together on the Saturday night to celebrate their 29-10 victory. There was no telephone call the next day. No message. No contact with the coach or the board.

Dorahy's response was as swift and direct as the swinging arm which had generated work for Edwards's dentist a few years before. He dropped Edwards to the replacements' bench and Offiah to the 'A' team.

Crucially, Dorahy received backing from the board and there would be many who would applaud his firm stance, which essentially was reminding his players that it was the club who paid their wages and that attending vital training sessions was not optional.

Yet although Offiah appeared to accept his punishment placidly and professionally, scoring a try in his second team outing at centre, inside he was seething. Mention Dorahy's name and the bile, even now, bubbles to the surface.

'It was definitely John Dorahy saying, "I am in charge", which I can appreciate and understand but there was a lot of posturing by him,' said Offiah, a Manchester United fan who likens Dorahy taking over at Wigan to David Moyes's ill-fated attempt to succeed Sir Alex Ferguson at Old Trafford.

'We felt we were players who had won Challenge Cups, won Lance Todds and what had he done? It was not like he was bringing anything great for us to learn. All that he was bringing we were rejecting.

'That is why it was hard when Sir Alex Ferguson retired. How was someone else supposed to come in when they had won the Premier League so many times? If someone comes in and changes things it is going to be a battle.

'John Dorahy should write a book on how not to manage a club, on how not to come into a successful club, because everything he did was wrong. I knew there was nothing to be gained by throwing my toys out of the pram and I was sensible and old enough to deal with it. I accepted it. I didn't agree with it. Do you think he would have done that to Ellery Hanley?'

The question hangs in the air, although Dorahy's response on hearing Offiah's criticism was 'absolutely'. Yes, he would have dropped Ellery Hanley in those circumstances.

'Had they contacted me I would not have had a problem,' said Dorahy. 'I have played an international and had to back up the next day in a competitive match, not just training. At Hull KR in 1986 we played ten matches in 23 days at the end of the season and were expected to turn up to training and recovery on the day after each match. Being professional, the decision was easy, just do it.

'Having that experience let me know if the player was fair dinkum or continuing to stir the pot.

'The captain and the board agreed to my response at the time and that puts the whole saga in perspective. John Monie or Wayne Bennett would not have put up with such petulance.

'I guess in this instance Shaun and Martin thought they were bigger than the team or club.'

Dorahy, however, accepts his attempt to instigate a new style of play was struggling to take root.

There were some notable victories such as a 26-14 triumph against Leeds at Headingley and a 27-12 win at Widnes but there was also a 46-0 defeat at Castleford and a 35-22 loss at Featherstone Rovers.

It was the Regal Trophy Final in January, however, which was to prove a pivotal moment in the Dorahy reign.

Not especially the fact that Wigan slumped to a 33-2 defeat to Castleford at Leeds, although that was humiliating enough.

It was what happened in the week before the match that caused a ragged and irreparable tear in Dorahy's credibility as a coach in the minds of a segment of the players. At one of the training sessions that week, Dorahy distributed blank team sheets to the squad and asked each player to write down the team he believed should play.

He asked them to name the position in which they believed they would be most effective and if they did not think they should play, then to nominate someone else in that position.

The unusual request caused murmurings of disbelief and discontent in the squad with young players such as Mick Cassidy unsure whether to comply with the coach's wish.

'We couldn't understand what he was thinking,' said Cassidy. 'Whether he wasn't confident of picking a winning team or whether he just wanted to get inside our heads and pick our thoughts.

'Three quarters of the senior blokes just did not put a team down. They just gave it back to him with nothing on it. I asked the senior guys what I should do as I was only young and they said, "You fill it in."

'There was a bit of a power struggle going on and the senior lads told us young ones to stay out of it. I think that was what put the final nail in the coffin for him. You don't just try to change something that has worked for many years. You have to try to understand it first. Definitely that was his downfall. So many of those stars had been so successful for a number of years. Why shouldn't there be player power?'

In hindsight, Dorahy accepts his 'Write your own team' initiative was a blunder.

It was perceived as weakness by some team members.

'It wasn't a smart move,' admitted Dorahy, whose son Dane also played full back or half back for Western Suburbs, Wakefield Trinity and Halifax. 'But it was nothing more than trying to get a feel for what the players were thinking. Some players don't like to voice their opinion in front of the squad. I said they didn't have to put their name on it, just the team. Some players thought it was a bit odd but as coaches we have different methods to try to achieve a result.

'There were a number of mistakes I made in my first time as a senior first team coach and that was one of them. Absolutely.'

Yet, strangely, with the passage of 20-odd years and minus the restricting pressure of collective responsibility, there are some players, such as Gary Connolly, prepared to admit that perhaps Dorahy was on to something.

'As a player you know which people you want to play alongside,' said Connolly. 'I would have done it privately, gone up to each individual and had a chat. The more input from players you get the better. I wanted to play with the best people. It was the wrong way he did it, but the concept was not too bad.

'I liked John. He wanted to change everything but I was new to Wigan so it didn't affect me. I thought, "He is talking sense here."

'The senior players, however, were saying, "We have won six Challenge Cups and seven league titles. Why are you changing everything? Just pick the side and we'll win everything for you." In kind words, that was what was said to him.

'I thought he was a decent coach with some good ideas, but other people wouldn't buy into it.'

That last sentence surely goes to the heart of a sporting coach's existence. Managing sporting excellence is all about views and opinions. It is full of theories and training manuals. It requires passion and commitment and knowledge.

But none of the above adds up to the proverbial row of beans if the coach cannot instil belief in himself and his methods in those he leads.

As renowned American football coach Vince Lombardi put it, 'It is essential to understand that battles are primarily won in the hearts of men. Men respond to leadership in a most remarkable way and once you have won his heart, he will follow you anywhere.'

Dorahy, it appears, as diligently as he strove to improve the squad, neither won the hearts, nor the minds, of the most influential senior Wigan players and his battle with Edwards suggests that it is far from easy for tough-minded former opponents to form close alliances at the elite level.

There was another character he failed to convince and whose chance comment somewhere over the North Sea on 13 October 1993 did little to bolster his confidence.

Dorahy had been invited by Dave Whelan, a subsequent owner of the club but a wealthy local businessman and club sponsor at the time, to join his private party of clients and staff who were flying from Blackpool to Rotterdam for England's ill-fated football World Cup qualifier against Holland.

As they were cruising over the North Sea, Whelan engaged Dorahy in a brief conversation.

'He said, "John, I wouldn't have chosen you as coach,"' recalled Dorahy, who admits to being somewhat taken aback by Whelan's directness.

'I said, "Why is that?" and he replied, "You don't have a high enough profile. You're not exactly John Monie, are you?"'

Whelan had enjoyed a close social relationship with the affable Monie during his four seasons with the club.

'No, I'm not John Monie at all,' agreed a perplexed Dorahy.

The altercation was left hanging and they went on to watch England lose 2-0 in the match which has become infamous for Graham Taylor's antics as England manager. A documentary camera captured Taylor sidling up to a linesman after Ronald Koeman had scored for Holland just minutes after he should have been sent off for a foul on David Platt.

'The referee's got me the sack, thank him ever so much for that, won't you,' said Taylor, somewhat economically. The match also contained Taylor's repeated use of the phrase 'do I not like that' which became something of a catchphrase and led to him being cast cruelly, as a 'turnip' in the English press with England failing to qualify for the 1994 World Cup.

Taylor, a caring, compassionate and intelligent man, who sadly died unexpectedly at the age of 72 in January 2017, subsequently resigned as England manager.

On the plane journey home late that night, however, Dorahy doubtless mused on the fickle nature of a sports coach as he mulled over Whelan's comments. Could he escape from the shadow cast by the sustained excellence of Monie? Would his face and, more importantly, his innovative ideas, ever really fit at Wigan? Those questions went deep to the core of the fissures manifesting themselves at Central Park.

Much of the angst came from Edwards, who had worked so well with Monie, sharing and honing ideas, but whose rough edge simply could not rub along with Dorahy's view of the sporting world.

Edwards's passion has never been in doubt. Neither has his cussedness to fight his corner when he is utterly convinced he is correct, without regard to the size or stature of the man in the firing line.

Even in the weight-pumping, giant-roaming world of rugby they do not come much bigger or tougher than former All Black Va'aiga Tuigamala. Yet even 'Inga the Winger', as he was known, felt the stinging lash of Edwards's tongue as early as his initial first team match at Central Park against Wakefield.

Wigan had scored a try and Tuigamala, who had made his debut away at Widnes 12 days before, was back near his own try line for the kick-off when the ball floated his way and he allowed it to sail over his head and bounce before crossing the dead ball line. Tuigamala, only recently converted from rugby union and not entirely up to speed with the rules, thought the restart would be by Wigan on the 20 metre line, as in union on the 22 metre line, rather than the less-advantageous league rule of a drop-out from under the posts.

A snarling Edwards apparently waved up to Dorahy who was sitting in the stand and then pointed accusingly at Tuigamala.

'He was mouthing, "Get this so-and-so off now," and in case I hadn't got the message he told the trainer to come and tell me as well,' said Dorahy.

Dorahy's response in the face of such flagrant confrontation was for Edwards to calm down. Tuigamala was inexperienced, he reasoned, and would learn from the incident.

Edwards, as befits his reputation in a game of brutal, head-on assault, would not let it go. Like a terrier on a hot day, snapping and yapping, Edwards spent the rest of the first half letting Tuigamala know what he thought of him.

The altercation continued as they walked down the tunnel at half-time, 12st Edwards verbally poking the 17st bear that was Tuigamala.

'Inga later said that if Shaun had not turned away and made for the dressing room he would have punched his lights out,' said Dorahy.

'That is the conviction Shaun had, wanting to be 100 per cent professional. It probably epitomises Shaun and the lengths he will go to. He probably doesn't realise he is going to upset someone and one day it might come back to bite him on the bum. Shaun would have ended up in St Helens if Inga had punched him, that's for sure. But I admire Shaun for that.'

It was not just Edwards, however, who proved to be a thorny character for Dorahy. When Dean Bell, the experienced and influential club captain, returned from an extended injury lay-off due to a troublesome groin, he sided with Edwards, who believed the changes in training, preparation and calls were adversely affecting the team.

'Wigan had always trained in a certain way,' said Edwards, recalling what was by some distance the most fractious period in his 14 years at the club. Short, intense sessions. It was the same way we coached London Wasps when we were winning championships with Warren Gatland, the same way we coached Wales when we won grand slams. Similar sort of concept. Make the training fast, vigorous, very, very intense, almost harder than the game but not for long periods.

'John Dorahy changed that. We were training for two hours at a time, stopping, talking, middle of winter, freezing. It was the first time I didn't enjoy playing rugby.

'I said to Dean, "It's all wrong, we don't train this way at Wigan."'

Edwards jumps out of his chair to emphasise the energy he was anxious to convey. Eyes darting, lightly jumping from foot to foot like a boxer, his words in the present tense and his mind busy and alive with the images of his sporting prime.

'This is the way we train at Wigan.

'Bang!' He thumps his right fist repeatedly into the palm of his left hand.

'Bang! Bang! Bang!'

'Fast. Intense. Powerful. Quick. Bang. No time to think. Fast, fast, fast.'

Edwards switches to a more languid stance, arms hanging limp at his side and affects a slow, dull monotone as he mimics what he claims was a typical training session under Dorahy.

'No, stop, slow down, take it easy. What do we do now? Oh we are in this part of the field. Oh, we've got three options. Duh!'

At the time Bell was also concerned for his own place in the team with Gary Connolly and Barrie-Jon Mather playing well in the centres.

Dorahy proposed slotting Bell in at loose forward, moving Phil Clarke and putting either Denis Betts or Andy Farrell on the bench.

'Dean said, "No, you don't want to do that," but at the end of the day you just have to ride some of those moments,' said Dorahy. 'And then look for the moment when you can dovetail them all together.'

Everywhere he turned, at times, it seemed there was a problem, a concern, a whinge, a conflict, something which needed fixing.

Quite how Wigan managed to renew their annual subscription to the Twin Towers for the seventh time in a row was something of a miracle considering all the infighting, especially as the cup run required one of the gutsiest comebacks in the club's history in the fifth round.

The date: Sunday 13 February 1994. The venue: The Boulevard, Hull. The score: Hull 21 Wigan 22.

Those are the salient statistics, but they hardly convey the drama of a match which deserves its treasured place in Wigan folklore. A match which required every last ounce of Wigan's champion heritage.

I listened to that match 200 miles away in deepest Bedfordshire with my seven-year-old son Michael, ears pressed to the Wigan Clubcall service on the telephone. No digital radio in those days, no internet streaming. Just parochial commentator John McDermott's flat vowels relaying the agony of a first half during which Wigan went 21-2 down, going in at half-time 21-6 thanks to a Barrie-Jon Mather try right on the half-time hooter.

Up in the stand, the story goes, chairman Jack Robinson turned to Va'aiga Tuigamala at that point and apologised for bringing him halfway around the world only to miss out on Wembley, only for Tuigamala to reply, 'God didn't bring me all this way to lose.'

What exactly was said in the Wigan changing room during that half-time interval has been fogged by the passing of time, but Kelvin Skerrett certainly exhorted his team-mates to greater efforts, Shaun Edwards tapped in to his bottomless pit of passion to find some choice phrases and Dorahy, never a ranter or a raver, spoke individually to players and employed a tried and tested motivational technique which had worked countless times during the past six years. The Wembley factor. As in, 'Who wants to be in the losing side that didn't get to Wembley?'

'It became personal at times like that,' explained Martin Dermott. 'Every Challenge Cup round was like a final because everybody wanted to get to Wembley. Dean Bell was usually a catalyst in that. He'd say, "Remember what it's like to play at Wembley. If you want that feeling again we have to win this game."

'Even at half-time if we were losing he'd say, "If you want to put that Wembley blazer on and go out in front of your friends and family, you know how good it feels, you have to turn it around." He was the driving force. You could take it from Dean because you knew he would go through a brick wall for you. He had the knack of being brutally honest with players.'

Bell was out injured on that particular day but his sentiments still resonated around the away changing room.

There was another factor at The Boulevard during that half-time interval which gave the players and fans hope. The wind. More accurately, a chill, biting, paint-stripping gale. It had howled into Wigan's faces during that first half. Now it was at their backs and Mather, with his second touchdown, and Sam Panapa took advantage to reduce the deficit.

With ten minutes remaining, however, Wigan still trailed 21-18.

Then, as so often in sport when pressure reaches tipping point, a player made a mistake. Poor old Daniel Divet probably wonders to this day why he tried to pass the ball after fielding a high ball on his goal line. Go down, play it safe, cherish the rugby ball. That is the drill in such circumstances.

But Divet let it go, the ball came loose, Wigan gained possession and Shaun Edwards and Ian Gildart combined to send 18-year-old Andy Farrell over in the corner. Farrell, as we have already established, went on to enjoy the sort of career rugby players dream of, eventually becoming a proud member of the Wigan hall of fame, but it is debatable whether he scored a more important try for his hometown club.

Wigan now were leading 22-21, but still excruciating drama remained when Hull winger Paul Eastwood lined up a penalty goal attempt in front of the posts with moments to play. The Wembley fairytale looked to have run its course.

Maybe it was the wind. Maybe it was the weight of responsibility resting on one clean strike of Eastwood's right boot. Maybe it was just the fact that Lady Luck, if she exists, flipped a coin and it came down displaying the Ancient and Loyal crest of Wigan.

Whatever the reason, the ball drifted wide, Eastwood sank to his knees in the mud and Wigan and Dorahy and the whole you-could-not-make-it-up potboiler, which was Wigan RLFC at the time, rolled on to the next episode.

The quarter-final against Featherstone Rovers was negotiated calmly enough, a 32-14 victory at Central Park, and the 20-6 semi-final win against Castleford at Leeds helped ease some of the lingering humiliation from that Regal Trophy Final defeat.

Wigan, despite all the acrimony, were at Wembley again. It was what happened shortly after that semi-final, however, which shines a light on the extent of the infighting within the club.

There was a knock on the door of Dorahy's house in Standish Lower Ground at around 9pm. It was Jack Robinson, the Wigan chairman.

A few pleasantries were exchanged and Robinson explained he had come direct from a club board meeting.

Dorahy recalls the conversation, 'He said, "I'm here to tell you, mate, I've got some challenges. It comes down to, it's either you or it's me. I'm the chairman, mate, so it's you. If I don't go, you go."'

Robinson went on to explain there was a power struggle raging for control of the club.

'He then said, "We have got to have a scapegoat,"' recalled Dorahy. 'He said, "Mate, you're the man. We've had some challenges this year. Our Regal Trophy loss wasn't good. A couple of the players have had problems during the year and you haven't had the best of relationships with your second team coach Graeme West."'

Dorahy defended his record. He pointed out that Wigan had beaten St Helens twice, they were back at Wembley, they were in good shape in the championship and the Premiership Trophy was still a possibility. He had succeeded in everything he had been asked to do at that informal interview back in May. Robinson, however, was not for turning, saying simply, 'We're not going to retain you after this year.'

Dorahy felt a sickening knot of disappointment deep in his stomach as well as a profound sense of unfairness, but he claims there was no animosity. No harsh words. They shook hands, Robinson left and Dorahy consoled himself with the fact that at least he had a Wembley appearance to look forward to.

At training next day, however, Bell was drafted in to take the session with Dorahy. The air of unease and uncertainty within the squad was palpable.

Who was in charge? Who would pick the team? Who would call the moves? Was Dorahy gone? Was Bell the new boss even though he was leaving at the end of the season to return to New Zealand?

There was talk of a bust-up between Dorahy and Bell and that Andy Platt had been asked to take over the captaincy.

The fine details of the conflict have been clouded by the haze of time but there is no doubt the whole Wigan Wembley experience was in danger of imploding.

'For a while there I thought I was in *Coronation Street*,' said Dorahy, recalling the political machinations which turned the run-up to Wembley into little short of a soap opera.

'There were things in there like bed bugs that kept biting you. You had to keep swatting them off to get on with the challenge.

'Following that training session Dean went to Jack Robinson and said he couldn't do this anymore. This isn't right. He said, "I shouldn't be doing this, it's not me." Dean told me that and I fully respected and appreciated that.'

So it was back to Dorahy, on his way out but still in charge with little more than a few weeks to go before Wembley. The atmosphere, however, was improved.

'I don't want to come across as a vindictive person towards John Dorahy,' said Edwards. 'All I can say is that when he chilled out, because he was made to chill out, it was better.'

It certainly appeared to be business as usual when, six days before Wembley, Wigan went to Watersheddings and ran in nine tries to beat Oldham 50-6 in the final league match of the season to clinch yet other championship.

But then something unnecessary and unfortunate, possibly even misunderstood, occurred which was to contribute to the general tenor of Dorahy's leaving.

As the team were celebrating their triumph and posing for team photos Dorahy was pounced upon by Sky Sports pitchside interviewer Bill Arthur, whose first sentence was more of a statement than a question.

'When you are winning in style like that it makes you wonder why there was any doubt and why you had the problems you had,' said Arthur.

At times like that, with the sound of joy and celebration all around and another trophy heading for the cabinet, there is almost always no mileage in being anything other than magnanimous.

Unfortunately, Dorahy, his mood doubtless coloured by the frustrations and disappointments of recent weeks and emboldened by the heady euphoria of the moment, chose a different course.

'I'd just like to say to all those doubters: Suck!'

A concerned Arthur thought Dorahy might have used the 'F' word. Off camera, Dorahy explained it was 'suck' with an 'S' and proffered the Australian definition.

'Bad luck, we won, see you later, carry on. A tongue-in-cheek version of "Get lost, we don't give a damn".'

It should be remembered the interview was live and the adrenaline was pumping and a character renowned for shooting from the lip such as Alex Murphy might have got away with it.

The point, however, is that to some it sounded churlish and unprofessional. It lacked generosity of spirit. It was not the Wigan way. It was not a phrase John Monie would have uttered.

Yet there was one more decision Dorahy took in the run-up to Wembley which was equally unfathomable to many and raises eyebrows to this day.

When Dorahy read out the 15 players, including substitutes, on his Wembley team sheet there was no place for Jason Robinson. Instead, Va'aiga Tuigamala was handed his Wembley debut.

It is not, however, a decision Dorahy lost any sleep over, either then or now.

'There were two reasons,' said Dorahy. 'One was I felt Inga would do a hell of a job. He was a big match player. Being an All Black I felt Inga could handle the occasion and help us win the match.

'The second reason was that Jason, in my estimation, wasn't in the right place at that particular time. There were certain elements in his demeanour off the field that just weren't in sync with the moment.

'They are difficult decisions. I would have loved nothing more than to have picked Joe Lydon. I counted him as a friend and a very good colleague, but I felt Sam Panapa covered more options on that particular day. But I was extremely happy to see what Jason achieved in rugby union after that.'

More than two decades on and after a stellar career in both codes, plus a head coaching stint with Sale, Robinson appreciates the trauma involved in making selection decisions as a coach and recognises Dorahy's dilemma.

'John Dorahy is a nice guy,' said Robinson. 'I don't have a problem with him. At the time I did, just because of the way he did it. If John had been straight with me and said I'm picking him over you, I feel he is better than you, you can take that as hard as it is.'

Robinson, however, claims he was given two reserve matches to prove he was ready for Wembley, in one of which he was man of the match and in the other scored three tries.

'So when I didn't get picked I was devastated,' said Robinson. 'I was annoyed because I felt it was almost as if he had me dangling on a string instead of just telling me. When I scored three times it was like, "Hang on a minute, what more can I do?" If he had made his decision before, then tell me. All I wanted was for him to be straight.

'I realise he had a tough decision to make. Tuigamala was a big signing, they had paid a lot of money for him and I was a young lad.

'At the time I was distraught and annoyed at John Dorahy but looking back now, he had such a difficult decision because there were so many good players.

'He might have been right in some ways. I just had it in my head that it was wrong the way he did it.'

Unwittingly, however, Dorahy might have been the catalyst in laying the foundations for the bond which was to grow between Robinson and Tuigamala, which culminated in Robinson becoming a born-again Christian and radically altering his lifestyle.

'If it had been anybody else but Inga it would have been ten times worse,' said Robinson. 'If someone takes your place in a team, as much as you are team-mates you can still be angry with him. But I remember Inga coming to me and talking to me about it. The way he did it I couldn't be angry with him.

'He is just such a nice bloke. He was almost like a big brother. He just put his arm around me and said something like, "Chin up, we're all in this together." Looking back, you really appreciate that.

'You couldn't not like Inga. He was a nice, happy guy, turned up every day with a smile from ear to ear. Played it hard, but always fair. One of those who would smash somebody and then put his arm around them and help them back up.

'But everybody who went to Wigan either as a coach or a player had huge pressure. It was all about performing. It was keeping the steamroller going. I am sure it was very tough coming in and dealing with all those different characters. I couldn't have done it.'

Neil Cowie, a replacement the Sunday before when the title was won against Oldham, also failed to make Dorahy's Wembley squad.

Which is why when the bulk of the team were talking excitedly about Wembley once more, Cowie, Robinson and a few others who had failed to make the final line-up headed off, quietly seething, in the direction of the snooker club on the corner of the approach to Central Park and proceeded to drown their fury with the mother of all benders.

The run-up to Wembley 1994 was anything but uneventful.

23

The Perfect Storm

MARTIN Offiah casually scanned the back page of the *Daily Mirror* and then flicked inside to find an action picture of himself in try-scoring mode on the inside spread.

It was not the picture, however, which caught his attention as he rubbed the sleep from his eyes and contemplated a leisurely breakfast on the morning of the 1994 Challenge Cup Final. It was the banner headline spanning two pages and proclaiming 'FINISHED'.

The article contained the thoughts and prejudices of one Alex Murphy, the former St Helens, Leigh, Warrington and Great Britain scrum half, a man of legendary status in the game of rugby league almost as much for his penchant for controversy as his playing acumen.

In the newspaper world his columns were often known as 'Murphy's Mouth'.

He had picked this particular morning to let rip at Offiah. It wasn't a full double-barrelled blast but rather a piece comparing Offiah with some of the great wingers of the past and arguing that there were no great wingers around in 1994 and Offiah was just the best of a bad lot. The phrase 'damned with faint praise' comes to mind.

Offiah set his jaw and his eyes smouldered with resentment as he read the *Mirror* prose. It was not just Murphy's rent-a-gob criticism that roused the ire in Offiah. Not really. It was the culmination of negativity that, despite his scintillating try ratio, had turned the previous 12 months into one ordeal after another. In essence, the player everyone perceived as having a career untroubled by any burden of humility had been suffering something akin to a personal meltdown.

He had been training hard, sometimes too hard. He had been putting on muscle in the gym and striving to improve every facet of his game.

He had been doing everything in his power to battle the demons, which he claims had been there since the day he switched codes.

'I always felt I wasn't good enough,' admitted Offiah. 'When I signed for rugby league I had a chip on my shoulder. Of all the players Doug Laughton signed at Widnes I was the only one who didn't have a students' cap. All the others such as Jonathan Davies, John Devereux and Paul Moriarty were full internationals, but I wasn't.

'They weren't paying me as much as Davies but in his first game for Widnes I scored five tries against Salford. He touched the ball once and all the column inches were about him and I'm thinking, "What the fuck do I have to do?", pardon my French.

'That is what fuelled my career. Every time I had something to prove. I took all the abuse, all the racism from spectators, because I was doing something I loved to do. But it all came crashing down on me. Do you know how hard it is to top the try-scoring charts every year? To do it again and again and again.

'Then Wigan have just signed an All Black winger, Va'aiga Tuigamala, and they've got Jason Robinson on the other wing and people who were glad I had come to Wigan, but didn't really love me, all began to surface. My own fans were shouting to get rid of me.'

Robinson has good reason to remember the torrid time Offiah went through, if only because he believes it deflected abuse away from him.

'It wasn't easy being a black man in professional sport at that time,' said Robinson. 'I know because I got a lot of stick myself over the years. In the early days you always got it.

'That's why I came off my wing because I always got abuse close to the touchline. I was always encouraged to come off my wing anyway and go looking for work and I thought, "Too right, I'm not staying here with this going on."

'It did change but in the early days it was brutal. Go to Hull or St Helens and, man, you got abuse. It was always great having Martin there because he took most of the abuse. Everyone wanted to have a go at Martin.

'And it was almost the goal of every player on the opposing side to smash him, which was great for a young black lad on the other wing because he was taking so much heat off me.'

Offiah can chart the low point to a match when a young Henry Paul, playing then for Wakefield, handed off his lame attempt at a tackle and inadvertently poked him in the eye on the way to scoring a try in a Wigan defeat at Central Park, leaving the jeers raining down on him.

It was after that a disconsolate, disaffected Offiah went out for a drink with Shaun Edwards and received a pep talk, the rousing nature of which he credits with turning his game around.

'Martin, you are already the best winger in the world,' Edwards told him. 'If it's not broken, don't fix it. Why are you always trying to add things to your game? Trying to be stronger, more powerful. Have some fun, relax a bit more. Turn up for training, train your bollocks off, go away and stop worrying about rugby all the time. I can tell it is on your mind all the time. I know, because I was like that myself when I was playing shit.

'When you get the ball in a game just run straight between two players. With your speed, even though you are only 14st you become 16st because you are so fast and powerful.'

Those words started to race through Offiah's mind as he read Murphy's column over breakfast and a steely determination began to take root in his soul.

The injuries, the dip in form, the crisis in confidence, had all taught Offiah that he was not invincible. That he could not be 'great' all the time, every match of every season. No one could. But if ever there was a time to make history and prove that there was no better rugby winger on the planet then it was now or never. At Wembley. Not far from where he was born. His spiritual home.

Offiah clung to that unexpected gift of inspiration from Murphy as the Wigan bus eased its way along Wembley way. And he thought to himself, 'I am prepared to die today. I have the mentality to put it all on the line.'

It helped that it was a perfect day for running rugby with barely a cloud in the bluest of skies and the temperature well into the 70s Fahrenheit by early afternoon.

The crowd sang 'Abide with Me', the players emerged to a kaleidoscope of cherry and white and blue and yellow, the Wigan team as usual heads down. No waving. Professional hats on. The opening salvos were tight. If anything, Leeds were controlling the play, physical and intimidating, pinning Wigan back close to their own line.

With 13 minutes gone, Frano Botica picked up from the play-the-ball in a central position five or so metres from Wigan's line and passed the ball to Offiah.

Twenty-three years on and sat in his Ealing home, Offiah beckons me over to the laptop computer on his lounge table and clicks the YouTube compilation of that final and scrolls to the exact point in time when he received the ball. It is not the first time he has watched this clip. It is not even in the first 1,000.

He rolls on the action slowly, almost a frame-by-frame analysis.

That first surge of acceleration was designed to gain as much ground as possible to clear Wigan's line. But Shaun Edwards's words ran through his mind. 'Run fast and hard and 14st becomes 16st.' There is a little swerve in his body shape as he powers into the defensive line. One defender aims for his legs and misses. Neil Harmon, the Leeds prop, lays a slight hand on him but gets a hand-off in the chest as Offiah bursts through the line.

'And then it was daylight and I went into autopilot,' explained Offiah, eyes dancing at the memory before pausing the action so that he could dwell on the mechanics which helped to throw open the gates to greatness.

'The only effort I had to do was to break that line. A forceful run and a step inside Harmon. As soon as I am through the gap I went into the promised land.'

He rolls the action again. A swerve to the left and then to the right and a couple of quick darts of his head as he checks there is no danger of a tackler from the defensive flanks.

Pause.

'I am now in the zone and tapping into my subconscious,' said Offiah. 'My brain is at a heightened level, it's reacting faster, at its optimum, so everything else seems slower. Everything was calm and surreal. All the times I had gone through and beaten players were going through my head.'

The action rolls on. Just Alan Tait, the Leeds full back, to beat. Offiah veers inside but Tait stays infield, offering him the touchline. It is as if a high-stakes negotiation is taking place at pace and with the winner of the 'this way or that way' conundrum taking all.

Pause.

'I had played Alan Tait many times and I knew what he did,' said Offiah. 'He gave players the outside and then mowed them down on his own terms. I knew that, so I used his strength against him. I did it on my terms. It was like having a race with somebody but I say, "Go!" I had a race with Alan and with all the posturing I did I set the race up. I said I'm faster than you and I'm going to say go. Who's going to win? I'm going to win.

'A lot of people break the line and then power all the way. The thing I learned as a sprinter is that you get up to speed and then you relax and coast and then go again.

'He was trying to jockey me and I was trying to jockey him and I knew if I got him in the right position I was going to win because I am faster than him. I had to judge it to perfection and I did because otherwise he could have tap-tackled me or I would have gone into touch. There was so much going on in my head but it was all in perfect motion.'

For a moment Offiah was not in Ealing. His voice was charged with emotion and he was back revisiting the best of his days, nerve endings tingling with the rush of excitement.

Experiencing the thrill of when he was the king of all he surveyed when it came to running fast and free on a rugby field. Reconnecting with the defining moment of his sporting life.

He rolls on the YouTube clip once more. This time he slides in for the touchdown and immediately jumps up and Tait, with a knowing look, one professional to another, gives him a tap of congratulation. Offiah sinks to his knees and his hands come up to hide his face as the enormity of the moment sinks in. It was almost as if even he could not believe just how good he had just been.

That image has been replayed thousands of times and used in newspaper articles, magazines and posters. Why, it is even now set in bronze outside Wembley as part of the tribute to the sport of rugby league, the statue also featuring Billy Boston, Eric Ashton, Gus Risman and Alex Murphy.

Offiah and Murphy, his unlikely inspiration on that fateful Saturday, entwined forever. How prosaic is that?

What was going through Offiah's mind as he knelt on the Wembley turf sucking in oxygen in the heat of 1994?

'Everything I have been trying to do I have done it, that is what I was thinking,' said Offiah. 'I had never felt that before. I had scored five tries in a semi-final. I had scored five tries on Jonathan Davies's debut. I had gone to Australia and scored in Test matches. I had scored ten tries in a Premiership semi-final. I'd won a Lance Todd Trophy before. But never had I done this.

'I didn't know I would have a statue of me in that pose outside Wembley a few years later but at that time I knew I had done something great. I can connect with that moment right now.

'Wow! And then all I was thinking was, "Let's not lose the game," because if we had lost then that moment was lost. Apart from my kids being born, from a personal moment that was the pinnacle. Everything else has been a correlation to that. Could I stay at that level? Am I as good as that any more?

'Every single year the Challenge Cup has been at Wembley since then that try has been shown.'

Every time Offiah meets Tait he reminds him mischievously of their duel in the sun, usually by taunting him with a snatch of Ray French's commentary, 'Now then, Martin Offiah, he's got Alan Tait to beat.'

In its own homespun way, French's BBC commentary that day was a work of verbal art for which perhaps he did not receive enough credit. Essentially plain and simple with a splash of colour in exactly the right places. An informative squiggle of a phrase here, a bold brush stroke of a comment there.

Not everything French has done could be classed in similar fashion. Some of his commentaries alongside Alex Murphy in the late 1980s were out of the Laurel and Hardy school of commentary, although that might have owed something to Murphy's apparent habit of switching channels at inopportune moments to search for the racing results.

'How do you fancy sinking your teeth into one of those?' I recall French once saying when the cameraman zoomed in to reveal the physio rubbing a prop forward's meaty thighs on the touchline.

'I'd rather have a Holland's pie if you don't mind, Ray,' Murphy replied. It was borderline puerile, but harmless and with a colloquial flavour.

French, who commentated on every Challenge Cup Final from 1982 to 2008, also had a penchant for unintended comedy by stating the obvious, as in, 'And he's got the ice pack on his groin there, so possibly not the old shoulder injury.'

Yet listen to his description of Offiah's try and appreciate how the rhythm and timbre of his voice effortlessly mirror the ebb and flow of the action.

'And Martin Offiah, trying to make some space. Now then, Martin Offiah. He's got Alan Tait to beat. On the outside. And surely he's going to go the full length. That is one sensational try. That must rank among the finest ever seen on this ground. Wigan were under pressure. Wigan almost had points against them and this man, Martin Offiah, the world's most lethal try scorer, the whole length of the field and they are in the lead. A month ago people were saying he was out of form. Well, there's his answer. Wonderful effort.'

Not Hemingway, it's true. But dramatic, distinctive, succinct and brilliant in its simplicity. And all in a voice which was perfectly in sync with the sport. A voice of earthy character, a semitone or two too high in pitch on occasions maybe, but that tremulous characteristic only served to lend it energy when the action soared to the sort of heights men such as Offiah were destined to take it.

Down the years, the BBC has been adept at finding, supporting and promoting voices synonymous with their chosen sport.

Think of Peter Alliss and golf. The mellifluous tones of Peter O'Sullevan and horse racing. John Motson and football. Bill McLaren, 'They'll be dancing in the streets of Hawick tonight', and rugby union. Richie 'good morning, everybody' Benaud and cricket. And Murray Walker, whose commentaries on motor racing really did sound uncannily at times like a set of squealing Formula One tyres negotiating Silverstone's Stowe Corner.

Think even of Eddie Waring in the 1960s and 1970s, a commentator who divided opinion in rugby league more than any other. Some thought of Waring as a charismatic and avuncular character from Dewsbury with a personable nature, whose Yorkshire tones typified the warm and friendly reputation of the north.

Others believed his voice did the game a disservice, simply confirming northern stereotypes, his trademark phrases such as 'oop and under' and 'he's goin' for an early bath' becoming northern clichés just as wearisome as flat caps and ferrets.

Despite the controversy, the BBC stuck with Waring until illness made it clear he was struggling to identify players and his last Challenge Cup commentary was in 1981.

The following season French took over and in contrast to Waring, who had no playing experience, the new voice from St Helens had the rare distinction of having played rugby union and rugby league at international level. To be precise, four matches for England as a lock forward in union's 1961 Five Nations Championship and four caps at second row for Great Britain's rugby league side, two in the 1968 World Cup, while playing for Widnes.

Even so, there were those who found French's commentaries too lightweight and lacking in cogent analysis. But no one could say they were not distinctive, forthright or evocative.

In retrospect, the most remarkable aspect of French's commentary on that Offiah try is that it did not include his trademark and most annoying phrase, 'He's going for the line.'

Yet perhaps that is because Offiah, as he is fond of saying these days, really did let the line come to him that day. There was too much going on, too much to think about, to worry about the try line.

The match, however, was not won with that try alone. French had much more descriptive work in front of him.

Unfortunately for Alan Tait there was more misery in store in the 27th minute when he failed to gather a high kick from Shaun Edwards and Andy Farrell accepted the gift to run in the second try and allow Wigan to go in leading 12-0 at half-time.

A penalty from Graham Holroyd and tries from Jim Fallon and Garry Schofield early in the second half, with just a penalty in reply from Frano Botica, brought Leeds back to 14-10.

Then came Offiah's second major contribution, this time aided by a couple of tidy steps and a scything break from Mick Cassidy in midfield. The replacement forward, wearing his trademark scrum cap, set off on a diagonal run towards the left wing and was about to be enveloped by the covering defenders when Offiah glided into perfect position on his outside. For a forward at the limit of his speed and with lungs bursting with effort, surely there could not have been a more welcome sight than Offiah lolloping along beside him in second gear.

'You just knew if you made a break at Wigan that Martin Offiah would be on your shoulder,' recalled Cassidy. 'I had a quick look to my left and gave it to him. I've got the picture in my study at home of him screaming for it and me passing the ball to him. He was in the best form of his life. My job was done.'

Five seconds later, after Offiah had eclipsed Fallon in a straight foot race, the ball was being touched down once again with Botica converting.

A Sam Panapa try and the inevitable Botica conversion made it 26-10 but, even then, Offiah was hungry for history, prowling across the line in search of his third try, which would have made him the first rugby player to score a hat-trick at Wembley.

The opportunity was there, too, if he had caught a dodgy long pass from Phil Clarke, instead of knocking on and allowing 17-year-old Leeds winger Francis Cummins to pick up the loose ball and sprint 90 metres unopposed for the touchdown which Holroyd converted.

It did not matter. Wigan were worthy 26-16 winners and the tally was seven. Seven Challenge Cups in a row. Head coach John Dorahy soaked in the joy rolling down the Wembley terraces, another cup and league double seemingly vindicating his appointment despite the challenges of the past 12 months.

As the players walked around Wembley on their lap of honour the photographers urged them to hold up seven fingers.

'I didn't,' said Gary Connolly, who had suffered at Wigan's hands in 1989 and 1991 while playing for St Helens. 'I was sticking one up saying this is my first. I was a bit jealous of them all.'

For Offiah there was the additional but cherished duty of picking up his second Lance Todd Trophy, the perfect end to the most idyllic of afternoons.

Offiah's career has taken copious celebrity twists and turns since then. He starred in the first series of BBC's *Strictly Come Dancing* and has appeared on quiz shows such as *The Weakest Link* and *Pointless* as well as *Big Star's Little Star* and *All Star Mr and Mrs* with his partner Virginia Shaw. Rarely, it seems, does a series of the BBC's *A Question of Sport* go by without him appearing.

He has also worked as a players' agent and as a pundit and presenter on Sky Sports.

But when the rugby is mentioned, 'that try' is the first topic of conversation.

There is even a bar named after it at the new Wembley, called simply 'The 1994 Bar', with the plaque reading, 'Named after the greatest try ever scored at Wembley.' No mention of Offiah. It simply is not required.

At this point in our interview Offiah walks over to the bookcase in the corner of his lounge and plucks a paperback from the shelf which bears his name as author.

He shows me the cover, which includes a picture of him with the Challenge Cup amid a montage of rugby league greats such as Clive Sullivan, Ellery Hanley, Wally Lewis and Jonathan Davies. The title? *50 Of The Best*. The subject? Offiah's choice of the greatest rugby league tries of all time.

Number one. You have guessed it. That try. Offiah scribbles a message on the inside cover, signs it and kindly hands it to me. A gift from the try that just keeps on giving.

Offiah admits that day is still never far from his thoughts, especially since the statue commemorating rugby league has been erected not far from the Bobby Moore statue at Wembley.

In fact, in the title of Offiah's Twitter feed he describes himself as 'retired rugby player with a statue at Wembley' with the hashtag line 'wowhowdidthathappen'.

He also makes the occasional detour so his children, Tyler and Phoenix, can see their dad in bronze, taking pictures of them sitting on the bronze knee of Alex Murphy.

The statue is not without controversy and many aficionados of rugby league would have included, at the expense of Offiah, the playmaking skills of Andy Gregory, who played in eight Challenge Cup finals, winning the Lance Todd Trophy twice, or Shaun Edwards, who played in a record 11 Challenge Cup finals, winning nine, or Ellery Hanley, who won the sport's prestigious Man of Steel award a record three times.

Offiah also deems himself fortunate to have been included alongside Boston, Ashton, Risman and Murphy.

'I really think I only got in because they wanted to give it a modern flavour,' admitted Offiah. 'I think the RFL and Wembley were quite keen for me to be on.

'Some fans will say, "Why him?", but you can't really argue against it when you think what I have done. There are so many people with credible reasons to be on that statue. If it was anywhere else but Wembley, say in Huddersfield, I wouldn't be on it. I am from London. That try connected the sport of rugby league to the general sporting world in London. I am on a statue at Wembley. I am in the rugby league hall of fame. I was in and out during my career, but the things I did connected with the sporting world. You can put my stuff on YouTube now and people can still go "Wow". I was ahead of my time.'

Even so, many disparate events were required to collide to engineer 'that try'. So many sliding doors had to open and shut in perfect sequence to bring Offiah to what he believes was his rightful destiny.

If Jason Robinson had been playing, as many people other than coach John Dorahy believed he should have been, then Offiah would never have been in the receiver's position to take the pass from Botica, as that was one of Robinson's specialities.

If Paul Eastwood hadn't missed that late penalty for Hull in front of the posts in the fifth round.

If Shaun Edwards's pep talk had not touched upon a receptive place deep in his psyche and soothed his crisis of confidence.

If Alex Murphy had not stirred his blood and sharpened his motivation on the morning of the match.

It was, as Offiah is fond of saying, 'the perfect storm'.

When Offiah was informed he was to be honoured by being included on the Wembley statue he was asked to come up with an inscription for an accompanying book. The line he chose probably summed it up best of all.

'Careers can be forgotten. Moments last forever.'

24

The Gospel According to John Dorahy

THE party after the 1994 final was like all the rest. Following the razzamatazz of Wembley, the Wigan squad travelled to the hotel their wives and girlfriends had been staying in and celebrated with a sumptuous dinner, including fine wine, copious beers, speeches and music.

They knew how to play hard. They knew how to party hard.

As the night wore on, however, the euphoria of Wembley and the realisation of a lifetime's dream began to give way to a feeling of simmering frustration for head coach John Dorahy.

Various sponsors, board members and players were invited by chairman Jack Robinson to say a few words, but Dorahy, the head coach who had just emulated John Monie by delivering the double of cup and league titles, was conspicuous by his absence at the microphone. The invite never came.

It tormented Dorahy for the rest of the night and he claims a succession of sponsors and dignitaries made a point of telling him they were dumbfounded by the omission.

The next morning the squad set off on the team bus, up the M1 and the M6, bound for Central Park and the usual chaotic homecoming party with the fans, which invariably culminated, as was customary, in the players trashing the dilapidated changing rooms.

As they approached the town the bus stopped at a convenient spot and the players, backroom staff and board, as was also the custom, switched to the open-topped double-decker bus which was to parade through the streets of Wigan town centre before arriving at the stadium.

It was at this point that Dorahy chose to speak to Robinson.

That bus journey has been the subject of copious stories, rumours and innuendo over the best part of a quarter of a century. Books and articles have been written and some of the more lurid tales from so-called witnesses would have us believe that Wigan's version of the 'Rumble in the Jungle' took place on the bus that afternoon with Dorahy and Robinson cast in the heavyweight roles of Muhammad Ali and George Foreman.

It is why, before recounting his version, Dorahy stretches out his hand palm down in front of him and tells me, 'I will give you the dead-set truth on the Bible.'

The gospel according to John Dorahy admits that he believed Robinson was 'extremely disrespectful and rude' not to invite him to speak the night before.

Which is why when he walked down the bus and saw Robinson sat next to fellow board members, Tom Rathbone and Jack Hilton, he slid in opposite the chairman.

'I said, "Look Jack, thanks for the opportunity, I have thoroughly enjoyed it, but I was hugely disappointed last night when you didn't invite me up to speak to the people who had helped. That was extremely rude. I didn't appreciate it. People here didn't appreciate it. My family didn't think it was right and it was certainly disrespectful."'

Robinson looked straight ahead and said nothing.

'I thought you were a pretty weak man,' Dorahy continued. 'I'm leaving at the end of the season and I think you're a weak man.'

Dorahy pauses to collect his thoughts and sift through his vault of memories, anxious to deliver the chronology of those events as accurately as possible despite the 23-year passage of time.

He insists he did not swear and was not offensive, although he admits using a metaphor which referenced Robinson's antiques business.

'I said, "Jack, you're like a second-hand furniture dealer. You are not standing up for what is right. You've painted a picture of me like old furniture and not as a true treasurer of what we achieved this year,"' recalled Dorahy.

With that Dorahy stood up and attempted to hop out of his seat, which was a cumbersome manoeuvre as it was one of those with a table attached.

'At that point he grabbed me by the forearm,' said Dorahy. 'He said, "Stop here." I pulled away and said, "I've had enough Jack, don't even try."'

Dorahy turned away and went up the stairs to the top deck where a bunch of players were drinking beer and waving to the fans.

Two minutes later Robinson appeared on the top deck.

'He came over and confronted me and I said, "Jack, I have nothing to say." He said, "I'll have more to say to you later," and started pointing his finger at me. He then turned and walked off.

'That is the top and bottom of it. Yes, there is a story which was written by the club captain that there was a punch-up, but I can categorically, hand on heart and hand on the Bible, say there was never an inkling of a punch-up from me or between Jack and I.

'I wouldn't demean myself or the chairman by even contemplating doing that. As a player, yeah, I used to get into the odd punch-up or throw the odd sly one, which is how I got Shaun Edwards when I knocked his tooth out, but as a man and as a person I have got a lot more to live up to than looking for fights off the park with someone who I felt had done wrong by me.'

Apart from the little matter of Martin Offiah, the world's most valuable player at the time, being dangled by his ankles from the top deck of the bus by two of Wigan's burliest forwards, all in good fun but in full view of an agitated police escort, the rest of the homecoming went to plan.

The plan involved thousands of fans revelling as usual on the Central Park pitch, Denis Betts crooning into a microphone on stage, thank-you speeches by the dozen from the players and inevitably thousands of photographs, one of which caught Dorahy with right hand holding the cup and left hand holding a sign to the fans and the cameras which read, 'For all you doubters. Suck.'

It was the same sentiment issued in that infamous interview on Sky television at Watersheddings a week before. Yet if that live TV comment could be put down to brain fog in the heat of battle then there was no doubting the premeditated intent of that stark sign, which was so out-of-kilter with the happy faces and joyous celebration all around.

The players eventually retired inside to perform the unfathomable club custom following a Wembley triumph of smashing up the changing rooms.

At which point the simmering frustration of Jason Robinson and Neil Cowie, in particular, at missing the final was vented in spectacular fashion.

Robinson admits taking a lump hammer to the wall while Cowie apparently ran from one end of the changing room to the other and headbutted the studded plaster wall so hard that his head went clean through into the adjoining corridor and, with his ears jammed, he was stuck there looking bemusedly right and left like a bull leaning over a farmyard gate.

'It was like a cartoon sketch,' said Robinson. 'The sight of a lump hammer in the changing room and the opportunity to smash it up was something I couldn't turn down. With some of the other guys who hadn't got picked we just went to town on those changing rooms. It was a way of venting our frustration.

'There was so much competition in there, everybody wanted to play and when you didn't play, naturally you were devastated. It was just a bit of an outlet for us.'

The season, however, was far from over. There was still the little matter of a Premiership Trophy quarter-final against St Helens due the following Sunday. Dorahy took training as usual on the Tuesday and then was called to a board meeting on the Wednesday.

He remembers his wife, Linda, sounding a prophetic warning before he left home for the short journey to Central Park, 'Whatever you do, just don't lose your job. It means too much and gives you an opportunity to go and get another job.'

He was careful to follow that advice when Jack Robinson brought up the 'second-hand furniture' incident on the bus and accused him of being 'disrespectful to the chairman'.

Dorahy was immediately contrite.

'Yes Jack, I apologise sincerely. In the heat of the moment you could take it that way, but it certainly wasn't meant to be derogatory.'

The board agreed Dorahy could see out the season and he queried whether that included taking the team to the World Club Challenge in Brisbane, which as an Australian had been one of his major ambitions.

'No, no, no, you can't do that,' said Robinson forcefully. 'Once the Premiership is over, that's it.'

Dorahy argued the point but the board were unyielding.

'I said, "I guess that's it then, see you later," that's the truth of it,' said Dorahy.

Even then the drama of a fraught 12 months was not quite over, however, as the statement released by the board explaining his instant dismissal gave the reason as 'gross misconduct'.

No detail was forthcoming to Dorahy, either publicly or privately, which led to intense speculation, although Dorahy believes his comments on the bus to Robinson, coupled with his ill-advised 'suck' comment on live TV almost two weeks earlier, were used as catalysts for his demise.

'I was absolutely gobsmacked, to use an English turn of phrase, and extremely disappointed,' said Dorahy.

'I used the word "diabolical" at the time because I thought, "Why the Dickens would they use such harsh, horrendous adjectives for what went on?"'

Dorahy immediately engaged a solicitor to ensure the remainder of his contract was paid up but believes the manner of his leaving was detrimental to his future career when chasing head coach jobs at the top clubs. He never landed the prestigious job he craved in Australia although he did turn up at Warrington two years later for another season, which ended prematurely in his resignation when results took a turn for the worse. And he did make peace with Jack Robinson, who struggles to communicate nowadays after suffering a serious stroke in 2010.

'I went to see him when I was with Warrington and had a chat and we shook hands and I said, "Sorry if I caused you any angst." We agreed to talk whenever we met and get on with our lives. I think what happened at Wigan coloured the Warrington challenge. We did well in 1996 but in 1997 we started slowly and it was an easy excuse for them to say you didn't finish it off well at Wigan. We don't want any episodes here, so we'll let you go.'

Dorahy admits talking through the events of those challenging, troubled, exciting, life-affirming times has been a cathartic experience, exorcising a few ghosts on the way as well as allowing him to reassess his time as an ambitious young coach who landed a dream job which perhaps proved beyond the realms of his experience.

It would be wrong, however, to run away with the idea that Dorahy was universally disliked in the Wigan changing room. He wasn't and isn't. He may not have been blessed with the engaging charm of Monie, nor possessed the aura of Graham Lowe, but considered reflection suggests he was a talented coach, arguably a good number two rather than an outstanding number one, who perhaps had the misfortune to be in the right place at the wrong time.

'He had some good thoughts and also some peculiar ones but I still admire him,' said Martin Dermott. 'He was a good friend of mine. I liked him as a person even if some of his methods didn't work with the players we had.'

Denis Betts supports that view.

'I was taken with John,' he said. 'He was good to me but the biggest problem he had was that he put the senior players in that group in the wrong place.

'He didn't have the support of the board. The players had the support of the board. That was ultimately what cost him.'

Andy Farrell has worked with some of rugby's biggest personalities as a coach with England and Ireland since hanging up his boots and he recognises the forces lined up against Dorahy all those years ago.

'It was awkward for me as a youngster seeing what happened,' said Farrell. 'It would have been a daunting place to come for your first job as head coach. It can be a lonely place as a coach and you have to make sure you have embraced it all and be ready for anything.

'I felt for John at the end. It was not that he was a bad coach, but it isn't just about tactics. It is how you make the team feel as a unit going forward together.'

Even Shaun Edwards, Dorahy's arch tormentor back in that 1993/94 season, views his tenure in more measured fashion following more than 15 years of his own as a top rugby union coach, with Wasps and as assistant to Warren Gatland with Wales.

He recognises the pitfalls of a coach overthinking strategy and trying to put his indelible mark on a team.

'John was a good bloke. He wasn't a bad fella. He just came and tried to change the way Wigan did things and that was a mistake,' said Edwards. 'Why would you try to change something that was not broken?

'A lot of coaches do that though. It's an ego thing. It can be, "This is the way I want us to play."

'It is like tackle technique. I give the Welsh lads some ideas about what they should do. I know these things work but, let's be honest, if they are doing something different but they are getting them down every time I couldn't give two hoots how they get them down, just get them down.

'It's not about me and my fantastic tackle programme. Just tackle the bastards. I have fallen into that trap a couple of times myself as a coach. It can be too much about your plan, about how you have outwitted the opponents. Sometimes you have to outwit them, but not all the time.

'Some of the technical things John Dorahy brought in were good. One particular thing, a double up, we used at Wasps, which was when two offensive players line up to one defensive player and you run and split up at the last second. I learned that off John Dorahy.

'Not everything he did was bad, but it was the monotony of training longer. We weren't used to that.'

For Dorahy's part, he does not look back in anger, but with a warmth which is commendable given the exacting circumstances.

'Me and my family had a great time in Wigan,' he said. 'We made some great friends and I stay in contact with a whole heap of people. We had a marvellous time. A winning time. I was fortunate to have a colts team coach in Ray Unsworth who understood the position I found myself in and he assisted me greatly throughout the season and was an ally in tough times. I have got nothing bad to say about Wigan. Jack was good to me until push came to shove.'

25

Regrets, I've Had a Few

THERE are some who believe what happened next was the greatest club feat in British rugby league club history.

Not Wigan winning the Premiership Trophy just 18 days after John Dorahy was sacked with a thrilling 24-20 victory against Castleford at Old Trafford, although that was a reassuring start for new caretaker head coach Graeme West.

No, the fact that they travelled to Australia and returned with the World Club Challenge Trophy after defeating Brisbane Broncos, Wendell Sailor, Steve Renouf, Chris Johns, Glenn Lazarus, Allan Langer and all, 20-14, in their own backyard.

That achievement is even more extraordinary when you hear Gary Connolly and Jason Robinson, in separate interviews, both describing that trip as 'more like a stag do'.

West, the former second-rower who was universally liked by the players, sensed the team needed a break. They required the pressure valve to be prised open to release the angst, the tension, the unremitting effort of a season which had seen them win three trophies and lose their head coach.

What better way to do that than a beery flight to the far side of the world and a few days on the Gold Coast with its shimmering beaches, wall-to-wall sunshine and ice-cold lager?

There is no evidence of the exact number of 'tinnies' consumed although there are tales suggesting a couple of the Wigan forwards did attempt to match the feat of colourful Aussie cricketer David Boon, who is said to have consumed 52 cans of beer during a flight between Britain and Australia in 1989.

There is also a story that on the way back, such was the enthusiasm to eclipse Boon's record, one Wigan player required wheelchair assistance to disembark the aeroplane when it stopped for refuelling.

Undeterred by the reluctance of the flight crew to serve him any more alcohol, on returning to the aircraft some of the players went into team mode, the story goes, ordering beer at the back of the aircraft and surreptitiously passing it forward so the 'record-hunter' could continue his mission.

Suffice to say, although at least one player I interviewed reckoned 58 tins were consumed by the 'record-hunter', the attempt never troubled the historians at Guinness World Records, who, understandably, are reluctant to ratify such behaviour for fear of encouraging imitation and potential mishap or disorder.

The Brisbane trip was memorable, however, for so many reasons.

'Westy had given us about four days to go and let our hair down,' explained Jason Robinson. 'We must have been Rapunzel the amount of hair we let down. It was fun.'

One particular night a bunch of players visited a casino because Billy McGinty had dreamed the night before about winning a small fortune.

The roulette wheels were whirring and the blackjack tables doing brisk trade throughout the evening when, in the early hours, Martin Dermott probed McGinty on the details of his dream and it emerged that '31 black' was key.

McGinty immediately wagered $20 on the premonition, only to see the number come up first time, winning the Wigan forward around $800 in total.

Dermott and McGinty jumped and embraced manically in celebration, much champagne was purchased, stretch limousines were hired and, as Robinson recalled, dawn was sidestepped neatly as the revelry continued.

'We were coming in at nine o'clock in the morning from the night before and the chairman thought we were going for breakfast, but actually we had just come in,' said Robinson.

'Martin Hall was even on Australian radio every morning with his own part in a radio show. He had this saying, "Ups-a-daisy, eggs and bacon." I don't know where it came from. But every morning he was on the radio and that was his intro: "Ups-a-daisy, eggs and bacon."'

It is safe to say the alcohol consumption was considerable until they called a halt to the festivities three or four days before kick-off and returned to warrior mode.

The Wigan team of that era possessed the ability to switch focus in an instant. Like turning on a light. One day they were acting like Club 18-30 members on a weekend blitz in Ibiza. The next they were hard-nosed professionals shedding buckets of sweat in a bid to prove they were the best rugby league outfit on the planet.

'The reality of what we were about to face kicked in,' said Robinson. 'We realised we could get really embarrassed if we did not get at it.'

So they ran out at the ANZ stadium, albeit with an under-strength team and second-rower McGinty being promoted to prop in his last match for the club, owing to Kelvin Skerrett having broken his jaw in the Premiership Trophy Final and Andy Platt being injured, and proceeded to demonstrate their mental toughness and physical quality in a match which was notable for many things, but two in particular.

First, and most important, it was the first and only time an English rugby league club side had travelled to Australia and left with world champion status.

Second, it saw Barrie-Jon Mather ignore the screams of Martin Offiah to run in for a first-half try which supplemented an early effort from Denis Betts and set the tone for a match in which Wigan were irresistible in attack and heroic in defence.

It took some nerve in those days to use Offiah as a decoy but that is what Mather did, selling the dummy to Wendell Sailor before galloping in for the touchdown.

This is how Channel Nine's Australian commentator, Ray Warren, described it, 'Mather stepping through, he's got support with Offiah, he runs away from Offiah and scores himself. Big Mather, all six foot seven of him, treated Martin Offiah with disdain. He looked at him and said, "You're joking. This is mine."'

It was Robinson who then ran in the try that proved crucial, picking up a loose ball and beating Sailor. And it was Shaun Edwards who completed a season of unremitting angst in harmony and style by taking the man-of-the-match prize.

There are those who believe the victory is the greatest moment in the history of the Wigan club, more glorious than any of their Wembley triumphs. Some go further, insisting it eclipses anything else in the history of British rugby league at club level.

Jason Robinson chews on both those contentions before concluding that it is about as close as any club side has come to achieving the impossible.

'Making my debut for Wigan was amazing, a great moment. So was playing at Wembley for the first time,' said Robinson. 'But Brisbane was the best from the north playing the best from the south and Brisbane at that time were huge. To play them in a full stadium after we had been written off because we didn't have a full strength team out, and win, was just an amazing feeling. Playing at Wembley was special but beating Brisbane away, the more I think about it, it shouldn't have been done.'

There is a look of awe on Robinson's face as he recalls the feat.

For McGinty there is also a mixture of awe at the 'incredible team ethic that night' and a sadness at leaving Wigan. The Brisbane match was McGinty's first for three months after having fallen out with John Dorahy.

It was also his last for the club because, although West wanted him to stay, he had already signed a binding contract with Workington for the following season.

'It has always been a big grind of mine the way it all finished at Wigan,' said McGinty. 'It was a real shame. I would have loved to have stayed there but I suppose it wasn't a bad game for your farewell. I can remember listening to the radio and everyone saying we would never get near the Broncos with so many players missing. We just wanted to prove people wrong. Neil Cowie put in an incredible stint that night. So did Gary Connolly and Jason Robinson. Nobody wanted to be the man to miss a tackle. Nobody wanted to be the person who didn't turn up to carry the ball.'

For Mather, a child of the 1970s who was named after Welsh rugby union fly half legend Barry John, that Brisbane achievement and his fleeting moments of brilliance in a Wigan shirt are a huge source of pride but also produce the ache of a man who knows if only fate and his own decision-making had taken a more considered course it could all have been so much better for so much longer.

Mather played in that 1994 Challenge Cup Final, where he had the dubious honour of marking Kevin Iro in the centres. He roomed with Dean Bell. The odd couple. A battered old warhorse who had been there and done everything and a bright but raw and shy 21-year-old beanpole, still studying at Liverpool University with it all in front of him.

'I didn't have a clue what to say to him,' recalled Mather. 'He had been my big hero growing up and even though we had played together all year I was still in awe. It was a great experience but I bet he thought, "he doesn't say much".'

The rest is a blur to Mather who watches the TV footage of that Wembley final from time to time at his home in Sydney where he is the football general manager of New South Wales Rugby League, if only so his children can have a laugh at the time their dad lifted the Challenge Cup trophy, only to dislodge the lid, which came crashing down on his head.

In some ways that is a metaphor for his playing career.

He was the lad born in Ince-in-Makerfield who moved to Blackpool as a youngster, but who was a steadfast Wigan supporter, cheering them on at Wembley as an 11-year-old in 1984.

He was the lad who wore the Wigan shirt around the house and whose biggest ambition was to pull on the first team cherry and white jersey more times than his grandfather Ronnie had done when amassing 211 appearances, scoring 11 tries, between 1950 and 1957.

All he ever wanted in his early days was to be the Wigan record holder in the family.

He might have accomplished that feat, too, if he had not also been the lad who let youthful impetuosity rule his head when he took Wigan to court in a protracted dispute after the club refused to release his registration without a transfer fee following him signing a contract with Western Reds in Australia. Mather's legal challenge was unsuccessful, but little more than 12 months after his starring roles at Wembley and Brisbane, his Wigan career was over. Sixty-seven matches and 35 tries. Not even close to his grandfather. The regrets are stacked up forlornly like books which have never been read.

'I made some bad choices,' Mather is candid enough to admit. 'Career-wise I let myself down. If I had stayed at Wigan and played with those better players for a while longer, rather than going to Australia, I would probably have done a bit more.

'I'm happy with what I did, but there is a bit of sadness tinged in there. I do regret leaving Wigan in the circumstances I did. I could have handled that differently and a lot better. You get advice and decide to take it and sometimes the grass is always greener. When I'd gone I realised what I had done.

'Sitting down with the club and being honest with each other would have been a better way to do it. But I was stubborn and Jack Robinson was stubborn and we never got to that stage. Looking back, it is one of my biggest regrets.

'When I first played for them I never wanted to leave and somewhere along the way it just turned into more of a business than a sport. I don't hold any grudges with Jack or anybody and hopefully they don't with me. Things happen, you move on and make the best of it.'

Which, in a way, is exactly what Mather did as any aficionado of pub sports quiz questions might know.

Who was the first Great Britain rugby league player to be capped by England at rugby union? The answer of course is Mather.

As if by serendipity it also happened to be at Wembley, in the last and most famous rugby union match played at the old stadium, Wales's 32-31 win against England on 11 April 1999, a game in which a last-ditch try from Scott Gibbs, another cross-code international, deprived England of a grand slam in the last-ever Five Nations Championship.

If you thought the cap Mather won for that first international union appearance is framed and hanging in pride of place in his Sydney home, you would be wrong. It went missing within an hour of the final whistle.

'Tradition was that everyone in the squad bought a drink for the new cap,' explained Mather. 'You had to drink them so I passed out and woke up at 9.30 the next morning, naked on the bed and no cap. I don't know where it is or who has got it.

'My mum has never forgiven me and hates me telling the story. "So embarrassing B-J. You were brought up better than that," she says. The next day I had to get a plane to Argentina to play for a World 15 and 13 hours on a plane when you have got the worst hangover in the world is the worst experience I have had in a very long time.'

The fact that it was the one and only international cap Mather won at rugby union only makes the story more poignant.

These days, despite the salutary tales, Mather cherishes the memories. The brilliance in Brisbane. The time he played for a team he believes was the best English rugby team of all time in either code, better than England's World Cup-winning rugby union squad of 2003.

The time he ran away from Martin Offiah, arguably the greatest winger in either code, plus the magical day he played for Wigan at Wembley.

Some years ago he was visiting a friend's house in Perth, Australia, and on the wall there was a picture commemorating that 1994 final.

'It was a photo of the two teams walking out,' said Mather. 'Behind my head there is a banner in the crowd saying "We love you B-J" with the "Love you" in the shape of a heart. All my mates from university had gone down to support me and to see that again was special.'

26

The Biggest Drinking Team
I Ever Played In

THE average committed rugby or football fan will put up with just about anything.

They have become almost immune to hardship. Traffic jams. Weird kick-off times. Ticket price hikes. Endless queues. Dodgy stadium food. Squalid toilet facilities. No pies. Hail, snow, you name it.

But there is one thing they seldom forgive. Betrayal. Or to be more precise, the perception of betrayal.

It is one of the reasons sports teams rarely sell to their fiercest rivals. There has not been a direct transfer between Manchester United and Liverpool, for instance, since Phil Chisnall left Old Trafford for Anfield in 1964. Anyone who does cross the Rubicon can expect jeers, whistles, verbal abuse and sometimes worse whenever they confront their former supporters.

To stretch William Congreve's famous quote, 'Heaven has no rage like love to hatred turned, nor hell a fury like a sports fan scorned.'

Which brings us to Gary Connolly.

Connolly never wanted to play for Wigan. He wasn't like Barrie-Jon Mather or Martin Dermott or Shaun Edwards or Andy Gregory, players born and bred in Wigan and whose entire life had been devoted to the idea of pulling on the cherry and white jersey, who were brought up to believe Central Park was the centre of the sporting universe.

Connolly was exactly the opposite. He was a St Helens lad through and through. The enemy. The rugby player with just two essential requirements written into his birthright. One, to beat Wigan on Boxing Day. Two, to beat Wigan on Good Friday.

That antipathy towards Wigan was not made easier by the fact that Connolly had played full back for St Helens in that humiliating 1989 Challenge Cup Final at just 17 years old when Saints were 'nilled' and again in 1991 when the result was closer and the Saints performance was much improved but ultimately it was still a defeat that remains a source of shame.

Even with the fearlessness and resilience of youth, those results hurt.

Connolly did not have a good game, especially in 1989, although he credits the experience of that defeat as 'critical in my career'.

What does rankle is that almost a quarter of a century after joining Wigan in 1993, at the zenith of their Wembley domination, he is reviled still in some quarters in his hometown of St Helens.

There is still the odd taunt of 'Judas'. There are still those who believe he was lured to Central Park purely by Wigan's ability to cough up a few more pounds than their neighbours across the East Lancs Road.

I met Connolly at his converted and beautifully refurbished farmhouse in Wigan, not far from the stately manor house at Haigh Hall where the team used to perform those gruelling hill runs with fitness coach Bill Hartley as part of their pre-season fitness training.

He had just finished a long shift at the care home where he works in St Helens. Time has frayed the edges of those boyish looks, which were so striking in those early Wembley finals, but he looked fit and strong, capable of pulling on a rugby shirt and putting in some hard yards even in his mid-40s.

Most of all, however, he was keen to set the record straight once more on that controversial transfer.

He explained how he had tried to renew his contract with St Helens at the age of 21 after four years with them and how he was prepared to sign for another five years. In fact, he wanted to stay there for the rest of his career.

St Helens, however, would not budge on the terms of his old contract but allowed him to go out on loan to Australia to play a stint of 15 matches with Canterbury.

Canterbury wanted to sign Connolly on a permanent deal and, having fallen in love with the lifestyle Down Under, he was prepared to oblige them. They even agreed personal terms.

Quite unexpectedly, Connolly then received a phone call from his agent.

'He said, "Saints have sold you to Wigan,"' recalled Connolly. 'I said, "I don't want to go to Wigan. What do I want to go to Wigan for?"'

The bottom line was that Canterbury could stretch to a fee of £80,000 to St Helens for Connolly's registration whereas Wigan were prepared to fork out £250,000. For St Helens it was a no-brainer and for Connolly, once he had overcome the shock of what amounted to 'consorting with the enemy', it also made sense.

'I knew I was going to a great side, the best side in the country,' said Connolly. 'I would win a lot of trophies and the change would do me good and probably improve my game because I would be playing with better people.

'What made it easier was that I had gone on the Great Britain tour in 1992 and there were 13 Wigan players on that tour so I got to know the entire Wigan side. It made my job easier going to Wigan, it wasn't so daunting.'

As far as the details of the transfer, however, Connolly felt he was in a catch-22 situation. He could not tell the St Helens fans the whole truth. That it was never his idea. That he did not manipulate the move. That it was not all about money. And he could hardly come out publicly and say he did not want to go to Wigan when the deal was done.

'You can't go into a dressing room full of superstars and say that,' said Connolly. 'So I kept my mouth shut and got ten or 15 years' shit from St Helens spectators saying I was a Judas and that I went for the money.

'The honest truth is I didn't. They sold me. But I loved playing back at St Helens. All I wanted to do then was beat them and shut them up and for the first four or five years that is what Wigan did to them.'

Connolly occasionally returns to visit St Helens for a big game and helps with the raffle on the pitch at half-time. The years have taken the edge off the fans' sense of betrayal, but even now there are little pockets of resistance.

'I still get some stick,' he admitted. 'Not as much, but I still get the funny looks and the "Judas" comments. But since I have retired I have done a few interviews and tried to get the message across that I wasn't to blame, but they do not believe me. Some Saints fans come up to me and say, "We've heard the tale, no way, you went for the money." I just say "Whatever."'

The statistics and the silverware, Challenge Cup and World Club Challenge winners' medals in his first year, are proof alone that it was the right move.

Connolly's background and his allegiance to the club's biggest rivals, however, give him a unique perspective when it comes to coldly analysing Wigan's sustained success during the latter part of British rugby's greatest club run of achievement.

He had no innate loyalty to the town; quite the opposite. No history of playing in the area's schoolboy age groups. No sense of youthful shared convictions. No sense of 'band of brothers' camaraderie.

The nearest he came to that was as a 12-year-old Wembley ball boy during the 1984 Challenge Cup Final between Wigan and Widnes when he had a close-up vantage point as Joe Lydon, playing for Widnes, sped by to score those two famous tries, up there with the finest long-range tries ever seen at the stadium.

From that day on he admits Lydon, born and bred in Wigan, became an inspiration.

He has told Lydon the tale and also provided evidence when the two were sharing a drink in a pub with the BBC's *A Question of Sport* programme playing on a television in the background.

From across the bar Connolly spotted a clip of Lydon setting off on a run for one of those tries.

'I pointed at the set and said, "This is you Joe, but watch, in a second when you run past there is a lad with a shock of blond hair on the touchline. That's me, Joe, that's me." And it was. He was my hero at the time.'

By the time Connolly joined Wigan, Lydon was nearing the end of his playing career. Yet neither Connolly's lack of local heritage, nor the opprobrium of his hometown fans, have ever prevented him from telling it straight.

'The best move I ever made was going to Wigan without a shadow of a doubt,' said Connolly. 'Players used to come to me and say I can get £10k more to go somewhere else. But I always used to work out that once tax was taken off and it was spread over a year they would be better off at Wigan.

'You could earn that much in match payments alone and your profile would be better at Wigan. I would never have advised any youngster to go somewhere else to get more money. I used to say, "It's the best club in the world. Stick here."'

Not that everything was sweetness and light at Central Park. It wasn't. The John Dorahy year had exposed the infighting at the club. It had also proved that whatever was thrown at a team, so long as the players were good enough and prepared to dig deep into their reserves of pride and courage, they could overcome any distractions.

Connolly had been accustomed to a team which bonded together as people as well as rugby players at St Helens. They were like minds. Friends as well as colleagues. They socialised together.

At Wigan it was apparent that was not always the case.

'There were a few cliques at Wigan,' said Connolly. 'They didn't hate each other, but they wouldn't socialise with each other. Rightly so, everyone doesn't have to get on.

'On a rugby field, though, they would die for each other, because they were all winners. If one player from one clique was in a fight in town on a Saturday night and a player from another clique was walking past I'm pretty sure one would walk off and leave the other one to it.

'But on a rugby field they would give 100 per cent because they were both winners and wanted the same thing.

'At Wigan I learned you did not have to be the best of mates. You just had to have the same desire to win.

'If the guy is beside you and you miss a tackle you are going to feel ten times shit if he hates you. You are not going to let it happen again. If it's your best mate and he puts his arm around you and says, "Don't bother about it," you might miss another one.

'If you both have the same will to win it doesn't matter if you are friends or not. I remember when Teddy Sheringham and Andy Cole came out at Manchester United and said they hated each other and I thought to myself, "This happened ten years before at Wigan."'

According to Connolly, it is also a misconception to hike down the well-trodden path which attributes Wigan's golden era to the fact that the club went to full professional status before most of the rest.

It is true that when Connolly was at St Helens he was supplementing his rugby earnings by working full-time as a bricklayer. When he arrived at Wigan in the latter part of 1993, no one was allowed to have a supplementary job. The club insisted the players kept fresh for the match at the weekend.

But it did not mean they did extra training. It did not mean they attended the club five days a week. It did not mean any more rugby. The one thing it did mean was that most players had much more free time on their hands.

'At Wigan no one had a full-time job,' said Connolly. 'We trained Tuesday night, Thursday morning and Saturday morning. You had time to do your own weights. You would do weight sessions and sprint sessions but you didn't have to turn up for them. You turned up because you wanted to do them.

'People say Wigan won things because they were fully professional but it was probably worse at Wigan because we had more free time and we were drinking more.

'That Wigan team was the biggest drinking team I ever played in because we had time. No one had a job, nobody had to get up the next morning. We were out every Sunday after a game and we were out every Thursday.

'When I was at Saints I was working on a building site. I was up at 7am. There was no way I could go out for a drink. I had no time for drinking because I trained Saturday morning at 10am. The only time for a drink was Friday nights. You used to turn up at Saints training with a bit of a hangover and you were playing on the Sunday. At Wigan we were out midweek and all sorts because we didn't have to get up for training.

'The truth is Wigan went full-time professional when everybody else went full-time professional. It was just that we were not allowed to have another job. We only had to be at the club two hours on a Tuesday, two on a Thursday and an hour on Saturday and game time. Five hours a week we were committed to be at the club.'

Connolly's explanation for the success is simple. The club bought the best players. They opened the cheque book and assembled a squad of full internationals at a time when there was no salary cap in place to render the sport a more level playing field.

That is undeniable. Connolly was one of those players. His analysis, however, fails to credit the conveyor belt of homegrown talent which was continuing to flourish at that time, including such esteemed characters as Andy Farrell, Mick Cassidy and Phil Clarke, with Kris Radlinski pushing to break through, another prodigy in the making.

The other hoary question which inevitably is churned out whenever that era is recalled is whether Wigan's success was good or bad for the game of rugby league.

There is no doubt it had reached a stage towards the mid-1990s when only a handful of clubs had any real prospect of reaching a Challenge Cup Final. Leeds, Wigan and St Helens were major forces but then it was a struggle to make a persuasive case for anyone else.

The salary cap changed all that.

'The gap between the top four clubs and the bottom four clubs back then was immense,' said Connolly. 'Now it is spread out. Everybody can beat anybody on the day because of the salary cap. There is no one club going out and signing all the best players. All the cream is not at the top.

'It was probably a wake-up call the game needed. People looked at Wigan and said, "How do we get better?" Copy Wigan. When it went to summer rugby everybody properly went full-time and it was a level playing field.'

That was also a culture shock for Connolly in that he went from spending five hours a week at the club to being required to spend five hours a day.

'My hourly rate took a heck of a tumble but it was the way the game had to go,' said Connolly. 'I wasted a lot of my youth not training as hard as I could. I have seen part-time and full-time but I wouldn't swap my career because I really enjoyed the early years. It wasn't as strict and serious as it is now, you could enjoy yourself a lot more.'

It was a career which also saw him land the coveted Lance Todd Trophy, not for Wigan, but for Leeds, and in unusual circumstances considering he found himself on the losing side in a 22-20 defeat against Bradford Bulls in a final played at the Millennium Stadium, Cardiff, in 2003.

As if to prove sometimes you cannot win whatever you do, Connolly received criticism for looking miserable and not celebrating when he was presented with the man-of-the-match trophy on the pitch, one of only ten players to have won the Lance Todd while playing for the losing side.

The reality was that he was bursting with pride inside but acutely aware that some of his team-mates were in tears after having lost the tightest and most dramatic of finals.

'People thought I wasn't respecting the trophy,' said Connolly. 'I was happy, it just wasn't the right time to show my emotions with my team-mates depressed and crying.'

The Leeds adventure lasted just 12 months before he fell out with head coach Tony Smith and found himself back at Wigan, playing for nothing.

'I got paid up by Leeds and phoned Andy Farrell to tell him I was retired,' recalled Connolly. 'While I was talking to him he phoned Maurice Lindsay at Wigan and after a brief chat came back to me and said, "You are training tomorrow. There is just one downside. They can't pay you because of the salary cap."'

At a loose end, Connolly went along to Central Park and helped out by playing a handful of games under Denis Betts as head coach.

There were no tries in his brief stint but plenty of memories were rekindled, considering it was almost exactly ten years since that 1994 Wembley final and arguably the most frantic 12 months of his life. The controversial transfer, the double of Championship title and Challenge Cup triumph, the brilliant World Club Challenge win in Brisbane and the final recognition when Wigan were awarded the Team of the Year prize at the BBC Sports Personality awards.

Let's face it, although rugby league and the Challenge Cup, in particular, have been loyally served by the BBC down the years, the sport has rarely featured when the most prestigious individual or team awards have been handed out in December.

Since Chris Chataway, the British middle- and long-distance runner most famous for being one of the pacemakers when Roger Bannister ran the first sub-four-minute mile, picked up the first individual award in 1954, no rugby league player has won the main award, with Jonny Wilkinson the only rugby player to do so after his World Cup-winning drop goal for England's rugby union side in 2003. In fact, only one rugby league player has ever been nominated for the award, Leeds's Kevin Sinfield finishing runner-up to Andy Murray in 2015. True, Mal Meninga, the former Australian captain who was courted by Wigan in the 1980s but signed for St Helens for a season in 1984, did land the Overseas Personality award in 1990.

Nevertheless, it seemed like a groundbreaking moment for the sport when Wigan actually won the BBC Team of the Year prize in 1994 and were invited down to London to receive the award.

Members of the team had attended the awards before in the Queen Elizabeth II Conference Centre but had always come away with little more than a few kind words and a lot of hangovers.

Martin Dermott recalls one occasion, in particular.

'Oh dear, I woke up the next morning with a fire extinguisher in the bed and it was all wet,' said Dermott.

'Me and some of the lads had been downstairs in the QE2 building after the event and there were some lady golfers and within a couple of hours they were wearing our Wembley kit and we were wearing their skirts and golfing blazers.

'Paul Gascoigne and Ally McCoist were there and they had a bottle of scotch and we were all in a circle drinking it and it just got wilder and wilder and before long I was wearing a dress and a blazer.

'I remember standing there drinking and thinking, "This is not happening. Gazza, McCoist, me and some golfing women. And I am just a lad from Wigan." It was snowing at the time and we went outside and had a snowball fight. It was bizarre.'

Yet while Dermott and co. were revelling in carefree fun and celebrating their dominance on the pitch, men in suits were plotting the biggest shake-up in the sport's history.

27

The Dawn of Summer

THE rugby league chairmen who sat around the Central Park boardroom on Saturday 8 April 1995, had no choice. Not really.

On the table was £77m over five years from Sky television magnate Rupert Murdoch to set up a European Super League and switch seasons from winter to summer. On the line was the future of their sport.

They chose unanimously to accept the cash and guarantee their survival.

The deal, which had been hatched hurriedly at a meeting between Rugby Football League chief executive and former Wigan chairman Maurice Lindsay and BSkyB chief executive Sam Chisolm four days before, was not quite as simple as it sounds.

Initially, it comprised a Super League of 14 clubs, including Bradford, Halifax, Leeds, London, St Helens and Wigan, plus Paris and Toulouse along with six proposed merged clubs, Calder, Cheshire, Cumbria, Humberside, Manchester and South Yorkshire.

The idea was to include as wide a demographic as possible while bringing together financially weak clubs to share economies and pool fan bases. It was a sound plan in theory, a non-starter in practice with the tribal nature of rugby supporters.

There were widespread demonstrations by fans, some resenting the move to summer and all the turbulence that entailed, others desperate to preserve the identity of names that had been supported for generations by their families.

Within hours, chairmen began to withdraw promises of mergers and three weeks later a new Super League plan was established which abandoned the proposed mergers, dropped the Toulouse club from the blueprint and formed instead a 12-club league comprising Bradford,

Castleford, Halifax, Leeds, London, Oldham, Paris, St Helens, Sheffield, Warrington, Wigan and Workington.

To ensure the deal encountered no more glitches, BSkyB threw in an additional £10m, making the move from winter to summer worth £87m.

There are still those who say it was a bad deal. Still those who preferred the soggy mud-heaps of November and December, when shirt numbers were virtually obscured by half-time, to the perfect hard pitches which encourage running rugby in June and July.

There are those who still pillory Lindsay for what they describe as 'selling the soul of the sport', even though Lance Todd had floated a similar idea in the 1930s.

In truth, summer rugby and the Super League had probably been inevitable since Wigan's Jack Robinson first coined the phrase in 1986 when 12 of the leading clubs had joined forces to demand a bigger share of the sport's cash.

At the time the levy on gate receipts was 15 per cent, which was collected from the First Division clubs and spread equally between all the clubs at the end of the season.

It was a vital source of income for struggling clubs and a threat by the top 12 to break away from the RFL resulted in the levy being cut to eight per cent. Financial pressures, however, continued to mount. The Bradford fire, when 56 people died at Bradford City's football stadium in 1985, resulted in ground improvements being made compulsory at sports stadia.

The tragedy of Hillsborough in 1989, which claimed the lives of 96 Liverpool football supporters, enforced more stringent measures, such as CCTV, electronic turnstiles, extra stewarding and policing.

It all came at a cost and concentrated the focus on change as a means of survival. Perhaps the most imaginative and intuitive club at the time was not one of the big boys. Instead, it was left to lowly Keighley, formed in 1876 but a club struggling to exist in an area hit hard by austerity and the decline of the textiles industry, to show the way.

In 1991, following a series of financial meltdowns, the club was taken over by a group of local businessmen who effected a creative makeover of stunning proportions.

The club was rebranded as Keighley Cougars. The owners introduced cheerleaders, on-field mascots, lively PA announcements, pre-match entertainment and loud music whenever the team scored, the sort of attractions commonplace in American sports and, to a lesser extent, in rugby league in Australia.

They courted the local schools to set up a youth academy, pumped cash into the team and appointed Great Britain coach Phil Larder. Crowds soared from the hundreds to 5,000.

So progressive and successful were the ideas that they attracted national attention with then Prime Minister John Major lauding them for their community involvement.

Little were they to know then that aspects of their model were not that dissimilar from the one put forward by Brisbane Broncos chief John Ribot in March 1994 when he met television magnate Rupert Murdoch to propose the formation of a Super League Down Under tailored to the demands of his television network.

It was a meeting which was to spark the so-called 'Super League War', as the Australian Rugby League had already promised rival TV tycoon Kerry Packer first call on its TV rights.

In true Murdoch style he began to sign up players anyway, hurling money beyond reason at them. But that was not enough. Murdoch also needed to take away the ARL's trump card with the players, which in essence was that, as the governing body, only they could offer international sport and the honours that went with it.

It was that 'card' which prompted Murdoch to sign up other rugby league-playing nations, including Britain, to his TV-funded new world, to cut off the ARL's power.

That was the turbulent back-story to why Lindsay sat around a table at Central Park with Britain's rugby league chairmen and urged them to do a deal which was the forerunner to the thriving domestic Super League of today.

Even those who lament the way it used to be would have to concede that rugby league did not lack courage when it came to preserving the sport in a volatile world.

It is a trait of which the sport rightly can be proud.

True, accepting Murdoch's money could be seen by some as courting the establishment and betraying the sport's cultural identity.

But what was British rugby league supposed to do? Remain on the sidelines? Retreat even further into its working class heartlands? Reject the inevitable? Or watch impotently while football took the Murdoch path to untold riches and rugby union dragged itself, without a hint of demonstration or protest, from its once-prized amateurism to national and international prominence in the realms of professionalism?

Sometimes, as the miners and print workers discovered in the 1980s, the tide of change is unstoppable and the only way to survive is to adapt and be flexible. Rugby league chose to adapt.

Unfortunately for Keighley, ironically the keenest of all to adapt, there was to be no happy ending. While the club succeeded in winning the Second Division championship in the 1994/95 season they were excluded from the Super League the following year.

The club which had shown the way with financial good management and resourceful imagination was denied the promotion it deserved. It is so often the way in sport. The rich wield the power, the poor play for the scraps.

Relentless change in the way the game was played, promoted, funded, marketed and televised was in the air.

For Wigan, however, there was at least one thing which remained constant. As the Super League deal was being finalised they were preparing to battle for their eighth Challenge Cup trophy in a row.

28

Medals and Memories

THE band was playing, the crowd were preparing to sing rugby
league's Challenge Cup anthem 'Abide with Me', kick-off against
Leeds on 29 April 1995 was minutes away and Jason Robinson
was lying in the Wembley changing room with all sorts of motivational
thoughts scurrying through his mind.

He remembered the gut-wrenching day just a few years earlier when
he had been turned down by Leeds, his hometown club.

He thought back to 12 months previously and the perceived injustice
of being left out at the last minute by John Dorahy and missing out on
Martin Offiah's inspired and glorious annihilation of the Yorkshire club.

He pondered on the dramas and concerns of the last few weeks when
he had broken a bone in his right hand and then one in his left foot, which
had threatened to deprive him once more of a chance to prove his talent
on the biggest stage to all who had doubted him.

The hand was bandaged. The foot, only partially recovered, was still
painful. Too painful.

Which was why, just minutes before kick-off time, Dr Ansar Zaman,
the Wigan club doctor, reached inside his medical bag and produced a
needle. Not just an ordinary needle. A needle so long and thick that it
could have been used to knit the Wigan scarves on sale around the stadium
concourse.

Rugby players are tough and uncompromising by nature, but the sight
of that needle was truly alarming.

Three or four of the backroom staff were enlisted to hold Robinson
still while the doctor performed what turned out to be quite possibly the
most important manoeuvre of the afternoon.

'The needle went through the base of my foot and because the skin there is so thick and because it had to be twisted to get it into the right positions the pain was just horrendous,' said Robinson.

'But suddenly I couldn't feel my leg. It was numb.'

He pulled on his socks and boots, walked into the tunnel behind the rest of his team-mates and as he was sucked into the vortex of noise and colour that greets the two teams he attempted to concentrate on the established protocols of being a Wigan rugby player at Wembley.

'Don't look into the crowd. Don't wave to your family. Don't get lost in the moment.'

This was Wigan v Robinson's hometown team. This was the opportunity to make history. More history.

It had been a remarkable 12 months under new coach Graeme West, who had been handed the permanent job following the brilliant World Club Challenge triumph in Brisbane, after which fans had campaigned for him to stay.

How could the board refuse? The fans loved West, the players respected and liked him, he was a former player and captain of renown and his easy and courteous manner made him an agreeable figure with the media.

The squad, bolstered by the arrival of Welsh rugby union star Scott Quinnell and Henry Paul, the latter as part of the deal that allowed Andy Platt to join Auckland Warriors, had responded in stirring fashion.

The Regal Trophy had been captured with a six-try, 40-10 demolition of Warrington at Huddersfield in January. Wigan had finished top of the Stones Bitter Championship by seven points from nearest rivals Leeds.

And now, here they were, back at Wembley, bidding for their eighth Challenge Cup in a row.

There had been just one scare on the way. That had come in their first match, the fourth round tussle with St Helens at Central Park. It was the 38th game of their remarkable cup adventure and with St Helens leading 12-6 at half-time as the rain fell, the run was in jeopardy.

Fortunately, Denis Betts scored a try after 48 minutes which Frano Botica converted to bring the scores level. But St Helens were the better, more controlled team and a penalty by Bobbie Goulding and a drop goal each from Goulding and Ian Pickavance made it 16-12 to Saints with less than ten minutes remaining. Enter Martin Offiah and some typical magic down the left to send Martin Hall in for the touchdown to level the scores again with Botica this time missing the conversion.

That is the way it stayed, 16-16, the only one of the 43 matches in the historic run that Wigan did not win and arguably one they should have lost, considering Goulding's attempt at a winning drop goal four minutes from the hooter rebounded off the post.

As if to prove that in sport 'carpe diem', or 'seize the day', is the most salient of mottos, the chance was gone for St Helens, who took Wigan back to Knowsley Road only to be steamrollered 40-24 in the replay with Offiah scoring a hat-trick and further tries coming from Phil Clarke, Gary Connolly, Henry Paul and Robinson. From then on the route to the final was laden with tries, 24 of them in three matches which saw them beat Batley 70-4, Widnes 26-12 and Oldham 48-20.

The preparations for Wembley could not have been smoother, unless, of course, you happened to have been Robinson with a plaster cast on hand and foot for the last few weeks prior to the final.

There was another player whose pre-match routine did not go according to plan, second-rower Mick Cassidy.

Ask any Wigan fan to name the most distinctive thing about Cassidy in a career during which he played 368 matches for his hometown club, scoring 52 tries, and the chances are they will tell you he was the head-down, hard-working guy with a tidy turn of pace and a shock of blond hair who always wore a scrum cap. He was never without that scrum cap. There were times he might well have worn it in the shower so moulded was it to his cranium.

Yet as they emerged from the Wembley tunnel Cassidy's blond mop stood out like autumn snow on Winter Hill.

Where was that cap?

'It was a big occasion, the normal routine wasn't the same and I just walked out without it,' said Cassidy. 'I had never done that before. I think the occasion got to me and I just forgot all about it.'

None of which would have mattered if the knee of Leeds second row forward Richie Eyres, the player sent off for his assault on Offiah in the 1993 final, had not connected with Cassidy's temple during an attempted tackle after nine minutes. Unfortunately, it did, quite accidentally, and suddenly the lights were extinguished on the Wigan man's 1995 final.

When Cassidy came to, he was lying on a bed in the old Wembley hospital underneath the concrete stand with intermittent and confusing roars in the background and a man in a suit, surrounded by medical paraphernalia, asking him impenetrable questions.

'Do you know where you are?'

'Er, no.'

'Do you know what is happening?'

'No.'

Cassidy leant up on the bed and looked around.

'I didn't have a clue where I was,' he recalled. 'I had no idea I was at Wembley and it was the Challenge Cup Final. The doc told me where I was and what had happened and I just said, "What's the score?"'

The answer was 2-0 to Leeds, courtesy of a penalty goal from Graham Holroyd.

However, by the time Cassidy had been escorted back to a seat in the Wigan touchline dugout, from where he watched his replacement and training partner, Andy Farrell, perform his duties for the rest of the game, Robinson had already scored the first of two quite brilliant tries which were to earn him the Lance Todd Trophy.

As an athlete, there is no doubt Robinson was a freak of nature. Players have tried to emulate his running style and England rugby union fly half Jonny Wilkinson once credited Robinson with teaching him, at England's Pennyhill Park training headquarters in Surrey, how to be a more elusive runner, taking short, staccato steps, enabling swift and unpredictable changes of direction.

Others might have tried to imitate, but there was only one Robinson.

'He made something out of nothing there,' was how BBC commentator Ray French described his first try against Leeds.

So he did. A spin and a fend-off to elude the clutches of Leeds winger Francis Cummins. A step off that numbed left foot to evade full back Alan Tait and the rest of the defence and then a trademark scamper to the line. Frano Botica added the conversion.

Seven minutes later Henry Paul took a pass from Phil Clarke and pirouetted through some weak tackling for another touchdown and with Holroyd and Botica slotting penalties before half-time Wigan went in with a 12-4 lead.

It was what happened five minutes after the interval which ensured Robinson would always own a key to the vaults of Wembley history.

The Wigan forwards conveyed the ball up the middle in routine fashion until, suddenly, Robinson arrived at dummy half on the halfway line. Instead of passing as the Leeds defenders retreated, Robinson scooted sideways, stepped off that numbed left foot once more and within the space of ten metres had scythed a passage through the entire Leeds defence.

Speed of thought. Fleetness of foot. They were the weapons which gave Robinson a clear, unopposed, delightfully carefree run to the line.

He was able to look right and left to ensure no would-be tacklers were in the vicinity and then, before touching down the ball between the posts, he blew a kiss to the crowd.

It was rugby's equivalent of a golfer walking up the 18th fairway at St Andrews, knowing he had won The Open Championship and savouring the moment by tipping his hat to the exultant galleries.

These days, Robinson's face grimaces with a mixture of embarrassment and disapproval as he recalls that moment of understandable indulgence. It does not sit comfortably with his modest demeanour.

'Looking back, I think, "Oh, just put the ball down and then celebrate,"' said Robinson. 'I suppose it was just the excitement of the moment. It is hard to contain. Nowadays, it gets drummed into players, don't be a clown, score the try and then do your celebrating. For me, though, scoring two tries at Wembley against Leeds, it couldn't get any better.

'I always had this thing about Leeds. I felt let down by them when they didn't sign me. It always seemed like I had to prove a point, it was always an incentive for me to do well.'

Robinson looks back on those two Wembley tries as vindication that he was in the right place at the right time and equipped with the talent to grace a team of undoubted rugby superstars.

Yet Robinson is unique in Wigan's glory years history in that arguably he is the only superstar of that era who could claim legitimately to have left Central Park and gone on to even greater achievements.

Eight years on from his Wembley heroics, Robinson was in Sydney, on a night of torrential rain, dripping with expectation, where he scored the lone England try as the men inspired by head coach Clive Woodward defeated Australia 20-17 to win the rugby union World Cup for the only time.

Jonny Wilkinson's famous last-gasp drop goal rightly has taken its place in English rugby folklore but Robinson's try, coming as it did just before half-time, was pivotal.

It is only natural that it has become the most iconic moment in Robinson's career, the moment he has been asked about most.

'The reason why 2003 is number one is just because of the magnitude of it,' said Robinson.

'But people say to me, "Which do you like best, rugby league or rugby union?" And sometimes it is hard because the games are so different, but I would have to say that rugby league is best at club level and rugby union best at international level.

'There are very few people that win a World Cup, especially the way that we did it in Sydney. But I have so many great memories at Wigan. People forget I played nearly ten years for Wigan and I played only seven years in rugby union and only five of them at international level. Even so, I get remembered for playing for England at rugby union more than anything else.'

Robinson, however, sees distinct parallels with the Wembley-winning teams he played in at Wigan and the greatest rugby union side England has ever produced.

'There are so many similarities in how driven the players were individually and how talented they were,' said Robinson. 'Maurice Lindsay played a big part, too, bringing in the best players. He was ahead of his time. I liken him to Clive Woodward, who put in place everything for the England players to thrive. But you have to have the players. You can have a great system, but if you haven't got quality players you are always going to struggle.

'Because Wigan had so many good players it just made all the other great players want to come. I look at those two teams, Wigan and England, in the same light. I have been blessed in having the best times at Wigan and the best times England rugby ever had.'

Robinson is in demand by sponsors and corporate bodies these days, either as a motivational speaker or by firms who calculate an association with the nostalgia of great deeds long gone can lend a glossy sheen to their products and their values.

Nothing, however, comes close to replacing the fabric of those past triumphs.

'There is no environment I have been in since that can recreate the unity, the bond, the team spirit, the banter that you get on a daily basis as a rugby player,' he said.

'Some of it is brutal. You couldn't place it in any other workplace otherwise you would get fired. When you are playing rugby it is so physical you have to look after each other. If you have an off-day you know your mate will support you. I don't think you have people covering for you in an office in the same way.

'It is a rough, tough game. It is almost like being on the savannah. If the "lion" spots you are trailing a bit of blood, the opposition will be on to you and pepper you all day.'

Wigan did not need to worry about such vulnerabilities in 1995 when the combined experience and confidence of seven Wembley wins in a row appeared to render them invincible.

Robinson's two tries, both of which he rates as technically better than his World Cup score in 2003, were followed by touchdowns for Martin Hall and Va'aiga Tuigamala. And while James Lowes scored a consolation try for Leeds with two minutes remaining, when the final hooter sounded the scoreline was a commanding 30-10 to Wigan who had won their fifth league and cup double in a row, as well as their eighth consecutive Challenge Cup at Wembley.

So, up the Wembley steps they clambered once more, this time led by Shaun Edwards, who had last performed the task of lifting the cup as captain seven years before in 1988, when he had stepped in for Ellery Hanley amid the feud with coach Graham Lowe.

For Edwards it meant a ninth winners' medal in ten Wembley appearances, a phenomenal record. He was to return to the Twin Towers just once more, when he led the London Broncos to defeat, ironically against Leeds, but he rates receiving the cup in 1995 from Prince Philip as among his finest achievements and the Wigan team that year as the best he played in.

Rugby league followers during that time will have their own opinions and gauging greatness is always a subjective exercise.

But a glance at the 1995 line-up makes it hard to disagree with Edwards.

Backs: Henry Paul, Jason Robinson, Va'aiga Tuigamala, Gary Connolly, Martin Offiah, Frano Botica, Shaun Edwards. Forwards: Kelvin Skerrett, Martin Hall, Neil Cowie, Denis Betts, Mick Cassidy, Phil Clarke. Subs: Paul Atcheson, Andy Farrell.

True, it did not boast the playmaking genius of Andy Gregory, although Edwards had undertaken that role with some aplomb for the past three years, and it did not contain Ellery Hanley, in his prime a player with few peers.

But undoubtedly there was a fine balance of homegrown players, Edwards, Cassidy, Clarke, Farrell, and overseas stars, New Zealand's Paul and Botica and Samoan Tuigamala, plus rugby greats such as Robinson and Offiah.

'That was the best Wigan team,' said Edwards. 'It was a relief really when we lifted the cup against Leeds that year because they had beaten us in the league the last time we had played and the massive Super League war had just started.

'We wanted to send out a message that we were still the top dogs and technically that was one of our best performances at Wembley.

'To dominate such a very, very good Leeds team with players such as Jim Fallon, an England "A" international, Craig Innes, an All Black, Kevin Iro and Garry Schofield and Ellery Hanley, was something special.

'I was particularly pleased with my own performance because there was a lot of pressure on me and I think I delivered. I was the youngest-ever captain in 1988 and played with a shattered cheekbone in 1990 but 1995, I think, was my proudest moment. I thought we were the best club team in the world at that time.

'Jason was particularly determined that year after being left out by John Dorahy the season before. Westy put his faith in him that day and he repaid Westy.'

Robinson, not surprisingly, picked up the Lance Todd Trophy, although it is not, as you might imagine, in pride of place on his mantelpiece.

'It's in a bag somewhere, with all my medals,' said Robinson. 'I have never been one for getting too carried away with trophies. None of my medals are on show.'

He taps his temple with the forefinger of his right hand.

'It is in here that is important. All the memories.'

Vivid. Heartwarming. Unforgettable memories. So many of them in the calendar year up to the end of May 1995 when Wigan won every trophy available to them, a grand slam which was completed three weeks after their Wembley triumph when they defeated Leeds once more, this time 69-12 at Old Trafford, in the Premiership Trophy Final.

It was a season when Edwards and Denis Betts each scored 20 tries, Robinson 23, Tuigamala 25, Gary Connolly 30, while the incomparable Martin Offiah weighed in with 53.

Has there ever been a rugby team so perfectly in sync? Or a sporting side so compellingly in touch with the essential values of industry and technique while displaying such freedom and panache?

Perhaps even more impressive was the appetite for glory week on week, month on month, year after year.

'The taste of success is addictive,' said Robinson. 'When you have never had it, you are not sure what it is all about, but when you have tasted it, you want more. You want to play again at Wembley, score another try. You want to play for your country or Wigan in the biggest games, compete against the best players, test yourself against the best in the world.

'Then you know where you are. It is all right doing it at a low level, but the real test is when you are playing against the best and performing. There is nothing better than doing that and getting the best of your opposite number. That year, 1995, was just unbelievable.'

Addicted to glory. It could be an epitaph for that entire team.

And when the all-conquering season was complete and every trophy shoehorned into the bulging Central Park cabinet, one of Wigan's hometown boys, Phil Clarke, thought back to a bitingly cold January day when, as a 12-year-old who lived and breathed rugby league, he attended, by himself, a John Player Special Trophy Final at Central Park involving Leeds and Widnes.

After the match, which Leeds won 18-10, Clarke joined the queue to catch a bus to the family home five miles away in Blackrod when a group of Leeds supporters, in high spirits after their victory, asked him who he supported.

'Wigan,' he said proudly and enthusiastically, although the team was still emerging from doldrums that had seen them recently having had to fight their way out of Division Two for the first time in their history. Also, they had not been to Wembley for 14 years and not won the Challenge Cup for 20 years.

The Leeds fans laughed, the sort of derisory chortles a young, impressionable, hopelessly besotted sports fan does not forget in a hurry. Or even a lifetime.

'I'll always remember that,' said Clarke, whose career was curtailed when he suffered a broken neck in his only season with Sydney City Roosters in 1996 and was advised by doctors to hang up his boots. He has forged a media career since as one of rugby league's most knowledgeable and eloquent pundits on Sky television.

'It was an amazing journey from being stood in that bus queue, for Wigan and for me. I always wonder if I could ever have bumped into those Leeds people after Wembley in 1994 or 1995.'

What would he have said to them if he had?

'We're not doing so bad now then, are we?'

29

Here's to You Mr Robinson

ALL empires fall. It is a truism of history, whether ancient ones of Rome and Persia or the more recent decline of the British Empire. Vast business enterprises rarely go on forever either, as Woolworths and British Home Stores have proved in recent years, disappearing from the British high street after being unable to adapt to changing times.

Great sporting monoliths are no different. Liverpool ruled English domestic football for 20 years in the 1970s and 1980s, only to then go on and sample the pain of more than a quarter of a century without a league title.

The phenomenal West Indies cricket team of the 1970s and 1980s, which comprised prodigious talents such as Clive Lloyd, Michael Holding, Viv Richards and Malcolm Marshall while winning back-to-back World Cups in 1975 and 1979, was sucked into decades of decline by neglect and poor governance.

The reasons empires and dynasties fail are many and varied. But almost always they include one or more of the following states of mind: too comfortable, too unwieldy, too ill-disciplined, too arrogant, too complacent.

The salary cap, which was instituted in 1999, did much to level the playing field in British rugby league, but complacency and a touch of arrogance were certainly part of the reason behind the fall of Wigan as undisputed cup kings after eight consecutive winning trips to Wembley.

There were other factors, too, not least the consequences of rugby league's leap into the unknown with the establishment of the Super League at the behest of Rupert Murdoch and his £87m inducement.

Murdoch's need to gain the upper hand in his battle for supremacy with the Australian Rugby League meant an unsatisfactorily rushed and truncated final season for English clubs, with Wigan winning the 100th season of rugby league by eight points from Leeds.

It also saw that season end for Wigan on 21 January 1996 with the new Super League season beginning at the end of March. Unfortunately, because Wigan were drawn in round four, a preliminary round of the Challenge Cup that year, it meant they were required to play Bramley on Sunday 28 January, just a week after the old season ended.

No matter, they eased to a 74-12 victory at Central Park, but tired limbs, a hectic blur of a season and the imminence of Super League then led head coach Graeme West to take a fateful and ultimately flawed decision.

He gave the players an extended break. Some went skiing. Others took to the sun in places such as Tenerife. The reasoning was sound. After all, the Super League was the new priority and West wanted his players fresh and hungry for the challenge. The timing, however, was awful, as a few days later Wigan were drawn to play Salford away on Sunday 11 February in the fifth round of the Challenge Cup.

Even though Salford were not one of the founder members of Super League, The Willows was always a tough venue, especially amid the heady mix of an emotional cup tie.

A tight ground, questionable facilities, an away changing room dubbed 'prehistoric' by Jason Robinson, who likened the rickety old chairs provided for changing purposes to 'something off the *Antiques Roadshow'*.

The fact that Wigan went into that game with some players still in holiday mode after the bars and temptations of Tenerife and without the full preparation of a focused training camp was also indisputably a factor in what was to follow.

But there were even more powerful factors at play, intriguing quirks of fate and circumstance which meant this was a match destined to examine the fitness and character of Britain's most successful rugby league club like no other.

One was the fact that the Salford head coach was none other than Andy Gregory.

It was almost four years since Gregory had left Wigan. He had not wanted to leave. Nothing would have pleased him more than to have fanned the smouldering embers of his playing career within the confines of his hometown club, especially as it had taken him so long, via spells at Widnes and Warrington, to realise his ambition of playing for them.

But the club, demonstrating top class sport and sentiment are reluctant bedfellows, had been unwilling to hand him an agreeable contract, the terms offered being considerably lower than Gregory had been led to expect as Wigan were convinced that he was becoming injury-prone. It was how Gregory found himself departing Central Park for Leeds in 1992, sold for just £15,000 and with a bitter taste in his mouth.

As it turned out, Gregory's stay across the Pennines in a team which comprised stars such as Ellery Hanley, Garry Schofield and Alan Tait, lasted just 18 months.

The grind along the frequently gridlocked M62 to training and a frustrating list of injuries took their toll and he never reproduced the form that had seen his talents light up eight Challenge Cup finals.

So it was, that, at around the same time that Va'aiga Tuigamala was joining Wigan for £400,000, Gregory was on his way to Salford, the team his father had played for, as player-coach for just £10,000. Or to put the numbers into words, a snip, a bargain. So much experience and inspiration for such little outlay.

At the time, he was asked if he would have returned to Wigan. His response shines a light on the commitment, determination and stubborn vehemence Wigan faced at The Willows that February day.

'I have to say that if Wigan had been the only team to make me an offer I would have packed the game in rather than go back there,' Gregory told *The Independent*.

'That's the way I feel about how I was treated. I've nothing against the Wigan players. Any resentment I have is towards one or two people sitting in the stand.'

The appetite for revenge in the Salford squad did not end there. In fact, Gregory's discontent with the power brokers in the directors' box at his hometown club was as nothing compared to that of Steve Hampson.

Like Gregory, the former Wigan full back had never wanted to leave Central Park. But it was the manner of his departure in 1993 which jolted not just his pride, but his pocket.

Hampson played 306 matches for Wigan. He was a firm favourite with the fans for his courage and his tenacity and in 1993 when he was informed that he was being released he was just four months short of having completed ten years with the club.

In normal circumstances that would have triggered his right to a testimonial which, for such a popular figure, almost certainly would have made him financially secure for the rest of his life. Wigan supporters knew how to reward their most trusted and admired servants. Invariably, they turned out in their thousands.

'When I got fired off by Jack Robinson I was annoyed,' said Hampson. 'Very, very disappointed. The reason I had not gone in asking for more money was that I thought I would get a testimonial and make some money to start a business with or go into coaching. I was one of the popular guys. I had always gone to events with the Knights of Central Park and other fundraisers to help out as many people as possible.

'People had been telling me I would have made at least £100,000 from a testimonial, which in 1993 was a lot of money.'

The ruthless timing upset Hampson. The dismay at the way he discovered his fate lingers to this day.

He was not at home at the time, so it was his girlfriend who picked up the phone at their home when the call came.

'To be kicked in the guts by doing it over the phone was bad enough, but it was not even to me,' said Hampson. 'They told her they would not be offering me a new contract. They did it all wrong. They didn't tell me to my face.

'They told my girlfriend over the phone while I was away. It was very amateur and when I got back he [Jack Robinson] wouldn't see me. That is the way it ended. I thought my career would end at Wigan on the coaching side of things, but I just got shafted.'

It meant Salford's coach, plus the club's most experienced player, had unfinished business to complete at The Willows. Yet there was even more history stacking up against Wigan.

Three more players in the Salford starting line-up that day, Steve Blakeley, Scott Naylor and Sam Panapa, had all been released by Wigan over the past few years. There were so many individual points to prove and a huge collective one in the fact that Salford had been excluded from the inaugural Super League even though they had finished the previous season as first division champions.

Ending the Wigan cup years would be the perfect way to confirm the folly of that exclusion.

Wigan could not have fielded a stronger side. Gary Connolly at full back, Jason Robinson and Martin Offiah on the wings, Henry Paul and Shaun Edwards at half back and Va'aiga Tuigamala and the blossoming Kris Radlinski in the centres.

As back lines go, that surely rivals some of the best in the history of the sport, but it was in the forwards where Gregory had identified a vulnerability.

Over the previous eight years, Wigan had been renowned for the pace and the athleticism of their pack. Against Salford they fielded Neil Cowie and Terry O'Connor as props, Martin Hall as hooker, recent rugby union convert Scott Quinnell along with Andy Farrell in the second row and Simon Haughton at loose forward.

A respectable six but the fact that they could account for a total of just seven Challenge Cup Final winners' medals between them during Wigan's glory years, just two more than Hampson had in his trophy cabinet, tells you this pack was not the stuff of dreams.

The lack of pace was the most crucial element.

'We knew that essentially they had four props playing,' said Hampson. 'Greg and I looked at that big set of forwards and decided to take them on down the middle.

'So we got the quicker guys like Steve Blakeley, who was quite rapid at the edge of the rucks, to try to beat their slower guys. It was a planned strategy to work around those rucks, make it a fast game and tire their forwards out. It worked.'

So much so that Blakeley, who had made just eight substitute appearances in his time at Central Park before being shifted on for £28,000, was man of the match, kicking five goals from five attempts and tormenting Wigan with his penetrating runs through the middle. The Wigan defence, which had been so meticulously constructed in the days of Graham Lowe and John Monie that it had proved impregnable for more than eight years of cup rugby, was suddenly creaking like a rusty old gate.

Who won the best supporting role behind Blakeley? None other than Scott Naylor, who scored two tries from centre against his former team-mates, one of them a 40-yard burst in which he lost a boot but sprinted on to secure the touchdown.

That is sport for you. Expect the unexpected. Fear the men on a crusade and the individuals with a point to prove. Blakeley and Naylor had arrived at Salford for less than a total of £50,000. Hampson had cost nothing.

Yet here they were masterminding the unthinkable. The pitch was a shade sticky but there was no biting wind, no low sun, no lacerating rain, none of the elements which had threatened Wigan's cup run at isolated outposts in the past.

No, there was nothing to detract from Salford's 26-16 victory. They were simply the better team on the day. Expertly drilled. More committed. Scott Martin and David Young supplemented Naylor's tries for Salford, while two tries from Va'aiga Tuigamala and one from Martin Offiah were scant consolation for Wigan.

The final hooter was greeted by hugs, home cheers and a mini pitch invasion and as Wigan's players manfully congratulated their victors before trudging off the pitch in a numbed haze, all the rancour Hampson had been bottling up since learning of that phone call to his girlfriend two and a half years before came swirling to the surface.

He could not help himself. He could not resist it. He ran down the touchline, adrenaline pumping, perceived injustice rising like red mist within. He stood in front of the stand, waving and whistling up to Wigan chairman Jack Robinson. The man who had shown him the door at Central Park. The man who had denied him a testimonial.

'You didn't want me, did you?' he shouted.

And he stuck two hands up, each with two fingers in the air.

Here's to you Mr Robinson.

'I probably shouldn't have done it,' admitted Hampson, despite a satisfying smile playing on his lips as the bitter-sweet memories of that day recharged their batteries deep in his mind after lying dormant for so long.

'But I gave him the Vs for what he did to me. Maurice Lindsay, who was the boss at the RFL then, saw me as he was walking across the pitch and he just said in his posh voice, "Now, now Steve, I saw what you did just then."

'I am sure Maurice would not have let it happen to me, not to someone who had broken most of the bones in his body and had his teeth knocked out and his nose splattered over his face for the club.'

As Salford rightly celebrated, Gregory was asked if he could go all the way to Wembley with his first division side.

Quick-witted as ever, he came up with the perfect riposte.

'I'm not saying we'll win the cup, but we've a better chance than Wigan,' he said. 'And there have not been many sides this last decade able to say that. When the final whistle went it matched anything I ever felt as a player. It was a tremendous feeling. It's the proudest moment of my career.'

By this time Shaun Edwards was back on the team bus, contemplating the strange feeling and the sour taste of defeat in the Challenge Cup for the first time since the 10-8 first round defeat at a windswept Oldham on 4 February 1987.

Nine years and one week exactly had passed since then, during which Wigan had remained unbeaten in 43 cup matches. And Edwards had played in every single one of them.

There are some, including Phil Clarke, who maintain Edwards pulled rank at times, as one of the club's most influential characters, to ensure he reached those eight finals in peak condition by maybe missing the odd match in the run-up to the showpiece occasion.

'I have never met anybody who is as strong a competitor as Shaun,' said Clarke. 'I really respected that and I like Shaun, but I'll tell you this, he didn't always play the week before the final. He would just deselect himself. That's a fact. He would say he was injured and we would all know he was at Robin Park running track doing a session of 8x200m at full pace.

'He was peaking and making sure he didn't miss the final, which was a bit of a touchy subject in the squad with people saying, "How come I have to play this week? I don't want to get injured either."'

Nevertheless, in a facet of life which is always striving for superlatives such as biggest, best, highest, strongest, fastest, longest, Edwards's 43-match achievement is up there with the most enduring of records.

In that time Britain and the world had seen relentless change. Britain's first woman Prime Minister Margaret Thatcher had been and gone, the Gulf War had raged, Downing Street had suffered a mortar attack, the Berlin Wall had fallen, the Soviet Union had broken up, Nelson Mandela had been released from 27 years in captivity, the Channel Tunnel had been completed, the English Premier League had become the most famous and exciting football league on the planet and websites such as eBay and Wikipedia had been launched as the technology revolution gathered pace.

And Wigan and Edwards had just rolled on and on, collecting cup after cup, defying the odds, winning match after match. Until now.

There was no hand-wringing inquest. No locked changing room door. No rants. No recriminations.

'I just got straight on the coach,' said Edwards, whose record is likely never to be eclipsed. 'I never liked going to the bar after a game because you are knackered. Win or lose, I wasn't really a person to go mingling. I was always shattered. I just wanted peace and quiet.

'Salford did a job on us. Our ball control wasn't good enough on the day, about 40 per cent, and they outworked us and we just lost.

'I wish we had gone to training camp. Westy, fair play to him, was always good at giving us time off. He did so not realising we were going to draw Salford away. We had a full Super League season in front of us with a championship play-off at the end. Half of us went on holiday for a week. In hindsight it was a mistake.

'But we were just outplayed. We always had trouble at Salford, never had an easy game. Never smashed them.'

Martin Offiah was one of the few players not to go on holiday that week. He stayed behind and trained. Not surprisingly, he believes the decision to give the players a break was flawed and would never have happened during the John Monie regime. Tough, focused, hard-edged professionalism had been allowed to slide, just a smidgeon, just enough for the cracks to show. A spot of complacency. A touch, perhaps, of arrogance.

'With Westy it was the tail wagging the dog,' said Offiah. 'He was in control, but not really. If the players wanted time off they got time off, which is never a good thing. Everyone tried on the day but we definitely contributed to it happening. We were not focused.

'But eight consecutive years at Wembley is a long time. It's almost in your all-present memory. It's like juggling a ball for eight years. It doesn't matter what the world record is, sooner or later you are going to drop a ball, aren't you?

'It's like holding your breath. I don't know what the record time is for someone holding their breath and someone might come along and break that record. But one thing we do know, you can't do it forever.

'In sport it's the same, no one can do it forever because everyone gets older. Things go up and down. It's cyclical. We knew it had to come to an end sometime. But the way it did come to an end was like we couldn't hold our breath any more.'

The one consolation Offiah takes from the defeat was that the run did not end at his beloved Wembley. That would have been unbearable. Losing in front of 10,000 people on a Sunday afternoon at The Willows undoubtedly hurt, but there was not the crushing disappointment that would have been attached to the world watching them let down themselves and the entire town on the sport's showpiece occasion.

'It would have been hard to stomach if the run had ended at Wembley,' said Offiah. 'The way it ended was the way it was meant to end. Everything ends, everyone dies, but no one wants to die on their wedding day or a big day. Better to pass away gently at night or on a winter's morning.'

In so many ways that is exactly what happened at The Willows.

No winning ugly in the mud as had been the case against Hull KR in round one in 1990.

No raging against the spectre of impending defeat as there had been against Halifax in the quarter-final in 1993 when Joe Lydon dropped the winning goal with 36 seconds to go.

No impossibly brilliant comeback as against Hull in round five in 1994.

By contrast, as if to highlight the unpredictable nature of sport, the best side of the entire Wembley run, at least in the eyes of Shaun Edwards, slipped to meek surrender.

In Salford. On a cold and bleak Sunday afternoon. Against lower league opposition. When it was least expected.

The Wigan empire would never be quite the same again.

30

The Time of Our Lives

WHEN great sporting achievements are considered, past seasons recalled and trophies, medals and photographs lifted from dusty drawers and appreciated once more, it is always the specific moments that linger most.

The emotions start to blur soon enough for players and fans alike. The relief and euphoria of a victory which seemed impossible fades quickly, the agony and despair associated with unexpected defeat less swiftly, but still it goes. Even scorelines play tricks on the memory down the years, defying accurate recall.

Yet the moments survive. Sharp and undiminished by time, protruding from the maze of action like stepping stones across a meandering river of history.

Everyone's moments will be different and personal and the memory of them might be triggered by a name, a chant, a snatch of music, a smell, a try, a celebration, a tackle.

Wigan's eight Challenge Cup victories were strewn with such moments and after studying those battles afresh with protagonists from each campaign I can offer only a personal collection.

Such as Henderson Gill's hip-swaying celebration by the corner flag in 1988, which seemed to epitomise so completely the swagger and joy of a sunny afternoon at Wembley when all was well in the world of sport.

Such as the ride down Wembley Way in 1989 in a friend's BMW, parting a sea of flag-waving Wigan supporters left and right and hearing one female fan, who quite possibly had visited the nearby Blackbird pub, shout sarcastically in broad Wigan tones as she leered through the window, 'Southern softies. Who does she think she is in a Bob Marley?' only for my wife Carole in the passenger seat and the 'shouter' to realise at the same time and with much merriment that they were once work colleagues at the same Wigan textiles firm.

Such as Mark Preston's long-range try in 1990, if only because a picture of him scoring that touchdown adorned my son's bedroom wall for the best part of ten years.

Then there is Andy Gregory's over-the-head pass to Ellery Hanley and, not surprisingly, Martin Offiah's solo try in 1994, when he ran into the history books and the same Wembley corner where I was sitting with my family and the whole stadium rose to acclaim one of the greatest moments in sport. Any sport.

The next time I witnessed anything remotely as stunning as that was six years later in Stadium Australia at the 2000 Olympic Games when Australia's Cathy Freeman, with the hopes and expectations of an entire nation on her shoulders, won the 400m gold medal and then sat on the track for a full five minutes oblivious to the celebrations of all around as she gulped in oxygen and tried to take in the enormity of the achievement and the realisation that her life would never be quite the same again.

Offiah's post-try introspection, on his knees with his head in his hands, the pose immortalised in the statue at Wembley, was not dissimilar.

Stupendous moments. Fabulous memories. The Wigan fans who regularly boarded coaches on an annual basis on Saturday morning outside the town's Gas Showrooms, opposite the old Market Square, with their crates of beer and boxes of Pooles pies for the trip down to Wembley, most of which were consumed before they reached Knutsford services, will have a multitude of their own.

Isn't that what belonging to a club is all about?

A sports club is not all about the team because that changes year on year. It is not about the players. Not really. They come and go and often balance their affections and sometimes their commitment on the size of their pay cheque.

A club is about those moments, handed down from father to son and mother to daughter and uncle to nephew and so on.

That is why the memory of Billy Boston, bursting down the wing, would-be tacklers bouncing off his iron-hard frame, is still revered in Wigan by fans who never saw him play.

It is why those eight years when Wigan made the Challenge Cup their own and Wembley a home from home are destined to remain forever in the hearts of rugby fans associated with the town.

The measure of just how phenomenal that achievement was can be gauged in the fact that, once that 43-match run evaporated, Wigan were to lift the Challenge Cup just once in the next 15 years.

The salary cap in Super League is often quoted as the reason why Wigan were reeled in from their lofty height by the rest of rugby league. And there is truth in that. But what kept the run going for so long?

For Denis Betts, as for so many players during that era, it was the fear of tasting the bitterness of defeat. It was a theme which recurred time after time.

'Winning was never as good as losing was bad,' said Betts. 'So you weren't in it to win, you were in it not to lose and that is what the finals were built on.

'It got to the point where it was more relief to not be the side that had lost. The joy of winning is no comparison to the pain of losing. Losing stays with you for ages, winning disappears tomorrow. Losing nags at you all day, all week, all year if you let it.'

Joe Lydon believes much of Wigan's impetus was supplied by antipathy towards the club during those years of plenty. The hatred from outside forged a determination within which turned into something akin to a force of nature.

'Because we became one of the most successful teams in Wembley history, everybody outside the Wigan community wanted us to lose,' explained Lydon. 'It actually fuelled us to want to win. We didn't want to be the team that stopped winning.

'To some people it may have looked like a degree of arrogance, but it actually fuelled something that was so special within. The pressure from outside was nowhere near as big as the pressure from inside. That was peer pressure. It was mutual respect and the understanding that we had something special going on.'

Lydon's rugby career did not end with his playing days. He was team manager at Wigan from 1994 to 1996 and performance director for the RFL until 2000 before switching codes to coach the England rugby union under-19 team. He became backs coach for the England senior side and then head of rugby performance and development for the Welsh Rugby Union and then head of international player development with England.

There is no doubt about it. Lydon has achieved much since hanging up his boots. He has walked the corridors of power in the rugby world as elegantly as he scored majestic tries in his youth, but the morning after we met I received a text from him which gave an insight into how much that unique cup run still means to the protagonists of that era. And how evocative those thrilling days remain in their lives.

He revealed he had not slept a wink that night because the memories of Central Park and Wembley, the defining moments of his sporting life, albeit in such a brief passage of time, had been ignited by our chat and were exploding like miniature firecrackers in his brain throughout the early hours.

Edwards, arguably, has achieved even more, claiming a place as one of rugby union's most celebrated coaches at club level with Wasps and at international level with Wales.

Yet the reflected gloss of those glory years, when he was so integral to opening the gates to history, has followed him wherever he has gone.

'When I first came to London I would get recognised, not because I had coached Wasps to a Heineken Cup or anything like that. Lads in their 40s or 30s used to say, "You played at Wigan didn't you, with Ellery and Martin." It was great.

'I have coached Heineken Cup-winning teams, been with Wales, won grand slams, but when they recognised me it was because I used to play for Wigan.

'I was a Wigan lad who came all the way through.'

Edwards's chest rises with pride at the assertion. For a moment his eyes seem to glaze with nostalgia as his mind filters more than 30 years of achievement, the extraordinary force of which have opened doors and opportunities he could only have dreamed of as a boy.

There are a few regrets, although almost too few and too insignificant to mention.

'I would have loved to have won the Lance Todd [Trophy],' said Edwards. 'But would I swap it for nine winners' medals at Wembley and the most-ever appearances in rugby league matches there? No.

'I lost in the World Cup Final, that's the biggest regret. Mainly I was just lucky I was fit and available at the right times.

'I looked after my body. I had an aromatherapist to recover from matches. The day after games I would go for jacuzzis. The only thing I didn't do were ice baths. That's the main thing from the modern era I wish I'd known about, that and cryotherapy.

'The worst part of training is warming down, so boring. With ice baths there is no warming down. You just sit there for ten minutes. Next day your legs feel great and you have no problems.'

It is nearing the end of our interview and Edwards's infant daughter toddles into the room. He lifts her up and she squeals as he puts her under his arm in the manner of a rugby ball and pretends to run down an imaginary wing.

It is a fleeting glimpse of the softer side of a man who is most often viewed by the public high up in a rugby stand with a hard-set face like the north side of the Eiger.

So, after a lifetime of high achievement, how does Edwards view himself these days?

'I see myself as a normal Wiganer even though I have met kings and princes,' said Edwards. 'I must have met Prince William lots of times, what a lovely fella he is. He's a belting bloke, really down to earth. He always calls me the quiet one because I am usually stood in the corner not saying much.'

Mixing with royalty, winning grand slams, touring with the British Lions. Edwards's life has been lived at the pinnacle of sport, at a height at which most sportsmen can only crane their necks to glimpse.

But eight of those years stand apart, namely the glorious season after glorious season Edwards and his team-mates pulled on the distinctive jersey of his hometown club before beguiling the sporting nation and holding the Challenge Cup trophy aloft at Wembley.

'We'll never get those times back,' said Edwards with a nostalgic shake of his head. 'We feel privileged we were there to be honest because it transcended its sport. They were special times, but I think everybody thinks that in Wigan, don't they?'

Truly, it was a question that required no answer.

Postscript

I F it seemed that it was never quite the same again then it really WAS never quite the same again.

For a start, Wigan changed their name in 1997, adding Warriors to their title as the sport, in its new Super League incarnation, imported all manner of American promotional gimmicks in an attempt to jazz up the image for satellite television viewers.

The team returned to Wembley in 1998 with John Monie back at the helm in his second stint as head coach. They were overwhelming favourites against the unfancied Sheffield Eagles.

Yet in one of the biggest Wembley shocks of all time Wigan lost 17-8. It should not be forgotten that they did win the first Super League Grand Final that year, defeating Leeds 10-4 at Old Trafford, so the entire edifice was hardly crumbling. The talent was still there. But that Wembley defeat suggested the Monie magic was not what it was. The never-say-die chemistry of old was no longer working.

Why? There is no catch-all explanation. But perhaps a story told by Phil Clarke, who, after retiring early following his serious neck injury, was chief executive at Central Park in 1998, hints at Wigan's lost spirit.

'One thing that used to irritate me and others was the number of people who used to get on the team photograph at Wembley,' said Clarke. 'There would be more and more each year. In the end one year there were more non-players than players on it.

'Personally, I didn't agree with it. I am all for support staff and they should be thanked in the right place but I didn't think they should be on the picture. Neither did one or two other players. There was a point where one or two didn't bother going on the photo as a silent protest.

'In 1998 I decided I was going to exert a bit of authority and sent out a memo to all staff saying if Wigan were successful at Wembley then the team photo is for the team and the coach and we would have a group photo when we got back to Wigan if we were successful.

'We went and lost the final so I didn't need to worry about it. I probably shouldn't have written the letter.'

It is difficult to imagine a letter such as that being written in the days when Bill Hartley, Keith Mills and Derek Jones were the source of so much respect and inspiration among the Wigan squad.

Change gathered pace. In 1999 Dave Whelan finally succeeded in buying the club and the team and the town's football club, Wigan Athletic, also owned by Whelan, moved to the newly-built JJB Stadium, as it was then named.

It meant leaving Central Park, the club's home since 1902, a decision that, despite its rickety seats, dilapidated toilets and limited catering facilities, alienated many fans who treasured memories of the famous old stadium on the banks of the River Douglas close to the centre of town.

It did not help that the land was bought by supermarket giants Tesco to build another faceless megastore and car park, on a corner of which now resides a giant bronze rugby ball, the only reminder of the life-affirming sporting deeds which once took place on that revered rectangle on a weekly basis.

The day of leaving was emotional, the final match being played against a St Helens side coached by Ellery Hanley. Happily, a typically effervescent performance of old, complete with solo try by Jason Robinson, helped Wigan triumph 28-20. The salary cap, the Super League levelling of standards and the crusade for a sport of universal quality have all meant Wigan's Challenge Cup domination has been consigned to history.

In fact, Wigan were bottom of the Super League and faced relegation in 2006 before appointing new coach Brian Noble and signing Stuart Fielden from Bradford Bulls for a record fee of £450,000.

They avoided the drop, but at the end of the season were found to be £222,314 over the salary cap budget and were subsequently docked points, a situation which led to chairman Maurice Lindsay, once the architect of so much success and by now in his second stint at the club, eventually stepping down.

Yet Wigan have also ruled, admittedly more fleetingly than in their golden days, at key moments since the turn of the millennium. They beat St Helens 21-12 in the 2002 Challenge Cup Final at Murrayfield while the new Wembley was being constructed.

They lost, 32-16, two years later to St Helens at the Millennium Stadium and Wigan's first victory at the new Wembley under new owner Ian Lenagan, who bought the club from Whelan in 2007, came in 2011 when they defeated Leeds 28-18.

Two years later they were victorious again, this time beating Hull 16-0 to lift the Challenge Cup for a record 19th time.

The club, Super League champions in 2016 for the fourth time, remains a vibrant force in the game. The most famous rugby league club of all with legends such as Sullivan, Boston, Ashton, Hanley, Gregory, Edwards, Offiah, Robinson, Farrell, Radlinski and Tomkins having formed a vapour trail of sublime achievement across the sport's history.

Even now at places such as St John Fisher School, where the rugby balls flying around the playground suggest Catholicism is not the only religion, and at amateur clubs such as St Pat's, the stars of rugby league's future are learning their trade and feeding off the inspiring legacy of those who went before.

Yet perhaps the last word should be left to Noble, the hooker from Bradford who bore the brunt of Wigan's domination more than most but who could not cross the Pennines quickly enough when he was offered the job of head coach of the Warriors for his three-year stint in 2006.

Noble not only played for the Bradford Northern side beaten 2-0 by Wigan in the first tie of their 43-match undefeated cup run in 1988, the game when his protestations against Joe Lydon's self-confessed cheating fell on deaf ears, he was also a loser to Wigan in four more of those cup fixtures; in the second round in 1989, the quarter-final in 1991, the semi-final in 1992, a 71-10 defeat when Martin Offiah scored five tries and which Noble described as the most 'embarrassing and humiliating match of my career', and also in the semi-final in 1993.

Few experienced more hurt at the hands of Wigan's golden era. Perhaps none are better placed to assess the extent of the phenomenon.

'Wigan were untouchable at times,' said Noble, who, as well as his role as a BBC pundit, has been instrumental in trying to extend the base of the sport in Canada in recent times as director of rugby at Toronto Wolfpack.

'They had the best players, first full-time organisation in the country. The odds were stacked in their favour but that doesn't take anything away. The level of talent and the superstars they had were awesome.

'I loved the people at Wigan. I went there on the back of those eight dominant years. They were coming to terms with parity. The Rugby Football League were all over them like a rash, the salary cap had come in so the best players were being shared out. They were struggling down at the bottom of the league.

'Thankfully, they rang me and one of the best years of my life was the struggle against relegation in 2006. I thoroughly enjoyed it. There was a spirit and a camaraderie around the Cherry and Whites which I have found it hard to replicate since.

'I adored my time there. The people were brilliant to me. Wigan is synonymous with the name of rugby league and rightly so.

'Their amateur set-up alone is unprecedented anywhere in the world. You have to go to somewhere like the hotbeds of Sydney rugby and Queensland rugby to replicate the amount of players they have playing.

'Look around the rest of the league and they still produce the majority of the top players in the country for other teams as well. I wish we had another 20 places like Wigan.'

From a player who was so often on the receiving end of Wigan's glory days, and a Yorkshireman to boot, that is some compliment.

Appendices

THE 43 MATCHES UNDEFEATED

1.

Saturday 30 January 1988. Central Park. Round One.

Wigan 2 Bradford Northern 0

Wigan – Backs: Steve Hampson, Richard Russell, Kevin Iro, Joe Lydon, Ged Byrne, Shaun Edwards, Andy Gregory. Forwards: Adrian Shelford, Nicky Kiss, Brian Case, Graeme West, Ian Lucas, Ian Potter. Replacements: Ian Gildart (for Lucas).

Bradford – Backs: Mumby, Ford, McGowan, Mercer, Simpson, Stewart, Robinson. Forwards: Skerrett, Noble, Hill, Heron, Fairbank, Redfearn.

Wigan Goal: Lydon.

Half-time: Wigan 2 Bradford 0.
Attendance: 9,825.
Referee: Brian Simpson.

2.

Sunday 14 February 1988. Central Park. Round Two.

Wigan 30 Leeds 14

Wigan – Backs: Hampson, Tony Iro, Kevin Iro, Lydon, Byrne, Edwards, Gregory. Forwards: Shelford, Kiss, Case, West, Potter, Andy Goodway. Replacements: Russell (for Lydon, 21 mins).

Leeds – Backs: Gurr, Morris, Schofield, Stephenson, Basnett, Jackson, Wilson. Forwards: Tunks, Maskill, Fairbank, Powell, Medley, Heron. Replacements: Brooke-Cowden (for Medley, 32), Lyons (for Wilson, half-time).

Wigan Tries: Tony Iro 2, Goodway, Case, Russell, Hampson. Goals: Russell 2, Hampson. Leeds Tries: Schofield, Medley, Tunks. Goal: Stephenson.

Half-time: Wigan 16 Leeds 10.
Attendance: 25,110.
Referee: Kevin Allatt.

3.

Saturday 27 February 1988. Central Park. Quarter-final.

Wigan 10 Widnes 1

Wigan – Backs: Hampson, Henderson Gill, Kevin Iro, Byrne, Tony Iro, Edwards, Gregory. Forwards: Case, Kiss, Shelford, West, Potter, Goodway. Replacements: Lucas (for Edwards, 77).

Widnes – Backs: Myler, Thackray, Currier, Wright, Offiah, Dowd, Hulme. Forwards: Pyke, McKenzie, Steve O'Neill, Sorensen, Mike O'Neill, Eyres.

Wigan Tries: Tony Iro, Hampson. Goal: Kevin Iro.
Widnes Drop goal: Myler.

Half-time: Wigan 0 Widnes 1.
Attendance: 18,079.
Referee: Jim Smith.

4.

Saturday 12 March 1988. Burnden Park, Bolton. Semi-final.

Salford 4 Wigan 34

Wigan – Backs: Hampson, Tony Iro, Kevin Iro, Ellery Hanley, Gill, Edwards, Gregory. Forwards: Case, Kiss, Shelford, West, Potter, Goodway. Replacements: Lucas (for West, 64), Dean Bell (for Shelford, 64). Shelford (returned to replace Potter, 70), West (returned to replace Case, 70).

Salford – Backs: Gibson, Jones, O'Loughlin, Bentley, Shaw, Cairns, Bloor. Forwards: Herbert, Moran, Disley, O'Shea, Blease, McTigue. Replacements: Glynn, Major.

Wigan Tries: Edwards 2, Tony Iro, Kiss, Kevin Iro, Hanley. Goals: Kevin Iro 5. Salford Try: Blease.

Half-time: Salford 0 Wigan 12.
Attendance: 20,783.
Referee: John Holdsworth.

5.

Saturday 30 April 1988. Wembley Stadium, London. Final.

Wigan 32 Halifax 12

Wigan – Backs: Lydon, Tony Iro, Kevin Iro, Bell, Gill, Edwards, Gregory. Forwards: Case, Kiss, Shelford, Goodway, Potter, Hanley. Replacements: Byrne (for Edwards, 74), Shaun Wane (for Potter, 76).

Halifax – Backs: Eadie, Ronson, Anderson, Wilkinson, Whitfield, Grogan, Robinson. Forwards: James, McCallion, Neller, Holliday, Dixon, Pendlebury. Replacements: Scott (for Holliday, 20), Fairbank (for Robinson, 46).

Wigan Tries: Kevin Iro 2, Gill, Lydon, Tony Iro, Hanley, Bell. Goals: Gregory, Lydon. Halifax Tries: Anderson, James. Goals: Whitfield 2.

Half-time: Wigan 16 Halifax 0.
Attendance: 94,273.
Referee: Fred Lindop.
Lance Todd Trophy: Andy Gregory.

6.

Sunday 29 January 1989. Tattersfield, Doncaster. Round One.

Doncaster 6 Wigan 38

Wigan – Backs: Hampson, Tony Iro, Kevin Iro, Lydon, Mark Preston, Byrne, Edwards. Forwards: Lucas, Kiss, Shelford, Denis Betts, Goodway, Hanley. Replacements: Gregory (for Byrne), Andy Platt (for Betts).

Doncaster – Backs: Potts, Roache, Evans, Pennant, Turner, Kevin Jones, Pickerill. Forwards: Hartley, Gibbon, Noble, Kevin Rayne, Keith Jones, Timson. Replacements: Carr (for Timson, 59), Parkhouse (for Pickerill, 66).

Wigan Tries: Lydon 4, Betts, Tony Iro, Edwards. Goals: Kevin Iro 5. Doncaster Try: Hartley. Goals: Noble.

Half-time: Doncaster 6 Wigan 8.
Attendance: 5,274.
Referee: Dave Carter.

7.

Sunday 12 February 1989. Odsal Stadium, Bradford. Round Two.

Bradford Northern 4 Wigan 17

Wigan – Backs: Hampson, Bell, Kevin Iro, Lydon, Preston, Byrne, Edwards. Forwards: Lucas, Kiss, Shelford, Betts, Platt, Hanley. Replacements: Tony Iro (for Preston, 40), Goodway (for Byrne, 51). Byrne (returned to replace Bell, 77).

Bradford – Backs: Mumby, Sampson, McGowan, Johnson, Mercer, Wilson, Harkin. Forwards: Skerrett, Noble, Hamer, Hobbs, Fairbank, Stewart. Replacements: Pinner (for Wilson, 51).

Wigan Tries: Edwards, Kiss, Byrne. Goals: Kevin Iro 2. Drop goal: Lydon.
Bradford Goals: Hobbs 2.

Half-time: Bradford 4 Wigan 7.
Attendance: 16,738.
Referee: Robin Whitfield.

8.

Saturday 25 February 1989. Watersheddings, Oldham. Quarter-final.

Oldham 4 Wigan 12

Wigan – Backs: Hampson, Bell, Kevin Iro, Lydon, Tony Iro, Edwards, Gregory. Forwards: Lucas, Kiss, Shelford, Platt, Goodway, Hanley. Replacements: Betts (for Lucas), Byrne (for Goodway).

Oldham – Backs: Platt, Lord, Hyde, McAllister, Robinson, O'Sullivan, Bates. Forwards: Sherratt, Ruane, Casey, Croston, Round, Newton. Replacements: Meadows, Morrison.

Wigan Tries: Edwards, Kevin Iro. Goals: Lydon 2.
Oldham Try: Lord.

Half-time: Oldham 0 Wigan 6.
Attendance: 9,402.
Referee: Dave Carter.

9.

Saturday 25 March 1989. Maine Road, Manchester. Semi-final.

Wigan 13 Warrington 6

Wigan – Backs: Hampson, Tony Iro, Kevin Iro, Lydon, Bell, Edwards, Gregory. Forwards: Lucas, Kiss, Shelford, Potter, Platt, Hanley. Replacements: Betts (for Lucas, 56), Goodway (for Potter, 48).

Warrington – Backs: Lyon, Drummond, Cullen, Darbyshire, Thorniley, Woods, Turner. Forwards: Roach, Roskell, Boyd, Thomas, McGinty, Gregory. Replacements: Richards (for Cullen, 78), Duane (for Gregory, half-time).

Wigan Tries: Lydon, Edwards. Goals: Lydon 2. Drop goal: Lydon (61 yards, world record).
Warrington Goals: Woods 3.

Half-time: Wigan 4 Warrington 4.
Attendance: 26,529.
Referee: Robin Whitfield.

10.

Saturday 29 April 1989. Wembley Stadium, London. Final.

Wigan 27 St Helens 0

Wigan – Backs: Hampson, Tony Iro, Kevin Iro, Bell, Lydon, Edwards, Gregory. Forwards: Lucas, Kiss, Shelford, Platt, Potter, Hanley. Replacements: Goodway (for Potter, 66), Betts (for Kiss, 72).

St Helens – Backs: Connolly, O'Connor, Veivers, Loughlin, Quirk, Cooper, Holding. Forwards: Burke, Groves, Forber, Dwyer, Haggerty, Vautin. Replacements: Evans (for Dwyer, 45), Bloor (for Loughlin, 63).

Wigan Tries: Kevin Iro 2, Hanley, Gregory, Hampson. Goals: Lydon 3. Drop goal: Gregory.

Half-time: Wigan 12 St Helens 0.
Attendance: 78,000.
Referee: Ray Tennant.
Lance Todd Trophy: Ellery Hanley.

11.

Sunday 28 January 1990. Craven Park, Hull. Round One.

Hull Kingston Rovers 4 Wigan 6

Wigan – Backs: Lydon, David Marshall, Kevin Iro, Bell, Preston, Hanley, Edwards. Forwards: Lucas, Martin Dermott, Platt, Betts, Gildart, Goodway. Replacements: Byrne (for Iro, 38), Phil Clarke (for Gildart, 38), Gildart (returned to replace Lydon, half-time), Lydon (returned to replace Gildart, 61).

Hull KR – Backs: Lightfoot, Clark, Fletcher, Austin, Sullivan, Smith, Bishop. Forwards: Niebling, Rudd, Ema, Botica, Thompson, Lyman. Replacements: Irvine, Armstrong.

Wigan Try: Marshall. Goal: Lydon.
Hull KR Goals: Fletcher 2.

Half-time: Hull KR 4 Wigan 6.
Attendance: 8,473.
Referee: Ray Tennant.

12.

Sunday 11 February 1990. Central Park. Round Two.

Wigan 30 Dewsbury 6

Wigan – Backs: Byrne, Marshall, Hanley, Bell, Kevin Iro, Edwards, Bobbie Goulding. Forwards: Lucas, Dermott, Platt, Betts, Gildart, Goodway. Replacements: Lydon (for Byrne), Gregory (for Goulding).

Dewsbury – Backs: Coen, Elsey, Graham, Howley, Batley, Shuttleworth, Johnson. Forwards: Burgess, Kelly, Cocks, Butler, Coughlan, Wilkinson. Replacements: Trembath, Bailey.

Wigan Tries: Edwards 2, Bell, Kevin Iro, Lucas, Betts. Goals: Goulding 2, Lydon. Dewsbury Try: Coughlan. Goal: Graham.

Half-time: Wigan 2 Dewsbury 0.
Attendance: 11,113.
Referee: Dave Campbell.

13.

Saturday 24 February 1990. Belle Vue, Wakefield. Quarter-final.

Wakefield Trinity 14 Wigan 26

Wigan – Backs: Hampson, Byrne, Lydon, Kevin Iro, Preston, Edwards, Gregory. Forwards: Shelford, Dermott, Platt, Betts, Goodway, Hanley. Replacements: Gildart (for Shelford, half-time), Goulding (for Dermott, 61), Shelford (returned to replace Gildart, 68).

Wakefield – Backs: Leuluai, Wilson, Eden, Mason, Fox, Lazenby, M. Conway. Forwards: Rayne, B. Conway, Thompson, Kelly, G. Price, R. Price. Replacements: Perry, Bell.

Wigan Tries: Edwards 2, Kevin Iro, Hanley. Goals: Lydon 5.
Wakefield Tries: Kelly, G Price. Goals: M Conway 3.

Half-time: Wakefield 10 Wigan 12.
Attendance: 8,033.
Referee: Dave Campbell.

14.

Saturday 10 March 1990. Old Trafford, Manchester. Semi-final.

St Helens 14 Wigan 20

Wigan – Backs: Hampson, Byrne, Lydon, Kevin Iro, Preston, Edwards, Gregory. Forwards: Shelford, Dermott, Platt, Betts, Goodway, Hanley. Replacements: Goulding (for Gregory, 31), Gildart (for Betts, 31). Gregory (returned to replace Goulding, 55), Betts (returned to replace Gildart, 62).

St Helens – Backs: Connolly, Hunte, Veivers, Loughlin, Quirk, Frodsham, Devine. Forwards: Forber, Groves, Mann, Dwyer, Haggerty, Cooper. Replacements: Bailey (for Frodsham, 62), Bateman (for Cooper, 53). Cooper (returned to replace Forber, 62), Forber (returned to replace Dwyer, 70).

Wigan Tries: Hampson, Byrne, Goodway. Goals: Lydon 4.
St Helens Tries: Devine, Quirk. Goals: Loughlin 3.

Half-time: St Helens 12 Wigan 6.
Attendance: 26,489.
Referee: Robin Whitfield.

15.

Saturday 28 April 1990. Wembley Stadium, London. Final.

Wigan 36 Warrington 14

Wigan – Backs: Hampson, Lydon, Kevin Iro, Bell, Preston, Edwards, Gregory. Forwards: Shelford, Dermott, Platt, Betts, Goodway, Hanley. Replacements: Goulding (for Dermott, 31), Gildart (for Preston, 70).

Warrington – Backs: Lyon, Drummond, Mercer, Darbyshire, Forster, Crompton, Bishop. Forwards: Burke, Mann, Harmon, Jackson, Sanderson, Gregory. Replacements: McGinty (for Bishop, 61), Thomas (for Jackson, 35).

Wigan Tries: Kevin Iro 2, Preston 2, Betts, Hanley. Goals: Lydon 6.
Warrington Tries: Gregory, Lyon. Goals: Bishop 2, Darbyshire.

Half-time: Wigan 16 Warrington 8.
Attendance: 77,729.
Referee: John Holdsworth.
Lance Todd Trophy: Andy Gregory.

16.

Tuesday 12 February 1991. Wheldon Road, Castleford. Round One.

Castleford 4 Wigan 28

Wigan – Backs: Hampson, David Myers, Kevin Iro, Bell, Frano Botica, Edwards, Gregory. Forwards: Lucas, Dermott, Kelvin Skerrett, Betts, Platt, Hanley. Replacements: Clarke (for Lucas), Ged Stazicker (for Platt).

Castleford – Backs: Ellis, Wray, Irwin, Anderson, Plange, Steadman, French. Forwards: Crooks, Beardmore, Sampson, England, Hardy, Joyner. Replacements: Smith (for Anderson), Clarke (for Sampson).

Wigan Tries: Botica 2, Kevin Iro, Edwards, Myers. Goals: Botica 4.
Castleford Try: Irwin.

Half-time: Castleford 0 Wigan 22.
Attendance: 6,749.
Referee: Jim Smith.

17.

Sunday 24 February 1991. Spotland, Rochdale. Round Two.

Rochdale Hornets 4 Wigan 72

Wigan – Backs: Hampson, Myers, Hanley, Bell, Botica, Edwards, Gregory. Forwards: Lucas, Dermott, Skerrett, Betts, Platt, Clarke. Replacements: Stazicker (for Dermott), Mike Forshaw (for Skerrett).

Rochdale – Backs: Whitfield, Garrett, Abram, Lord, Nixon, Brogan, Holding. Forwards: Cowie, M. Hall, Humphries, O'Neill, Marsden, R. Hall. Replacements: Pitt, Gormley.

Wigan Tries: Hanley 6, Botica, Bell, Betts, Lucas, Edwards, Myers. Goals: Botica 12.
Rochdale Try: M. Hall.

Attendance: 6,492.
Referee: Brian Galtress.

18.

Sunday 10 March 1991. Central Park. Quarter-final.

Wigan 32 Bradford Northern 2

Wigan – Backs: Hampson, Myers, Kevin Iro, Bell, Botica, Edwards, Gregory. Forwards: Lucas, Dermott, Skerrett, Betts, Platt, Hanley. Replacements: Lydon (for Myers), Clarke (for Platt).

Bradford – Backs: Simpson, Cordle, Shelford, McGowan, Gumbs, Barnett, Pendlebury. Forwards: Richards, Noble, Hamer, Medley, Fairbank, Hobbs. Replacements: Marchant, Croft.

Wigan Tries: Dermott, Gregory, Kevin Iro, Bell, Botica. Goals: Botica 6.
Bradford Goal: Hobbs.

Half-time: Wigan 8 Bradford 2.
Attendance: 17,734.
Referee: John Holdsworth.

19.

Saturday 23 March 1991. Burnden Park, Bolton. Semi-final.

Wigan 30 Oldham 16

Wigan – Backs: Hampson, Lydon, Kevin Iro, Bell, Botica, Edwards, Gregory. Forwards: Lucas, Dermott, Platt, Betts, Clarke, Hanley. Replacements: Myers (for Lydon, 60), Goodway (for Lucas, 25).

Oldham – Backs: D. Platt, Irving, Foy, Anderson, Henderson, Clark, Ford. Forwards: Donegan, Ruane, Fieldhouse, Round, McAllister, Russell. Replacements: Duane, Atkinson.

Wigan Tries: Edwards, Hanley, Goodway, Iro, Botica. Goals: Botica 5.
Oldham Tries: Henderson, McAllister, Ford. Goals: Atkinson 2.

Half-time: Wigan 20 Oldham 0.
Attendance: 19,057.
Referee: Jim Smith.

20.

Saturday 27 April 1991. Wembley Stadium. Final.

Wigan 13 St Helens 8

Wigan – Backs: Hampson, Myers, Kevin Iro, Bell, Botica, Edwards, Gregory. Forwards: Lucas, Dermott, Platt, Betts, Clarke, Hanley. Replacements: Goulding (for Dermott, 60), Goodway (for Clarke, 22).

St Helens – Backs: Veivers, Hunte, Ropati, Loughlin, Quirk, Griffiths, Bishop. Forwards: Neill, Dwyer, Ward, Harrison, Mann, Cooper. Replacements: Connolly (for Veivers, 8), Groves (for Neill, 26).

Wigan Tries: Myers, Botica. Goals: Botica 2. Drop Goal: Gregory.
St Helens Try: Hunte. Goals: Bishop 2.

Half-time: Wigan 12 St Helens 0.
Attendance: 75,532.
Referee: Jim Smith.
Lance Todd Trophy: Denis Betts.

21.

Sunday 2 February 1992. The Willows, Salford. Round One.

Salford 6 Wigan 22

Wigan – Backs: Hampson, Botica, Bell, Gene Miles, Martin Offiah, Edwards, Gregory. Forwards: Lucas, Dermott, Skerrett, Betts, Billy McGinty, Clarke. Replacements: Neil Cowie (for Lucas, 54), Lydon (for McGinty, 23), Lucas (returned to replace Betts, 72).

Salford – Backs: Gibson, Evans, Gilfillan, Williams, Birkett, Reid, Cruickshank. Forwards: Young, Lee, Stazicker, Hansen, Blease, Burgess. Replacements: Fell, Cassidy.

Wigan Tries: Edwards, Botica, Betts, Lydon. Goals: Botica 3.
Salford Try: Williams. Goals: Birkett.

Half-time: Salford 0 Wigan 10.
Attendance: 11,173.
Referee: Jim Smith.

22.

Sunday 16 February 1992. Central Park. Round Two.

Wigan 14 Warrington 0

Wigan – Backs: Hampson, Botica, Lydon, Miles, Offiah, Edwards, Gregory. Forwards: Lucas, Dermott, Skerrett, Betts, McGinty, Bell. Replacements: Platt (for Lydon, 28), Cowie (for Skerrett, 61). Lydon (returned to replace Hampson, 61), Hampson (returned to replace Betts, 73).

Warrington – Backs: Lyon, Drummond, Rudd, Bateman, Kenyon, Shelford, Crompton. Forwards: Harmon, Mann, Sumner, Jackson, Mercer, Cullen. Replacements: Sanderson, Thorniley.

Wigan Tries: Skerrett, Offiah. Goals: Botica 3.

Half-time: Wigan 6 Warrington 0.
Attendance: 21,736.
Referee: Brian Galtress.

23.

Saturday 22 February 1992. Knowsley Road, St Helens. Quarter-final.

St Helens 6 Wigan 13

Wigan – Backs: Hampson, Botica, Bell, Miles, Offiah, Edwards, Gregory. Forwards: Lucas, Dermott, Skerrett, Betts, Platt, McGinty. Replacements: Cowie (for Dermott, 32), Lydon (for Platt, 29). Platt (returned to replace Hampson, half-time).

St Helens – Backs: Veivers, Hunte, Connolly, Ropati, Sullivan, Griffiths, Bishop. Forwards: Ward, Groves, Mann, Nickle, Dwyer, Cooper. Replacements: Riley (for Connolly, 77), Forber (for Groves, 52).

Wigan Tries: Hampson, Edwards. Goals: Botica 2. Drop Goal: Botica.
St Helens Try: Connolly. Goal: Bishop.

Half-time: St Helens 2 Wigan 6.
Attendance: 16,018.
Referee: John Holdsworth.

24.

Saturday 28 March 1992. Burnden Park, Bolton. Semi-final.

Bradford Northern 10 Wigan 71

Wigan – Backs: Lydon, Botica, Bell, Miles, Offiah, Edwards, Gregory. Forwards: Lucas, Dermott, Platt, Betts, McGinty, Clarke. Replacements: Cowie (for McGinty, 27), Skerrett (for Lucas, 27). Lucas (returned to replace Betts, half-time), McGinty (returned to replace Platt, 71).

Bradford – Backs: Green, Cordle, Shelford, Simpson, Gill, Summers, Iti. Forwards: Grayshon, Noble, Hamer, Hobbs, Medley, Fairbank. Replacements: Richards, Croft.

Wigan Tries: Offiah 5, Miles 2, Botica, Betts, Lucas, Lydon, Edwards, Bell. Goals: Botica 9. Drop Goal: Gregory.
Bradford Tries: Shelford, Gill. Goal: Hobbs.

Half-time: Bradford 0 Wigan 25.
Attendance: 18,027.
Referee: Robin Whitfield.

25.

Saturday 2 May 1992. Wembley Stadium, London. Final.

Wigan 28 Castleford 12

Wigan – Backs: Lydon, Botica, Bell, Miles, Offiah, Edwards, Gregory. Forwards: Skerrett, Dermott, Platt, Betts, McGinty, Clarke. Replacements: Hampson (for McGinty, 27), Cowie (for McGinty, 64). McGinty (returned to replace Gregory, 48).

Castleford – Backs: Steadman, Wray, St John Ellis, Blackmore, Nelson, Anderson, Ford. Forwards: Crooks, Southernwood, England, Bradley, Ketteridge, Nikau. Replacements: Smith (for Anderson, half-time), Sampson (for Crooks, 33).

Wigan Tries: Offiah 2, Edwards, Hampson. Goals: Botica 5. Drop Goals: Lydon 2.
Castleford Tries: Blackmore, England. Goals: Ketteridge 2.

Half-time: Wigan 19 Castleford 0.
Attendance: 77,386.
Referee: Robin Whitfield.
Lance Todd Trophy: Martin Offiah.

26.

Sunday 17 January 1993. Central Park. Preliminary round.

Wigan 40 Hull 2

Wigan – Backs: Hampson, Sam Panapa, Bell, Andrew Farrar, Offiah, Botica, Edwards. Forwards: Cowie, Dermott, Gildart, Betts, McGinty, Clarke. Replacements: Jason Robinson, Lydon.

Hull – Backs: Gray, Eastwood, Grant, Rob Nolan, Donkin, Gale, Henjak. Forwards: Dannatt, Lee Jackson, Walker, Wilson, Anthony Jackson, Sharp. Replacements: Jones (for Walker, 29), Divet (for Wilson, 29). Wilson (returned to replace Dannatt, 69).

Wigan Tries: Betts 2, Offiah 2, Botica, Edwards. Goals: Botica 8.
Hull Goal: Eastwood.

Half-time: Wigan 20 Hull 2.
Attendance: 12,420.
Referee: Russell Smith.

27.

Sunday 31 January 1993. Mount Pleasant, Batley. Round One.

Dewsbury 4 Wigan 20

Wigan – Backs: Hampson, Robinson, Bell, Farrar, Lydon, Botica, Edwards. Forwards: Skerrett, Dermott, Platt, Panapa, McGinty, Clarke. Replacements: Gildart (for Dermott), Paul Atcheson (for McGinty).

Dewsbury – Backs: Graham, Rombo, Hughes, Rogers, Bailey, Squires, Shuttleworth. Forwards: Worthy, Kelly, Cocks, Glen Bell, Flearey, Haigh. Replacements: Coughlan (for Worthy, 28), Pearce (for Flearey, 63).

Wigan Tries: Lydon 2, Botica. Goals: Botica 4.
Dewsbury Try: Rogers.

Half-time: Dewsbury 0 Wigan 6.
Attendance: 4,156.
Referee: Paul Crashley.

28.

Saturday 13 February 1993. Central Park. Round Two.

Wigan 23 St Helens 3

Wigan – Backs: Hampson, Robinson, Bell, Farrar, Offiah, Botica, Edwards. Forwards: Skerrett, Dermott, Platt, Betts, McGinty, Clarke. Replacements: Lydon (for Hampson, 32), Cowie (for McGinty, 60), Hampson (returned to replace Dermott, 68).

St Helens – Backs: Lyon, Hunte, Connolly, Loughlin, Quirk, Ropati, Cooper. Forwards: Ward, Dwyer, Mann, Harrison, Nickle, Joynt. Replacements: Griffiths, Veivers (for Ward, 60).

Wigan Tries: Bell, Clarke, Edwards. Goals: Botica 4. Drop Goals: Lydon 2, Offiah.
St Helens Goal: Loughlin. Drop Goal: Lyon.

Half-time: Wigan 6 St Helens 1.
Attendance: 21,191.
Referee: Russell Smith.

29.

Sunday 28 February 1993. Thrum Hall, Halifax. Quarter-final.

Halifax 18 Wigan 19

Wigan – Backs: Hampson, Robinson, Lydon, Farrar, Offiah, Botica, Edwards. Forwards: Skerrett, Dermott, Platt, Betts, Clarke, Bell. Replacements: Panapa (for Offiah, 49), Cowie (for Skerrett, 30), Skerrett (returned to replace Cowie, 57).

Halifax – Backs: Wilson, Bentley, Hallas, Austin, Preston, Bailey, Bishop. Forwards: Harrison, Southernwood, Stuart, Lord, Perrett, Divorty. Replacements: Fieldhouse (for Bentley, 39), McLean (for Stuart, 63).

Wigan Tries: Bell, Panapa, Lydon. Goals: Botica 3. Drop Goal: Lydon.
Halifax Tries: Hallas 2, Austin. Goals: Bishop 3.

Half-time: Halifax 6 Wigan 6.
Attendance: 9,841.
Referee: John Holdsworth.

30.

Saturday 27 March 1993. Elland Road, Leeds. Semi-final.

Bradford Northern 6 Wigan 15

Wigan – Backs: Hampson, Robinson, Lydon, Farrar, Offiah, Botica, Edwards. Forwards: Skerrett, Dermott, Platt, Betts, Clarke, Bell. Replacements: Panapa (for Bell, 14).

Bradford – Backs: Watson, Simpson, Marchant, Shelford, Anderson, Summers, Fox. Forwards: Hobbs, Noble, Hamer, Powell, Fairbank, Medley. Replacements: Heron (for Medley, 25).

Wigan Tries: Hampson, Farrar. Goals: Botica 3. Drop Goal: Edwards.
Bradford Try: Simpson. Goal: Hobbs.

Half-time: Bradford 0 Wigan 0.
Attendance: 20,085.
Referee: John Holdsworth.

31.

Saturday 1 May 1993. Wembley Stadium, London. Final.

Widnes 14 Wigan 20

Wigan – Backs: Hampson, Robinson, Lydon, Farrar, Offiah, Botica, Edwards. Forwards: Skerrett, Dermott, Platt, Betts, Clarke, Bell. Replacements: Panapa (for Lydon, 30), Farrell (for Skerrett, 55).

Widnes – Backs: Spruce, Devereux, Currier, Wright, Myers, Davies, Goulding. Forwards: Sorensen, P. Hulme, Howard, Eyres, Faimalo, D. Hulme. Replacements: O'Neill (for Faimalo, 28), McCurrie (for Currier, 55), Faimalo (returned to replace Sorensen, half-time).

Wigan Tries: Skerrett, Bell, Panapa. Goals: Botica 4.
Widnes Tries: Eyres, Sorensen. Goals: Davies 3.

Half-time: Widnes 12 Wigan 14.
Attendance: 77,684.
Referee: Russell Smith.
Lance Todd Trophy: Dean Bell.

32.

Sunday 30 January 1994. Central Park. Round Four.

Wigan 24 Wakefield Trinity 16

Wigan – Backs: Lydon, Robinson, Panapa, Gary Connolly, Offiah, Botica, Edwards. Forwards: Skerrett, Mick Cassidy, Platt, Mather, Gildart, Clarke. Replacements: Wright (for Mather, 63), McGinty (for Gildart, 34), Gildart (returned to replace McGinty, 54), McGinty (returned to replace Skerrett, 74).

Wakefield – Backs: H. Paul, Christie, Mason, Flynn, Wilson, Spencer, Conway. Forwards: Durham, Fuller, Marlow, Bell, Woods, Slater. Replacements: Brown (for Marlow, 69), Allen (for Spencer, 74).

Wigan Tries: Panapa, Wright, Connolly. Goals: Botica 6.
Wakefield Tries: Mason 2, Wilson. Goals: H. Paul 2.

Half-time: Wigan 12 Wakefield 6.
Attendance: 12,404.
Referee: Stuart Cummings.

33.

Sunday 13 February 1994. The Boulevard, Hull. Round Five.

Hull 21 Wigan 22

Wigan – Backs: Lydon, Robinson, Mather, Connolly, Offiah, Panapa, Botica. Forwards: Skerrett, Dermott, Platt, Cassidy, McGinty, Farrell. Replacements: Edwards (for Platt, 33), Gildart (for McGinty, 27).

Hull – Backs: Gay, Eastwood, Nolan, Grant, Sterling, Hasler, Hewitt. Forwards: McNamara, Dixon, Street, Doyle, Sharp, Busby. Replacements: Divet (for Busby, 19), Walker (for McNamara, 33).

Wigan Tries: Mather 2, Panapa, Farrell. Goals: Botica 3.
Hull Tries: Divet, Hasler, Sharp. Goals: Eastwood 4. Drop Goal: McNamara.

Half-time: Hull 21 Wigan 6.
Attendance: 11,117.
Referee: Dave Campbell.

34.

Sunday 27 February 1994. Central Park. Quarter-final.

Wigan 32 Featherstone Rovers 14

Wigan – Backs: Atcheson, Va'aiga Tuigamala, Mather, Connolly, Offiah, Botica, Edwards. Forwards: Skerrett, Dermott, Platt, Cassidy, Farrell, Panapa. Replacements: McGinty (for Tuigamala, 16), Gildart (for Platt, 33), Platt (returned to replace Gildart, 55), Gildart (returned to replace McGinty, 68).

Featherstone – Backs: Gibson, Butt, Calland, Ropati, Simpson, Pearson, Daunt. Forwards: Molloy, Gunn, Casey, Gary S. Price, Gary H. Price, Tuuta. Replacements: Roebuck (replaced Gary S. Price, 18).

Wigan Tries: Mather 2, Botica, Connolly, Panapa. Goals: Botica 6.
Featherstone Tries: Calland, Gibson, Ropati. Goal: Pearson.

Half-time: Wigan 16 Featherstone 4.
Attendance: 16,019.
Referee: Stuart Cummings.

35.

Saturday 12 March 1994. Headingley, Leeds. Semi-final.

Castleford 6 Wigan 20

Wigan – Backs: Atcheson, Robinson, Mather, Connolly, Offiah, Botica, Edwards. Forwards: Skerrett, Dermott, Platt, Cowie, Cassidy, Farrell. Replacements: Bell (for Platt, 32), Panapa (for Cassidy, 25).

Castleford – Backs: Steadman, St John Ellis, Blackmore, Anderson, Middleton, Kemp, Ford. Forwards: Crooks, Russell, Ketteridge, Morrison, Smales, Nikau. Replacements: England (for Ketteridge, 26), Hay (for Morrison, 26).

Wigan Tries: Botica, Atcheson, Offiah. Goals: Botica 4.
Castleford Try: Kemp. Goal: Crooks.

Half-time: Castleford 0 Wigan 18.
Attendance: 17,046.
Referee: Stuart Cummings.

36.

Saturday 30 April 1994. Wembley Stadium, London. Final.

Leeds 16 Wigan 26

Wigan – Backs: Connolly, Tuigamala, Bell, Mather, Offiah, Botica, Edwards. Forwards: Skerrett, Dermott, Platt, Betts, Farrell, Clarke. Replacements: Panapa (for Platt, 59), Cassidy (for Farrell, 52).

Leeds – Backs: Tait, Fallon, Kevin Iro, Innes, Cummins, Holroyd, Schofield. Forwards: Harmon, Lowes, Howard, Mercer, Eyres, Hanley. Replacements: Vassilakopoulos (for Hanley, 69), O'Neill (for Harmon, 62).

Wigan Tries: Offiah 2, Farrell, Panapa. Goals: Botica 5.
Leeds Tries: Fallon, Schofield, Cummins. Goals: Holroyd 2.

Half-time: Leeds 0 Wigan 12.
Attendance: 78,348.
Referee: Dave Campbell.
Lance Todd Trophy: Martin Offiah.

37.

Saturday 11 February 1995. Central Park. Round Four.

Wigan 16 St Helens 16

Wigan – Backs: Henry Paul, Robinson, Tuigamala, Connolly, Offiah, Botica, Edwards. Forwards: Skerrett, Hall, Cowie, Betts, Farrell, Clarke. Replacements: Atcheson (for Paul, 62), Cassidy (for Cowie, 23).

St Helens – Backs: Prescott, Hunte, Gibbs, Lyon, Sullivan, Veivers, Goulding. Forwards: Neill, Cunningham, Pickavance, Joynt, Nickle, Cooper. Replacements: Dannatt (for Pickavance, 22).

Wigan Tries: Tuigamala, Betts, Hall. Goals: Botica 2.
St Helens Tries: Pickavance, Hunte. Goals: Goulding 3. Drop Goals: Goulding, Pickavance.

Half-time: Wigan 6 St Helens 12.
Attendance: 15,714.
Referee: John Holdsworth.

38.

Wednesday 15 February 1995. Knowsley Road, St Helens. Round Four replay.

St Helens 24 Wigan 40

Wigan – Backs: Paul, Robinson, Tuigamala, Connolly, Offiah, Botica, Edwards. Forwards: Skerrett, Hall, Cowie, Betts, Farrell, Clarke. Replacements: Atcheson (for Tuigamala, 59), Cassidy (for Farrell, 12).

St Helens – Backs: Prescott, Hunte, Gibbs, Lyon, Sullivan, Veivers, Goulding. Forwards: Neill, Cunningham, Pickavance, Joynt, Nickle, Cooper. Replacements: Ella (for Gibbs, 24), Dannatt (for Neill, half-time).

Wigan Tries: Offiah 3, Clarke, Connolly, Paul, Robinson. Goals: Botica 6.
St Helens Tries: Goulding, Joynt, Nickle, Pickavance. Goals: Goulding 3, Prescott.

Half-time: St Helens 8 Wigan 32.
Attendance: 17,300.
Referee: John Holdsworth.

39.

Sunday 26 February 1995. Mount Pleasant, Batley. Round Five.

Batley 4 Wigan 70

Wigan – Backs: Paul, Robinson, Tuigamala, Connolly, Offiah, Botica, Edwards. Forwards: Skerrett, Hall, Cowie, Betts, Cassidy, Clarke. Replacements: Atcheson (for Offiah, 48), Scott Quinnell (for Cassidy, 49).

Batley – Backs: Moxon, Thornton, Gilfillan, Irvine, Walker, Wilson, Tomlinson. Forwards: Parkinson, Scott, McWilliams, Mirfin, Child, Cameron. Replacements: Middleton (for Cameron, 16), Grayshon (for Gilfillan, 23).

Wigan Tries: Offiah 3, Paul 2, Cassidy, Clarke, Connolly, Edwards, Skerrett, Tuigamala. Goals: Botica 10, Paul 3.
Batley Try: Thornton.

Half-time: Batley 0 Wigan 46.
Attendance: 3,800.
Referee: Colin Morris.

40.

Saturday 11 March 1995. Naughton Park, Widnes. Quarter-final.

Widnes 12 Wigan 26

Wigan – Backs: Paul, Robinson, Tuigamala, Connolly, Offiah, Botica, Edwards. Forwards: Skerrett, Hall, Cowie, Betts, Cassidy, Clarke. Replacements: Atcheson (for Cowie, 29), Mather (for Atcheson, 63).

Widnes – Backs: Broadbent, Green, Devereux, Wright, Hadley, Hammond, D. Hulme. Forwards: Ireland, McCurrie, Makin, Collier, Myler, P. Hulme. Replacements: O'Neill (for Makin, half-time), Singleton (for Myler, 72).

Wigan Tries: Offiah, Hall, Betts, Cowie. Goals: Botica 5.
Widnes Tries: Hammond, Makin. Goals: Hadley 2.

Half-time: Widnes 12 Wigan 14.
Attendance: 6,981.
Referee: Russell Smith.

41.

Saturday 25 March 1995. McAlpine Stadium, Huddersfield. Semi-final.

Oldham 20 Wigan 48

Wigan – Backs: Paul, Robinson, Tuigamala, Connolly, Offiah, Botica, Edwards. Forwards: Skerrett, Hall, Cowie, Betts, Cassidy, Clarke. Replacements: Mather (for Offiah, 25), Farrell (for Skerrett, 34).

Oldham – Backs: Gibson, Belle, Topping, Abram, Ranson, Marsh, Crompton. Forwards: Sherratt, Stephenson, Temu, Lord, Faimalo, Kuiti. Replacements: Bradbury (for Ranson, 33), Richards (for Sherratt, 34).

Wigan Tries: Connolly 3, Betts 2, Tuigamala 2, Edwards, Mather. Goals: Botica 6.
Oldham Tries: Belle 2, Bradbury, Sherratt. Goals: Marsh 2.

Half-time: Oldham 4 Wigan 20.
Attendance: 12,749.
Referee: Russell Smith.

42.

Saturday 29 April 1995. Wembley Stadium, London. Final.

Leeds 10 Wigan 30

Wigan – Backs: Paul, Robinson, Tuigamala, Connolly, Offiah, Botica, Edwards. Forwards: Skerrett, Hall, Cowie, Betts, Cassidy, Clarke. Replacements: Atcheson (for Skerrett, 53), Farrell (for Cassidy, 9).

Leeds – Backs: Tait, Fallon, Kevin Iro, Innes, Cummins, Schofield, Holroyd. Forwards: Howard, Lowes, Faimalo, Mercer, Eyres, Hanley. Replacements: Mann (for Howard, 30), Harmon (for Faimalo, 53).

Wigan Tries: Robinson 2, Paul, Hall, Tuigamala. Goals: Botica 5.
Leeds Try: Lowes. Goals: Holroyd 3.

Half-time: Leeds 4 Wigan 12.
Attendance: 78,550.
Referee: Russell Smith.
Lance Todd Trophy: Jason Robinson.

43.

Sunday 28 January 1996. Central Park. Round Four.

Wigan 74 Bramley 12

Wigan – Backs: Connolly, Robinson, Tuigamala, Kris Radlinski, Offiah, Paul, Edwards. Forwards: Cowie, Hall, Terry O'Connor, Quinnell, Cassidy, Simon Haughton. Replacements: Rob Smyth (for Radlinski, 49), Farrell (for Haughton, 26). Radlinski (returned to replace Paul), Haughton (returned to replace Cassidy, 72)

Bramley – Backs: Creasser, Francis, Pickles, W Freeman, Stead, Long, Ashton. Forwards: Gary Hall, Blankley, Thornton, Jewitt, Dean Hall, Hill. Subs: G Freeman, Fella.

Wigan Tries: Quinnell 2, Connolly, Offiah 4, Radlinski 2, Robinson, Farrell 2, Cowie, Tuigamala. Goals: Paul 4, Hall 5.
Bramley Tries: W Freeman, Stead. Goals: Creasser 2.

Half-time: Wigan 32 Bramley 12.
Attendance: 4,627.
Referee: Paul Lee.

THE END GAME

Sunday 11 February 1996. The Willows, Salford. Round Five.

Salford 26 Wigan 16

Wigan – Backs: Connolly, Robinson, Tuigamala, Radlinski, Offiah, Paul, Edwards. Forwards: Cowie, Hall, O'Connor, Quinnell, Cassidy, Haughton. Replacements: Skerrett (for O'Connor, 27), Andy Craig (for Haughton, 50), O'Connor (returned to replace Cowie, 50).

Salford – Backs: Hampson, McAvoy, Naylor, Martin, Rodgers, Blakeley, Lee. Forwards: Young, Edwards, Eccles, Forber, Savelio, Panapa. Replacements: Burgess (for Panapa, 18), Davys.

Wigan Tries: Tuigamala 2, Offiah. Goals: Paul, Farrell.
Salford Tries: Naylor 2, Martin, Young. Goals: Blakeley 5.

Half-time: Salford 14 Wigan 4.
Attendance: 10,048.
Referee: Dave Campbell.

The Players' Record

Record of the 53 Wigan players who appeared in the 43-match unbeaten Challenge Cup run, listed in order of total number of appearances.

	APPEARANCES				SCORING		
Name	*Starts*	*Subs*	*Total*	*Tries*	*Goals*	*DG*	*Pts*
Shaun Edwards	42	1	43	21		1	85
Denis Betts	29	3	32	12			48
Andy Platt	27	2	29				
Joe Lydon	22	6	28	11	26	7	103
Frano Botica	27		27	12	135	1	319
Steve Hampson	26	1	27	7	1		29
Dean Bell	25	2	27	8			32
Martin Dermott	25		25	1			4
Kelvin Skerrett	23	1	24	3			12
Andy Gregory	21	2	23	2	1	3	13
Phil Clarke	20	3	23	3			12
Martin Offiah	22		22	24		1	97
Kevin Iro	19		19	13	13		78
Ian Lucas	17	2	19	3			12
Ellery Hanley	17		17	12			48
Jason Robinson	15	1	16	4			16
Andy Goodway	11	5	16	3			12
Neil Cowie	9	7	16	2			8
Adrian Shelford	13		13				
Gary Connolly	12		12	8			32
Mick Cassidy	9	3	12	1			4
Billy McGinty	9	2	11				
Ged Byrne	8	3	11	2			8
Ian Gildart	4	7	11				
Nicky Kiss	10		10	2			8
Andy Farrell	6	4	10	4			16
Sam Panapa	5	5	10	6			24
Va'aiga Tuigamala	9		9	6			24
Tony Iro	8	1	9	6			24

THE PLAYERS' RECORD

Name	APPEARANCES				SCORING			
	Starts	Subs	Total	Tries	Goals	DG	Pts	
Henry Paul	7		7	4	7		30	
Martin Hall	7		7	3	5		22	
Ian Potter	7		7					
Barrie-Jon Mather	5	2	7	5			20	
Paul Atcheson	2	6	8	1			4	
Mark Preston	6		6	2			8	
Andrew Farrar	6		6	1			4	
Brian Case	5		5	1			4	
Gene Miles	5		5	2			8	
David Myers	4	1	5	3			12	
Bobbie Goulding	1	4	5		2		4	
Graeme West	4		4					
Henderson Gill	3		3	1			4	
David Marshall	2		2	1			4	
Ged Stazicker		2	2					
Richard Russell	1	1	2	1	2		8	
Scott Quinnell	1	1	2	2			8	
Kris Radlinski	1		1	2			8	
Terry O'Connor	1		1					
Simon Haughton	1		1					
Mike Forshaw		1	1					
Rob Smyth		1	1					
Shaun Wane		1	1					
Nigel Wright		1	1	1			4	

Bibliography

Moorhouse, Geoffrey, *A People's Game – The Official History of Rugby League, 1895–1995* (Hodder & Stoughton, 1995).

Hanson, Neil, *Blood, Mud and Glory. The Inside Story of Wigan's Year* (Pelham Books, 1991).

Radlinski, Kris, *Simply Rad: The Kris Radlinski Story* (Vertical Editions, 2010).

Robinson, Jason and Folley, Malcolm, *Jason Robinson. Finding My Feet: My Autobiography* (Hodder & Stoughton, 2003).

Offiah, Martin with Spires, Philip, *50 of the Best – Fifty of the Greatest Rugby League Tries of All Time* (Libros International, 2009).

Collins, Tony, *Rugby League in Twentieth Century Britain: A Social and Cultural History* (Routledge, 2006).